LET ME TELL YOU WHERE I'VE BEEN

Let Me Tell You Where I've Been

NEW WRITING BY WOMEN OF THE IRANIAN DIASPORA

Edited by PERSIS M. KARIM

The University of Arkansas Press
Fayetteville • 2006
In Association with the Iran Heritage Foundation

00 09 08 07 06   5 4 3 2 1

Designed by Liz Lester

⊗ The paper used in this publication meets the minimum
requirements of the American National Standard for Permanence
of Paper for Printed Library Materials Z39.48-1984.

LIBRARY OF CONGRESS CATALOGING-IN-PUBLICATION DATA

　　Let me tell you where I've been : new writing by women
of the Iranian diaspora / edited by Persis M. Karim.
　　　　p.　　cm.
　　ISBN 1-55728-819-4 (alk. paper) — ISBN 1-55728-820-8
(pbk. : alk. paper)
　　1. American literature—Iranian American authors. 2. Iranian
Americans—Literary collections. 3. American literature—Women
authors. 4. American literature—21st century. 5. American
literature—20th century. I. Karim, Persis M.
　　PS508.I69L48　　2006
　　810.8′092870899155—dc22

　　　　　　　　　　　2006003032

ACKNOWLEDGMENTS

The editor would gratefully like to acknowledge the following authors and the publications in which their work first appeared:

Gelareh Asayesh, "The Break," from *Saffron Sky: A Life Between Iran and America*. Copyright 1999. Reprinted by permission of Beacon Press.

Susan Atefat-Peckham, "Autumn Letter," "Avenue Vali Asr," "Fariba's Daughters," and "For Tradition," from *That Kind of Sleep*. Copyright 2001. Reprinted by permission of Coffee House Press, MN.

Tara Bahrampour, excerpt from *To See and See Again: A Life in Iran and America*. Copyright 1999. Reprinted by permission of Farrar, Straus and Giroux, LLC.

Firoozeh Dumas, "With a Little Help from My Friends," from *Funny in Farsi: A Memoir of Growing Up Iranian in America*. Copyright 2003. Reprinted by permission of Villard Books, a division of Random House, Inc.

Mahru Elahi, "Ajun," from *Fireweed* 75 (2002). Reprinted by permission of the author.

Parinaz Eleish, "Masouleh," from *Literary Review* 40 (Fall 1996); "How Lucky Persimmons Are," from *International Poetry Review* (Spring 1997); "Summer Day," from *Louisville Review* (Spring 1993). All poems reprinted by permission of the author.

HAALE. "Green World through Broken Glass," from *ratapallax* 8 (2002). Reprinted by permission of the author.

Haleh Hatami, "The woman has veto power" and "Cardamom and Hell," from *Faultline* (Spring 2005); "Lost Karbala," from *Kennesaw Review* (Spring 2003). All poems reprinted by permission of the author.

Zara Houshmand, "Invitation to the Hungry Ghosts" and "Unpacking," from *Caesura: The Journal of the Poetry Center San Jose* (Fall 2005); "Another Day and Counting" and "Home Stories," from *West Coast Line* (Winter 2003); "Mandala at Manzanar," from *[Two] Factorial* (Summer 2003). All poems reprinted by permission of the author.

Esther Kamkar, "Words to Die For," from *Hummingbird Conditions*. Copyright 2001. Reprinted by permission of Zibapress, Palo Alto, CA.

Persis M. Karim, "Axis of Evil," "Baba's Passing—February 2005," and "The Execution of Atefeh," from *Caesura: The Journal of Poetry Center San Jose* (Fall 2005); "Dawn on the Fall Equinox," from *Orchard Valley Review* (Winter 2005); "Ode to the Eggplant," from *di-verse-city* (Spring 2005); "Pomegranates," from *Reed* 58 (Spring 2005). All poems reprinted by permission of the author.

Azadeh Moaveni, "Love in a Time of Struggle," from *Lipstick Jihad: Growing Up Iranian in America and American in Iran*. Copyright 2005. Reprinted by permission of Public Affairs, a member of Perseus Books, LLC.

Farnoosh Moshiri, "On the Rooftop," from *The Crazy Dervish and the Pomegranate Tree*. Copyright 2004. Reprinted by permission of Black Heron Press, Seattle, WA.

Layli Arbab Shirani, "Captions," from *Suitcase* (2000). Reprinted by permission of the author.

Katayoon Zandvakili, "The Eglantine Deal," from *ratapallax* 8 (2002); "The World Was a Couple," from *Caesura: The Journal of Poetry Center San Jose* (Fall 2005).

With them the seed of wisdom did I sow
And with mine own hand wrought to make it grow:
And this was all the harvest that I reap'd—
"I came like water, and like wind I go."

—OMAR KHAYYAM

In loving memory of my Baba,
Alexander Karim—who instilled
in me a passion for learning and
a love of life and poetry.

and

In memory of Susan Atefat-Peckham,
whose voice rings clear and beautiful—
And was silenced much too soon.

CONTENTS

Acknowledgments   v

Foreword by Al Young   xiii

Gratitudes   xvii

Introduction by Persis M. Karim   xix

Home Stories

Autumn Letter by Susan Atefat-Peckham   3

Home Stories by Zara Houshmand   5

Dokhtar-e Amrika-i by Farnoosh Seifoddini   7

Dokhtar-e Irani by Farnoosh Seifoddini   9

Separation by Farnaz Fatemi   11

The Sun Is a Dying Star by Niloofar Kalaam   13

En Route to Persepolis by Amy Motlagh   23

Timing by Sheila Shirazi   25

Against the Kitchen White Wall by Michelle Koukhab   27

Road Trip by Shahrzad Zahedi   29

The Break by Gelareh Asayesh (from *Saffron Sky*)   31

Home by Shadi Ziaei   38

Persian Princess Insania by Leyla Momeny   40

Naderi by Amy Motlagh   42

Where Does My Language Lie? by Zjaleh Hajibashi   43

Inheritance by Mitra Parineh   44

Revolution 1979 by Tara Bahrampour   52

Portland, Oregon 1979 by Tara Bahrampour   53

With a Little Help from My Friends by Firoozeh Dumas
(from *Funny in Farsi*)   56

Another Quiet New Year by Nika Khanjani   61

My Brother at the Canadian Border by Sholeh Wolpé   64

1979 by PAZ   65

Captions by Layli Arbab Shirani   71

Arrivals and Departures by Sharon L. Parker   77

Excerpt from *To See and See Again* by Tara Bahrampour   86

For Tradition

For Tradition by Susan Atefat-Peckham   95

Sister by Farnaz Fatemi   96

Twin by Farnaz Fatemi   98

The Persian Bath by Michelle Koukhab   100

A Love Song by Parinaz Eleish   101

Pomegranates by Persis M. Karim   102

Passover by Amy Motlagh   105

ajun by Mahru Elahi   106

Next Year in Cyprus by Tarssa Yazdani   112

Recovery by Nasrin Rahimieh   117

Baba's Passing—February 2005 by Persis M. Karim   129

Joys of a Simple Meal by Esther Kamkar   131

Raw Walnuts by Negin Neghabat   132

The Camel and the Cantaloupe by Michelle Koukhab   135

Ode to the Eggplant by Persis M. Karim   137

Torches by Susan Atefat-Peckham   139

Woman's Duty

Avenue Vali Asr by Susan Atefat-Peckham   143

Woman's Duty by Tara Fatemi   145

The Next Day Is Always So Still by Nika Khanjani   146

Waiting for Ulysses by Laleh Khalili   148

The woman has veto power by Haleh Hatami   149

On the Rooftop by Farnoosh Moshiri   151

If You Change Your Nose by Leyla Momeny   161

Iranian Women by Mojdeh Marashi   163

Love in a Time of Struggle by Azadeh Moaveni
(from *Lipstick Jihad*)   166

Becoming a Woman by Elham Gheytanchi   180

The World Was a Couple by Katayoon Zandvakili   182

The Gift by Marjan Kamali   183

The Execution of Atefeh by Persis M. Karim   194

Bad by Sanaz Banu Nikaein   196

Summoning by Haleh Hatami   197

Masouleh by Parinaz Eleish   198

Words to Die For by Esther Kamkar   199

Fariba's Daughters by Susan Atefat-Peckham   201

Axis of Evil

Lower Manhattan by Susan Atefat-Peckham   205

Another Day and Counting by Zara Houshmand   207

Axis of Evil by Persis M. Karim   209

How Lucky Persimmons Are by Parinaz Eleish   211

Mamaan-bozorg by Farnoosh Seifoddini   213

In the Gutter by Sanaz Banu Nikaein   214

The Witness by Roxanne Varzi   216

American Again by Parissa Milani   220

Butcher Shop by Sholeh Wolpé   221

Iranians v. Persians by Sanaz Banu Nikaein   222

Invitation to the Hungry Ghosts by Zara Houshmand   224

When Toys Are Us by Beatrice Motamedi   225

As Good as Any Other Day by Parinaz Eleish   229

Dawn on the Fall Equinox by Persis M. Karim   230

Instilling Shock and Awe by Farnoosh Seifoddini   232

Summer Day by Parinaz Eleish   233

Beyond

Sestinelle for Travelers by Susan Atefat-Peckham   237

The Best Reason to Write a Poem Is Still for Love
    by Farnaz Fatemi   239

Perfectly Parallel Mirrors by Laleh Khalili   241

Money Buys by Sanaz Banu Nikaein   243

Once by Zjaleh Hajibashi   244

Excerpt from *Stones in the Garden* by Layla Dowlatshahi   246

Stripes by Katayoon Zandvakili   253

Magical Chair of Nails: Becoming a Writer in a
    Second Language by Roya Hakakian   256

Us Four by Sanaz Banu Nikaein   259

The Eglantine Deal by Katayoon Zandvakili   260

The Sandcastle by Firoozeh Kashani-Sabet   263

Ghazal by Mimi Khalvati   267

Mandala at Manzanar by Zara Houshmand   268

Beyond by Persis M. Karim   269

Only the Blue Remains Unchanged by Parinaz Eleish   270

Tales Left Untold

Night Conversations (Deep Are These Distances)
    by Susan Atefat-Peckham   273

Do You Miss Me? by Roya Hakakian   275

Lost Karbala by Haleh Hatami   277

Sing by Farnoosh Seifoddini   278

Earth and Water by Zara Houshmand   279

Tales Left Untold by Aphrodite Désirée Navab   281

Because of Hands and Bread by Esther Kamkar   295

Soleiman's Silence by Mehri Yalfani   296

Standing in a Mosque Contemplating Faith by Farnaz Fatemi   301

Sabze by Zarreh   303

Years Later by Parinaz Eleish   304

Native by Amanda Enayati   306

Unpacking by Zara Houshmand   308

Blessing by Mimi Khalvati   309

Green World through Broken Glass by HAALE   311

A Return by Kandi Tayebi   312

Blood by Azin Arefi   313

13 Days by Parissa Milani   332

Ari by Mahru Elahi   333

Let Me Tell You Where I've Been by Persis M. Karim   335

Cardamom and Hell by Haleh Hatami   337

Nazr by Zara Houshmand   338

Contributors   339

FOREWORD

Praise to the emptiness that blanks out existence.
Existence:
This place made from our love for that emptiness!

Yet somehow comes emptiness,
this existence goes.

Praise to that happening, over and over!
For years I pulled my own existence out of emptiness.

—RUMI

from "This World Which Is Made of
Our Love for Emptiness," translated
by Camille and Kabir Helminski

❧

Like the children and grandchildren of Holocaust survivors, women of the Iranian diaspora—mothers, daughters, sisters, wives, girlfriends, aunts, cousins—have inherited the heartbreak and hurt of the émigré, the immigrant, the exiled, the disconnected, the misunderstood and unwelcome; in a word: the uprooted.

In these tender and not-so-tender pages you'll find the barely tellable story of what really happens to dreams deferred. Through the vivid, sometimes spellbinding accounts they provide, these gifted writers speak powerfully to the subject of displacement.

As you reach the close of one chapter-length story to begin the next (and the many poems gathered here tell big stories as well), you could easily number or label every last one of them Chapter Zero or Chapter One.

Whether composed or intended as a story, a memoir, a poem or prose poem, a fantasy, an essay, or an unblinking assessment, each piece in this eye-opening collection unlocks something more than "that long iron latch across the front door." Each insight unlocks a mind or, rather, a mindset. Moreover, now that the complex interplay of zeroes and ones has linked us up digitally—finger by finger, toe by toe—the genie of interconnectedness can never again be bullied back into its jar. And who can overlook gender, that most primal of binary codes?

Why has written history focused so doggedly on conquest, power, aggression, subjugation, genocide, destruction, and betrayal? Why such a narrow range of fixed perspectives and viewpoints? Is it only because most of history's official storytellers have been men? Such questions may bubble up again and again as you delve into the streamlets that feed the ocean of this crucial, arresting history-in-progress. Crucial? Yes, nothing less than the future of democracy hangs upon how U.S.-Iranian relations eventually are balanced. When an Iranian newcomer to twentieth- or twenty-first-century Amrika (Persian for the United States of America) is shocked to discover that students don't rise and stand respectfully for teachers who enter a classroom, Americans need to take notice. We need to take notice when it troubles such a new-comer that kids born in the States remain contemptuously ignorant of global geography, neither knowing nor caring where on the globe Iran actually sits, to say nothing of her long-reaching history, her plentiful culture, or her tricky, even treacherous political relationship with the United States.

Shocking, too, is the big picture these pages paint of what the United States has become. In an apparent, centuries-late determination to rule the world, it plans to trash nation after nation—each of them oil-rich or bulging with raw resources, and none of them ethnically European or white; Amrika, once portrayed as the fruitful end of the rainbow for freedom-seekers, now would have its nominally naturalized citizens know that they'll remain here only as long as the country retains its patience and tolerance for foreigners with funny names and faces.

"We Play Cowboys and Iranians," one heartland bumper sticker reads. Who can help but laugh when poet Zara Houshmand describes the way "Tonight my cheeseburger arrives / with a flag poked proudly in the bun. / The tiny paper stars and stripes seem far away, / victory through the wrong end of the telescope, / moon-landing on the circle of my plate"?

Images and icons roll up, no matter who's doing the telling. To absorb even the most compressed history of the Iranian women's movement, which dates all the way back to 1850, would require the same hours or days you'd need to read celebrated physicist Stephen W. Hawking's *A Brief History of Time*. Who can tell us that the bodies of human organisms moving through space-time don't behave like sub-atomic particles? Simultaneity, a term useful to physicists in describing Albert Einstein's famous 1926 perception, wraps it up. Buddhists call it inter-origination. What it all boils down to is this: everything happens at the same time. When you bring in the subjective, you've got observers to deal with.

Moving at different temporal and personal velocities, each of the fifty-two observer-contributors to *Let Me Tell You Where I've Been* dramatically presents altered notions of simultaneity. Thankfully, they weigh in oddly, waywardly. We readers get their reassuring drift. Life goes on, no matter what. Hope stays alive. Crushing events in Iran send Iranians fleeing to the United States, the U.K., Canada, Australia, New Zealand, Sweden, France, Germany, and other Western-aligned countries. The paradox, the irony of this course is that the most powerful of those Western countries, the United States, often holds Iran's leadership hostage.

Still, émigrés rarely lose touch with their country of origin. That the voices we hear sound the same unmistakable cultural touchstones tells us where these women have been by reminding us—to snuggle into American usage—where they (or those closest to them) are coming from. Whichever generation sounds the note, cries or moans the blues, you'll have no trouble making out the physical and sensual references as they surface again and again: Tehran, Shiraz, Esfahan (poet Shahrzad Zahedi even speaks of Los Angeles's Iranian community as "tehrangeles"), tea (*chai sonati*) and tea-houses, Turkish coffee, sweets, pomegranates, backgammon, perfume, the smell of Gilani straw mats, the body-cloaking *chadors* that devotional city and country women wear, the *howz* (a household garden pool), walnuts, *mazeh* (bar snacks), scarves, Persian rugs, cardamom ("the sweet sharp / musky / green smell / that lurks in the back of kitchen cupboards"), hand-holding, the innumerable ways in which women admire and adore one another, social expectations, the carrying out of daughterly duties (for Baba as well as Maman). Such natural detail delights as much as it pinpoints.

Poetry, stories, music, drama, paintings, dance—all art helps dissolves base ignorance. The paths along which art and soul proceed still buzz and hum with traffic. How can we look at, listen to, touch, hear, or inhale the scent of anything or anyone from any distance and still not sense the vastness of this intimacy we share? For proof that culture crosses borders to make a home in territories for which armies have no maps, look no further than the book you now hold in your hands. In *Let Me Tell You Where I've Been,* Persis M. Karim has handed us not just one but a whole ring of keys to unlatch the many doors and windows that shut out air and light; the breath and vision of two nations that ideally will one day shake hands on some mutually rewarding goals.

Meanwhile, this singular anthology will give the world an urgent idea of where we need to go to meaningfully refill the gap, the grand, building-block emptiness against which all life continuously re-creates and invents itself anew.

AL YOUNG
Poet Laureate of California
October 2005

GRATITUDES

This collection reflects the vision and vibrancy of so many people. I would first like to thank all the writers who entrusted me with their poetry and prose and allowed me to gather their individual work in this symphony of women's voices. It is my hope that they will continue to write and to find avid readers and supportive publishers for their work.

I owe special thanks to Parissa Milani, who first proposed the idea for this collection. Over the several years it took to gather the writing in *Let Me Tell You Where I've Been,* Parissa helped push the project along and believed in it even when I lost some of my ambition to motherhood. Her inspiration and warmth are everywhere in these pages.

I would also like to thank some of the wonderful students who passed through my classes and then through my office doors, helping me with the long process and busywork of compiling and organizing this anthology. The energy and devotion of Deepthi Welaratna and Tara Coburn were invaluable in the early stages of this project.

Jahanshah Javid, the founder, creator, and editor of Iranian.com, an online magazine dedicated to serving the Iranian diaspora community, has been an indispensable part of this project. Without Jahanshah's support over the past decade, many of these writers would never have developed the confidence to write as much or as well as they do today. His magazine has launched many a writing career.

I would like to thank Joel Peckham for generously contributing some of Susan Atefat-Peckham's more recent, unpublished poems to this collection. Her voice adds so much to this collection, and I am honored to have it expressed so strongly here.

Without the diligence, devotion, and insight of my friend Destiny Lewis, this project might have lain dormant another year in my desk drawer. She was as dedicated to this book as any of these writers are to their craft. Similarly, Jacob Coltrane Burris's involvement in the final stages of editing helped create a coherence and order through the entire collection.

I have been blessed to have the support and faith of my family, particularly my lovely, late father, Alexander Karim, my dear mother,

Evelyne Karim, and my two sons, Niko and Kyle. Their love, and the love and nudging of my superb editor-husband, Craig Strang, make me a better person and writer.

Many thanks go to Carol Sickman-Garner, whose passionate interest and careful editing made this an even stronger manuscript. Finally, every book needs a visionary editor/publisher, and it is thanks to Larry Malley and the folks at the University of Arkansas Press that projects like this see the light of day. I am grateful for their enthusiasm and their support of literature that all too often is marginalized and compromised in the world of publishing.

INTRODUCTION

Long before the taking of hostages at the American Embassy in Tehran in 1979, the United States and Iran had a complicated relationship. Until Uncle Sam's ill-fated friendship with the Shah, most Americans hadn't even heard of Iran. Those who had, knew it as "Persia," a vague spot on the globe associated with carpets and cats. Few Americans knew that the CIA had instigated a military coup d'état in 1953 that ousted and imprisoned the popularly elected Mohammad Mossadegh, who in only a year went from being *Time* magazine's "Man of the Year" to being cast on the scrap heap of history by the U.S. government. The 1979 revolution that led to the establishment of the Islamic Republic, however, would make Iran a household name for many Americans.

The images and headlines of the 1980s—angry protesters, fist-waving students, bearded ayatollahs, captors and hostages, war—increased the distance and animosity between the two countries. Iran became a place largely defined by its restrictive political and religious identity, and in the eyes of Americans who had seen their society transformed by the free speech movement, the civil rights movement, and the sexual revolution, it seemed nothing short of otherworldly. While Americans were experiencing the effects of American feminism, Iran's post-revolutionary Islamic identity was being rigidly defined by perceptions about women and their appropriate social and sexual conduct. While Iran expressed its post-revolutionary ideology in part through its policies toward women, Americans became fixated on the veil as an icon of the essential identity of Iranian women. While women in Iran were limited in their opportunities and in their ability to vocalize dissent, Americans too participated in their silencing by assuming that they had little or no agency and were uninvolved in dissent.

Ironically, one of the most interesting by-products of Iran's revolution has been the explosion of women's writing both in Iran and abroad. While women in Iran may have been confined to a less public role, they have sought quieter places to express their individual identities, aspirations, and resistance. Women have developed successful and clever ways to respond to and maneuver around the forbidden spaces drawn by their government and society. Writing has been one of the public arenas to which they have been drawn. Even while they have had to endure harsh government censorship, Iranian women have, since the 1980s, written and published in unprecedented numbers. Over the past decade, Iran's best-selling fiction lists have been dominated by women. According to Majid Eslami, a critic and editor of the literary and art magazine *Haft,* "Women writers have become the avant-garde of Persian literature" (*New York Times,* June 28, 2005).

This outpouring of written expression has extended to women in the Iranian diaspora as well. My first encounter with this phenomenon occurred when I compiled and edited the first-ever anthology of writing by Iranian Americans, *A World Between: Poems, Short Stories and Essays by Iranian-Americans.* The number of submissions that my coeditor and I received for the book was phenomenal in itself—but we were surprised to find that 85 percent of the submissions came from women authors. On more than one occasion, I have been asked why so few Iranian men in America have been published. Perhaps in conforming to the expectations of their parents and the exigencies of immigrant life, they have been too busy becoming engineers and doctors to write poetry and memoirs. But it is more likely that the dramatic increase in the number of women writing and publishing outside of Iran is an outgrowth of Iranian women's specific experience; they have felt compelled to respond to the view of Iranian women purveyed by both the Islamic Republic and the Western media. Women writers of the Iranian diaspora have had an experience parallel to that of their counterparts living in Iran—they have found themselves having to reshape their identities to fit the new reality of their lives. In Iran, after the revolution, that meant women confronting a system that disenfranchised them and also made available new opportunities through education (a by-product of segregated educational institutions) and self-sufficiency after the devastating effects of the eight-year Iran-Iraq War.

Women who were part of the post-revolutionary immigration or were born in the West have also felt a need to reshape and define themselves. Writing is a way to wrestle with and name the chaotic experiences that define revolution, war, immigration, and the reconciliation of two distinct cultures. Poets and writers also use their work to counteract the barrage of visual images that has simultaneously been part of the Islamic Republic's campaign to Islamicize Iranian society after 1979 and of the Western media's fixation on veiled women and women's repression. Iranian women and their "Iranian American" counterparts have found both a voice and an audience for their work in the "in-between-ness" of Iran and America, or in some cases, Iran and other countries.

The increased writerly presence of women abroad may also have something to do with changes in the tradition of writing in Iran. Until the second half of the twentieth century, Iranian women were actively discouraged from and/or criticized for writing. Iranian poets such as Forough Farrokhzad, Simin Behbehani, and novelist and short story writer Simin Daneshvar achieved nominal success in Iran, but their work was often scrutinized and criticized more harshly than that of their male counterparts. Writing that expresses women's autonomy, sexual desire, or even political opposition has not been accorded the same respect or interest as the work of male intellectuals and writers. Iran's long and rich literary tradition has historically been the domain of men. Women writers who left Iran after 1979, however, found themselves in the new literary landscapes of Europe and the United States. They perhaps felt more liberty in expressing themselves, even while some may have lost their Persian-speaking readers by choosing to write in English or another European language. For the generation of young Iranian women who immigrated to the West or received their university education abroad, writing held entirely different possibilities than it had previously in Iran. Similarly, for young women born outside Iran, writing was no longer bound up in the predominantly male literary traditions of Iran. The urgency of their writerly mission grew out of the self-imposed silence of the Iranian exile experience and the struggle to acquire a voice and identity as Iranian Americans. For many of these writers, the English language became the best possible or only means of expressing themselves and their hyphenated identities.

I began the process of compiling the material for *Let Me Tell You Where I've Been* four years ago almost by accident. After the publication of *A World Between*, I received countless letters and email submissions from young writers (again almost all women) asking if there would be a second anthology. Many of these writers sent me their work and asked for advice about publishing. In a strange way, I found myself a kind of accidental literary midwife—helping to give birth to the literature of this Iranian diaspora. I had made it my personal mission to promote *A World Between* after it was published because I felt it offered a positive public identity for Iranians who had struggled to free themselves from the shadows of the hostage crisis and the inadvertent silence and shame that it caused for the Iranian community in the United States, only to be subsequently buffeted back into hiding by the acceptable racism that accompanied the Persian Gulf War in 1991. As I traveled to San Francisco, San Jose, Berkeley, Walnut Creek, San Diego, Los Angeles, New York, Chicago, and Austin, where I organized readings from the book with some of its authors, I was amazed and impressed at the public response. Those readings may have had more of an impact than the book itself. They became a curious and moving type of performance, created a stage from which we could announce our arrival, and publicly captured the multiplicity of voices and histories of Iranians of the diaspora. The experience of reading from and speaking about the book, and most of all, of watching my young and passionate coauthors gather their conviction by taking the stage, helped me to see just how hungry Iranian Americans were for a literary voice. In this book they sought a literature that was different from that of Iranians writing and publishing in Persian. In a sense, writers and readers were all looking to understand the experiences and reflections of Iranians in North America, separate from those of Iranians in Iran.

One of the interesting conversations that emerged from the publication of *A World Between,* and the subsequent readings in the United States, focused on what we might actually call ourselves. I intentionally used "Iranian-American" in the title of *A World Between* to identify the experiences of Iranians who migrated to North America in large numbers after the 1979 revolution. I now use "Iranian American" in part to identify the experience of migration and assimilation that connects this ethnic group to other immigrant groups that have struggled with their own identification with the homeland and the host country. People of Mexican heritage are a good example of this parallel; depending on their generation or their location in the United States, they refer to themselves as "Latino," "Mexican," "Chicano," and so on. These terms represent different stages of the immigrant experience and are influenced by the political and cultural context in which individuals are living. The search for a name or label represents the complex and dynamic process by which immigrant groups stake out cultural and political ground.

Throughout the 1980s and 1990s, many Iranians referred to themselves as "Persians" (a linguistic distinction) in an effort to distance themselves from the actions and policies of the Islamic Republic of Iran. The term "Iranian American"★ has proved to be complicated for the many Iranians living in multiple contexts—those living in America, in Europe, and those who seem to gravitate back to Iran even after long periods of time in the United States. It is for this reason that this collection casts a wider net and includes writings by women of the Iranian diaspora who live in several locations. This book, like *A World Between,* reflects literary and cultural expressions shaped by experiences of exile, immigration, otherness, and assimilation and by the complexity of these experiences, rather than the singular or stereotyped images that have been promulgated by the media. This book also represents the idea that any so-called ethnic literature simultaneously participates in and resists the boxes and ghettoes that are constructed by publishers, readers, and even those editors who, like me, compile anthologies from a single category or group of writers. My goal here is to present what I consider to be some of the most recent and compelling poems and narratives by women of the Iranian diaspora (written in English) that I have had the pleasure of

---

★ Another interesting by-product of the conversation that emerged around *A World Between* is that some people of Iranian descent in the United States (both first and second generation) have suggested a level of ill-ease with this term. For those who came as adults from Iran (even if they have lived here for more years than in Iran), the term suggests a level of assimilation that they don't feel they have experienced. For many Iranians, the experience of immigration was involuntary. They left as exiles and refugees, expecting to return after a period of stabilization. The discomfort with "Iranian American" can also be partly attributed to the fact that this group experienced a demonization of their country and people after the hostage crisis; while at certain points that demonization subsided, it was renewed by the Persian Gulf War, the events of September 11, 2001, and George W. Bush's "Axis of Evil" speech in January 2002.

I have heard repeatedly from young people who were born and raised here that they "are neither Iranian nor American"; instead they speak of being "from Iran, but not Iranian," or of being "born and raised in the United States, but culturally more international than the term 'American' allows." It is difficult to solidify the use of these labels for one's identity when the state of U.S.-Iranian relations remains so problematic.

reading. No doubt, I will be criticized for omissions of some well-known writers and for inclusion of less experienced ones.

The selections in *Let Me Tell You Where I've Been* represent what I consider the next step in the "literary maturation" of Iranian diaspora writing. Because women have emerged as the driving force of Iranian American literature, I decided to make women the focus of this collection. Since the late 1990s, several memoirs have been published in the United States that reflect the experiences of Iranian women in America. Books like Tara Bahrampour's *To See and See Again: A Life in Iran and America* (1999), Gelareh Asayesh's *Saffron Sky: A Life Between Iran and America* (1999), Azar Nafisi's *Reading Lolita in Tehran: A Memoir in Books* (2003), Firoozeh Dumas's *Funny in Farsi: Growing Up Iranian in America* (2004), Roya Hakakian's *Journey from the Land of No: A Girlhood Caught in Revolutionary Iran* (2004), and Azadeh Moaveni's *Lipstick Jihad: Growing Up Iranian in America and American in Iran* (2005) have met with remarkable success in part because they complicate our notions of Iranian women and articulate the ways that women respond to, remember, and utter their "Iranian-ness"—on more than one continent and in more than one political and social context.

Let Me Tell You Where I've Been shares some of the sentiments expressed in these recently published memoirs but brings together a large and diverse collection of writing by women poets, novelists, and nonfiction writers. Some of the authors included in *Let Me Tell You Where I've Been,* such as Zara Houshmand, Katayoon Zandvakili, Firoozeh Kashani-Sabet, and Nasrin Rahimieh, have been published widely in journals and other anthologies, including *A World Between;* the current collection reflects their more recent work.

One of the most satisfying experiences of editing *A World Between,* however, is that it introduced me to so many wonderful writers and poets. I came to know Susan Atefat-Peckham, for example, after she read that earlier anthology; over nearly two years, we had a series of wonderful, thoughtful exchanges via email about poetry, writing, and Iranian-ness. She was very supportive of my efforts and generously offered some of her work for this collection. I have included here some of her previously published poems that appear in her collection *That Kind of Sleep* (2001), for which she was named winner of the 2000 National Poetry Series. Atefat-Peckham's writing reveals a sensitivity to language and experience in the context of both Iran and the United

States. Sadly, her prolific and successful writing career was cut short in 2004 by a car accident that killed her and her young son, Cyrus, in Jordan, where she was teaching on a Fulbright fellowship. Joel Peckham, Susan's husband and a fine poet in his own right, has also generously given me permission to include four of her previously unpublished poems: "Night Conversations," "Sestinelle for Travelers," "Lower Manhattan," and "Torches." I am pleased and proud to include her poems here. As a kind of homage to her life and work, each of the six sections of the book opens with one of her poems.

By bringing together the work of more accomplished writers with that of younger, less experienced writers, this anthology presents for the first time a chorus of women's voices within Iranian diaspora literature. In part, this collection aspires to be a kind of barometer for the emerging literature of the Iranian diaspora. While the collection highlights those who write in English, other countries that have sizable Iranian populations, such as Sweden, France, and Germany, have also seen the emergence of Iranian diaspora literature.

The idea of an emerging literature of the Iranian diaspora is suggestive of the way that the common experiences of Iranian immigrants and second-generation writers can be articulated in a collection of this breadth. These writers do have experiences in common, but because of where they were born, where they were raised, or the circumstances of their or their family's immigration, there are also notable differences among them. This is partly what makes this a literature in the process of emerging and what makes it interesting to witness at this juncture.

Because of Iran's powerful poetic tradition, it is not surprising that writers of the diaspora have gravitated toward this genre. This collection, dominated by poetry, reflects the long and rich poetic tradition of the Iranian people. Because of the explosion of memoirs by Iranian American women, I also include excerpts from memoirs authored by Tara Bahrampour, Firoozeh Dumas, Gelareh Asayesh, and Azadeh Moaveni. The trend toward memoirs reflects an interest in first-person writing, which historically has been suspect in the Iranian literary tradition. Diasporic women writers have embraced this genre in part to signal a kind of agency that heretofore was off-limits to them and perhaps to reflect the new realities of negotiating identity in a non-Iranian context.

In lieu of a more conventional organization by genre, *Let Me Tell*

You Where I've Been presents the poems and prose writing through a loose categorization of themes that includes notions of exile, home, and unhomeliness *("Home Stories"); family, tradition, and ritual ("For Tradition");* women's roles, experiences, and resistance *("Woman's Duty");* politics, resistance, and war *("Axis of Evil");* spiritual and writerly movement beyond Iran and Iranian culture *("Beyond");* and longing and love *("Tales Left Untold").* Many of the poems and the fiction and nonfiction pieces fall into a number of thematic categories; this organization reflects my desire to make the individual pieces sing together and engage in a kind of literary conversation.

In the section called "Home Stories," writers like Farnoosh Seifoddini struggle in the context of their alienation from both Iranian and American culture, as in the poems *"Dokhtar-e Amrika-i"* and *"Dokhtar-e Irani."* One important sentiment reflected in many of the recent memoirs authored by Iranian American women is a preoccupation with moving between the two nations of Iran and the United States. This increased movement to and from Iran, either for the first time or on repeated occasions, suggests something important about the hold that Iran continues to have on the diaspora community. The lure of Iran as cultural motherland and yet a place too difficult to live in on a daily basis is something that a number of these writers express in their work, as in the excerpt from Tara Bahrampour's *To See and See Again.* The return journey or "pilgrimage" to Iran—for those born and raised there during part of their childhood or for those who have never lived there but who consider themselves "Iranian" or "Iranian American"— is an interesting negotiation and a topic that seems to preoccupy a number of these authors. Memoirs by Americans who lived in Iran during their childhood also reflect what I consider an element of the diaspora experience. While Sharon L. Parker is not Iranian by birth, she reflects a part of the Iranian diaspora experience: she spent her formative years in Iran, and it profoundly influenced her personal and professional perspective. Her essay "Arrivals and Departures" speaks to the nostalgia that Americans who lived in Iran share with Iranian nationals who were forced to leave the country after 1979.

In "For Tradition," I gather together writing that generally addresses family, tradition, and rituals. A poem such as Amy Motlagh's "Passover" highlight the importance of retaining the rituals of Jewish Iranian identity while observing the American, Christian rituals of Easter—the holidays of each of her parents. Other selections, such as Negin Naghabat's "Raw Walnuts" and Esther Kamkar's "Joys of a Simple Meal," highlight the importance of certain foods in Iranian culture, foods that help us maintain a connection to that culture and to family rituals and memories. Other poems are suggestive of strong familial connections, such as Susan Atefat-Peckham's poem "Torches," about the passing of her grandfather, and Farnaz Fatemi's poem "Twin," about her twin sister, Tara Fatemi, whose poetry also appears in this collection.

Some of the writing in "Woman's Duty" addresses the complexity of navigating womanhood in Iran and elsewhere. Poems like Leyla Momeny's "If You Change Your Nose" deal with the standards of beauty in Iranian culture and young Iranian American women's defiance of them. Elham Gheytanchi's "Becoming a Woman" documents her coming-of-age experience just after the revolution and identifies the shrinking spaces available to her as a woman in Iran. Mojdeh Marashi, who immigrated to the United States after the revolution, writes of the psychological impact of returning to Iran and confronting the different ways of constructing her womanhood in Iran and America. Azadeh Moaveni's "Love in A Time of Struggle," an excerpt from her memoir *Lipstick Jihad*, tackles a similar issue as Moaveni observes the dating rituals of young Iranian women and her own perspective as a young Iranian American female journalist who has a measure of freedom from these practices.

In "Axis of Evil," poems such as Parissa Milani's "American Again" and Zara Houshmand's "Another Day and Counting" articulate some of the layered anxiety and discomfort associated with Iranian self-identification. A number of these poets and writers speak to the shame and silencing that has resulted from major historical events involving or appearing to involve Iran and Iranians: the hostage crisis; the Iran-Iraq War; the Oklahoma City bombing; the Persian Gulf War; the tragedies of September 11, 2001; the ongoing war in Iraq; and the more recent vilification of Iran as a potent nuclear threat. Lamentations of the violence and human loss associated with the Iran-Iraq War and the current occupation and war in Iraq are expressed in Roxanne Varzi's "The Witness," Parinaz Eleish's "Summer Day," and Persis M. Karim's "Dawn on the Fall Equinox."

In the section entitled "Beyond," writers pay homage to the spaces between. Some of these poets and writers move beyond the knowable worlds of nations and cultures and use their work to confound, question, and challenge their backgrounds; they take their readers to new spiritual and cultural possibilities. An important element of this collection is the interest of these authors in creating literature that genuinely reflects something of both cultures. In some cases, writers express this duality through their choices about language and writing style, as in Roya Hakakian's essay "Magical Chair of Nails: Becoming a Writer in a Second Language," which addresses the necessity of the author unlearning her Iranian education. Other writers consciously make strategic use of Persian language, idioms, and names in their work to convey the beauty of Persian and the difficulty of translating some of their experiences and ideas into English. This is particularly evident in poems like Laleh Khalili's "Perfectly Parallel Mirrors," Zjaleh Hajibashi's "Once," and Katayoon Zandvakili's "Stripes." Mimi Khalvati's poem "Ghazal" employs the traditional Persian *ghazal,* and its Iranian poet extraordinaire, Hafez, through a modern spiritual rendering of this poetic form in English.

"Tales Left Untold," the last section of this book, brings together expressions not only of nostalgia for Iran but also of a deep psychic longing for home, for love, for belongingness. Anyone familiar with the classical Persian poets such as Hafez and Rumi knows that these poet-philosophers wrote beautifully about their desire for connection —whether connection to God, a lover, or nature. I cannot help but think that some of that same desire for connection, expressed in a contemporary, poetic sensibility, is carried on in writers of the Iranian diaspora. Poems like HAALE's "Green World through Broken Glass," Haleh Hatami's "Lost Karbala," and Susan Atefat-Peckham's "Night Conversations" are suggestive of this irrepressible longing and desire for connection.

Let Me Tell You Where I've Been presents to readers a variety of voices and a diversity of women's experiences in an emerging literature. This literature of the Iranian diaspora is complicated by the ongoing difficult relationship of Iran and the United States and the ease with which events and people associated with September 11 and with violent conflict in the Middle East generally are conflated with

Iran and Iranians. This anthology is concerned with the ways that Iran, Iranian culture, the Persian and English languages, and the dual identities of these authors are represented and expressed in the West. One could say that these authors are engaged in a sort of literary dialogue that is available nowhere else.

Some of the selections have no direct concern with Iran or Iranian culture but are brought together here because of their literary merit and to acknowledge that Iranian Americans needn't be typecast as writers who must represent and always write about the Middle East. Without a doubt, all of the writers in *Let Me Tell You Where I've Been* convey a passion for literature as a means of working through their complex feelings about the spaces and states where they live, whether as rooted, homeless, or diasporic subjects. This literature also conveys the powerful hold that Iran and Iranian culture exercises, not just on these writers but also on America and other societies that host significant Iranian immigrant populations.

It is my hope that this book adds an interesting and powerful literary voice to American literature and diaspora literature generally, perhaps fostering a more sincere and respectful dialogue between cultures. Iran and the United States continue to be bound up with each other. Perhaps the wisdom and beauty of this connection are more evident in literature than in the confused and conflicted headlines of the morning newspaper. I hope you find a little of that wisdom and beauty here in these pages.

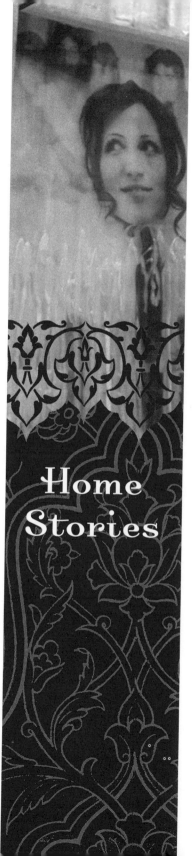

Home
Stories

Autumn Letter

∝

SUSAN ATEFAT-PECKHAM

For Mother

Mother always had her way
with words, squinting at my page
to find herself, to catch my foreign
breath and let it linger, see it blister
in lines and die a full death. Ey,
she said when I teased her
for the hours she would spend,
for calling the flower, Gerumium,
for the way she spelled, Esnickar,
Ey, she said, *Na Cun*. And *she*
once corrected *my* English.

Dying trees stretch their bones
up and forward like hungry men,
the red spreading top—first, the wet
falling. Her broken words leave
traces in iced fossils of leaves,
her drying body in a rose
I clipped with the blunt tip
of my thumb.

I gather leaves
with my husband, saying, I need
a red one, or, I need the one
that has no tears. Now they crunch
in pages of Khayyám. I think

of the letter I just read with words
cut out and rewritten. Circled above,
then scribbled, *Daddy says like this.*

She says a letter makes its way
to me. She says I ought to see
what words she's spelled this time.
I won't tell her what I write, but she
asks. Snow crowds a windowpane.
Frost blooms and fingers names.
Nebraska wind cuts quick. I've moved
geraniums in for winter. My aching
bones long for mother's words,
dried earth, blistered lines of green.

Home Stories

∞

ZARA HOUSHMAND

Fifty years ago, New York
my father to be
unfurled his carpet on your airport floor
and prayed his way through customs.
Hah! The last time *he* ever knelt,
and for all I know the last he ever prayed,
at least to show.

He polished his English
watching Cyrano
over and over on the silver screen
and like his hero, hid
his protruding foreign parts
in the fabric of his dreams,
hid his accent in the fist of his words,
and danced his way to the California coast,
Coyote from the East, yes, my dad
was Cyrano de Bergerac.
My dad
was not your Lucy's Desi.
Coyote of the West, too obsessed
to claim his difference as his own—
different only in being the best
and eager to do the work of four men to prove it.

I was born in fifty-three.
Berkeley. The year that everything started.
The man of the year on the cover of *Time*

was Mossadegh,
another fine coyote
pouring sugar in your gas tank,
pissing proudly on the oil machine
while the dark fuzzy thing in the stroller
parked at the back of the class
piled wet diapers on the great doctor dream
and the money, blocked, stopped coming from home.

Home? What home?
Hey, Great Satan, *Sheitan-e-Bozorg,*
better the devil you know.
Better the stories we tell ourselves
than the story we've been sold.

Dokhtar-e Amrika-i★

⁀

FARNOOSH SEIFODDINI

I

At the dinner table
We talk politics
I say we shouldn't go to war
We are hated around the world.
My mother laughs:
Akh! akh! Fekr mikoneh Amrika-ist!†

2

In middle school
with brown skin and toothpick curves
their eyes watch me
Camel jockey!
Vanessa, with her soft milky skin
and gold tinted hair
reassures me:
You'll bloom in college,
everyone will be after you.

3
At some bar
he walks towards me
two drinks in hand
his brow arches

★ American girl.
† Oh! Oh! She thinks she's American!

over pale blue eyes
he asks my name
then asks where I'm from
I say: the Axis of Evil.

4
In my dreams
things aren't punctuated properly
I wear Amrika on my head
a turban of red, white and blue
stars and stripes stream behind me
as I ride through the amber waves of grain
glide over the fruited plains:
on my camel.

Dokhtar-e Irani*

∝

FARNOOSH SEIFODDINI

I

I help my mother with the greens. Snap thick
stems off parsley for *khorosht-e sabzi*.† Snap snap.
Her fingers are getting less pretty but still soft.
Leila is pregnant, she's keeping it. Snap snap. *Her
poor mother.*

2

Albums reveal sexy happiness in pre-revolution
Iran. Several olive-skinned girls with shiny raven
curls wear dresses with dipping necklines. New
Year's Eve, 1962—heels high skirts short.

3

*Akh . . . Akh . . . Leave your home, your people, bring
your children into this culture.* Snap snap.

4

My first appointment with the gynecologist. My
mother insists on talking to the doctor before
she leaves me alone. *My daughter is a virgin, please
be careful when examining her.*

---

* Iranian girl.
† Persian dish with greens.

5

Snap snap. Those photos document torn hymens.

6

Another appointment. The doctor pulls on rubber gloves. Snap snap.

7

Leila! Leila! Iranian girls don't get pregnant!
Khodah omret bedeh!★

★May God give you life!

FARNOOSH SEIFODDINI

Separation

Farnaz Fatemi

When I am a child, my grandmother is pulled
across the ocean twice yearly
hovering above two cities, tongue divided
between English and Farsi.
She leaves my home many times
before I ever will, returning to say
Dellam khalee tang shodeh.
I learn this means *I missed you.*

In the other language we speak—
conversations of eating
hide and seek, and our expressions
in the crowd of family—
she never talks to me of leaving.
I am absorbed by her pink face
when I miss a joke
because it's in Farsi
her restrained laughter
betrayed by the edgeless smile
I will memorize

Dellam khalee tang shodeh
one of the few I repeat back to her.
Years later I discover it literally—
My heart is shrinking for you.
It must expand in our reunions.
Depth I hadn't imagined.

I have learned too much
about movement, not enough about
how the heart can translate
the language of separation into words.

FARNAZ FATEMI

The Sun Is a Dying Star

⤨

NILOOFAR KALAAM

I .

I dress with the same care some would use to polish a weapon. Not that it matters, I lost this battle at birth. But I shade the hollows with mystery, and coax pain into disdain. A flashing ghost of a doubt, a microscopic prick to their convictions—that's all I ask.

Tom walks in as I start on my eyes.

"This fuckin' long weekend is a fuckin' drag," he complains.

"Take it easy, baby," I coax, hoping that the check will arrive in the mail as promised, that the club will in fact pay him for the gig.

In the mirror, I watch surprise alter his face. "Goin' out?" he asks.

"Yep."

I move the inverted milk crate that acts as my dressing table and get closer to the mirror.

"Where to?"

"My uncle's."

Shock unfolds as confusion and spirals into a low chuckle. The kind that says, "Shit! I've been conned."

"You know," he tells me, "I keep forgetting you have relatives here."

I know he has been the sole support of my gloom. And it has been heavy.

"So do I," I reply.

He's sprawled across the old Guitar Chair. *Stop watching me. Please.* My hands shake.

"What's the occasion?"

"His in-laws visiting from Iran."

"Fu-un."

"His sister-in-law's my age," I offer.

We found it up the road and christened it the Guitar Chair because the left arm was missing. Perfect for holding the guitar.

"Her name's Meena."

"Your uncle's a doctor, isn't he?"

"Isn't that a pretty name?"

"What is it with immigrants, Laila? Why do they go so fuckin' straight when they come here?"

In the mirror I watch my jaw tighten. I watch the left side of my mouth twitch. I say nothing.

He strums, softly, absently, his gaze fixed on my reflection. Then he starts singing.

> "Surrender to the power of the Dollar.
>
> Work, buy, owe, work.
>
> Another VCR, a faster car.
>
> What do I care?"

He puts down the guitar and says, "You guys had a fuckin' revolution for fuck's sake."

He waits for me to respond. I don't. He picks up the guitar and plays some more. "For God's sake, can you say something?"

I can't. It is not that I don't want to, or that I have nothing to say. It is just that I can't find that first word. That first word that can lead to the many, the multiple, the dense cluster of words that have fused together, that have fused into silence.

In silence we weave the boundaries of our disparate spheres.

"Am I being racist?"

He is standing behind me now, his hands warm on my shoulders, his breath a tickle of apology. "Do you think your uncle would even talk to me?" He lifts my wrist to his lips.

In the mirror our eyes meet. From the aqua turbulence of his to the dark pits of mine, we trace our common despair.

"Let your hair down," his tongue on my wrist zigzags.

I shake my head, *no*. His hands slide up, searching for the pins that hold my dignity.

"I don't want to go," I say.

His fingers swim happily in the weight of my hair. "Don't."

Then the tears start, rolling dents in my armor. Before I can say, "I have to," our lips meet. We taste the heat and the flesh and the salt, and we stumble into security. My last thought before the world dissolves completely is that I will be late.

2 .

"Laila," my aunt flashes her latest Chanel smile, "you're finally here. We had just about given up on you."

It is as it always is. The women together, weary with preparations and strains of social interaction, the men elsewhere.

I whirl from one perfumed space to another, extending my greetings. I am really here to see Meena, but I comply with convention and leave her—the youngest—until last.

We embrace. And I am carried to the gardens of my youth.

The *howz** has the dimensions of a large looking glass. It reflects me and the willow tree behind me, even the rose bush on the other side. Twin cherries decorate my ears, jasmine hangs around my neck, falls between my breasts, twin bee bites swollen with their first strides towards womanhood. There are fish in the water, bright orange against turquoise tiles. Around and around and around they swim, day after day. Sunshine dances off their scales, burns through my skin. So hot that sun, and more powerful than anything I've ever known. Sweet scent of rose and jasmine in my nostrils. Headspin. I dip my fingers, red with rose petals, and drip water on my bare arms. Cool against heated flesh. One drop. Two. Drop. Drop. Such patience the fish have. And me, with my whole life ahead of me . . .

"Oh my god, Laila! Where have you been?" I wince as Meena's fingers dig into the silk that covers my wrists. "I've been dying to see you. You look wonderful. So creative. I love these scarves."

Her voice pulls me back, drags me, to the present, the party, my uncle's house.

---

* Small, shallow pool found in many Persian gardens.

"Do you remember me much?" I ask.

"No, not really."

She's grown into the beauty she has, oozing feminine grace over my tough hide. I watch her hands, soft and smooth and delicate. Nails well tended, fingers ringed in gold.

"I remember you. We played together sometimes." I feel brittle next to her. "Do you still have that *howz* in your garden?"

She cocks her head to one side and looks at me. "You really are different, aren't you?"

She moves her hands as she speaks. Small, graceful movements. And a ring on her middle finger catches my eye.

"I mean," she continues, "of all things, you remember the *howz!*"

I raise my eyes and smile. Then I look deliberately at the ring on her left middle finger. Instinctively, she covers it with her other hand. It is a cheap ring, coarse, with the initial *R* engraved upon it.

"So?" I ask, indicating the ring.

She giggles and her eyes sparkle. "So what?"

"So, what's his name?"

"Laila, you should see Meena's fiancé," my aunt's voice interrupts. "He is so handsome. Bring Babak's pictures, Meena."

A slow blush seeps through Meena's makeup. "Reza," she breathes in my ear as she rises to obey her older sister.

⚭

The women drool over Babak's picture. Meena smiles, an embarrassed smile. She doesn't say much. I try to join in for the heck of it, but find nothing to comment on in the heavily retouched photograph.

Instead I watch their faces lined early with bitterness, and wonder how many of them pinched a taste of passion before they chose security. The air around me turns heavy with the stench of unfulfilled desire, the reluctant knowledge of opportunities lost, the will to slash others' lives as they have slashed their own.

I rise from my seat. "Where is Amou?"★ I ask. As if I didn't know.

★ Paternal uncle.

3 ·

I join the men outside, where alcohol smoothes the kinks of unconsummated rebellion, and my uncle's voice warms an abandoned spot inside me.

"We're still looking for the right house. It's a toss-up between comfort and investment. My wife wants comfort, you know how women are, and I think of investment . . .

"Laila, *chosaky*,★ where've you been?" My uncle seems to think swear words can build a bridge between us. Then he engulfs me in arms so familiar, I can lose my wits and think I'm home.

"I'm telling you, I would've been fuckin' mad if you didn't show up."

Curious male glints invade our union. "This is my niece Laila," my uncle explains. I watch their glances shift from speculation to surprise, their thoughts converge to identical questions: Are you new here? How come we've never met?

"Laila's not an ordinary person," my uncle intervenes. "Don't look at her appearance, so sweet and delicate. Hard as a rock, this girl. More of a man than any of us here."

Brittle, Amou. Brittle, not hard.

"Laila's following in my footsteps. She's a medical student."

My mouth opens in automatic denial, only to clamp shut when I encounter my uncle's gaze. It holds a warning: Don't dare contradict me. It holds a bribe: see how I stand behind you in spite of . . . ?

The faces around me light up in admiration. Before I either choke or unleash my response, Amou pulls my hand.

"Come. I have something for you."

A bowl of cut lime, a saltshaker and a bottle of tequila. He's caught me off guard. My breath trips. I cough and tears lubricate my eyes.

"Is tequila alcoholic?" I ask softly.

His smile holds a warmth only alcohol could bring. "You were so young then, I worried about you."

Once at a Noruz party my uncle found me doing tequila shots with a bunch of guys. I watched his face, watched his jaw tighten,

---

★ Little fart.

watched the left side of his mouth twitch. He pulled me to one side. "Where are the other girls? Have they all stepped into the ladies' room and left you alone with the boys? And what is that you're drinking?"

"Tequila," I replied.

"Is tequila alcoholic?" he asked.

He pours us another shot and says, "You must accept that men and women are expected to act differently in our society."

Amou taught me how to swim. I was five years old and we were vacationing by the Caspian Sea. I was afraid of the water that swallowed the sun as though it were a child's orange candy.

"You are a lion," he told me. "What is fear to a lion? Nothing. You are afraid of nothing." Then he threw me into the waves. I sank and gulped, sank and gulped, until my eyes stung red, and my stomach filled with brine, and I had no choice but to declare I had no fear of water.

We drink to the silent desire that the bond between us will always remain this simple. Then others demand his attention. My uncle is a busy man, cream of the crop in a community of refugees and recent immigrants.

I fade into the background, noticed only by the covert looks of men in frigid wedlock. It dawns on me that Meena might like her drinks spiked.

4 ·

"We are having a hard time finding the right house. We want something spacious and cozy. Something that catches a lot of light, you know what I mean. Something like the houses we grew up in. Like the houses in Iran." My aunt's eyes dilate with pride, like a child awaiting applause. With no one looking I tip my glass into Meena's. "After all, we are Iranian and we have our own customs. We can't give them up, no matter how long we live here. We can't stop loving our homeland." I lean back against a wall. My aunt's eyes catch mine. She has clearly not expected me to be in the room. Her reaction makes her words register. She blushes and her eyes cloud with uncertainty, pulling us both to memories best forgotten.

∾

"You have a lot to learn here, Laila," my aunt and uncle told me the first night I arrived. "Europeans have a saying, 'He who is not an activist in youth has no heart, he who is still an activist in middle age has no brain.'

"Do you realize, Laila, what agony you have caused your parents? What agony you have caused us all? We each aged ten years for every year you spent in jail.

"From today on you must forget about that country and its politics. It is a lost cause."

Their words were redundant. All I had packed in my bag was the desire to make it up to my parents, to make the best of the opportunities life might offer me. In other words, all I desired was to enter medical school as I had always been expected to.

"Laila is a true patriot," my aunt says now.

I squeeze my eyes to hold back the flood of memories. Behind the blindfold in solitary you see nothing. Nothing. Not even a blank wall. But sometimes, sometimes—

"She's taken to Western ways now," my aunt continues, "but no one loves Iran the way Laila does. Isn't that true, Laila?"

The wall feels cool and solid against my back.

Of course times change, histories change. And what was a matter of life and death itself dies. Becomes a parcel for memory to toss around as it pleases. Like an old and feeble patriarch it retains a phantom authority: from time to time people feel obliged to ask it perfunctory permission.

"Laila?"

I push my weight off the wall. No, I will not make it too easy for them.

"I don't know, Auntie. After all, that country is a lost cause."

In the washroom I splash cold water on my eyes and face. In the mirror my face looks bloated with things unexpressed, inexpressible.

Things lost in silence, ingrown, infected. "Who are you?" I ask my reflection. "Who?"

Tom seems far away now, as though he belongs to a different life. Water rolls down my forehead, cheeks, nose, the sides of my chin. I know that no amount of cold water, no amount of tequila, can wipe this look away. I wonder how it is that no one ever seems to notice.

5.

"It's really too bad about Laila. She could have done anything she chose. Medicine, law, engineering. Anything at all. She's very smart, you know . . ."

I put an arm around each of the two women—my aunt and her mother—and flash my brightest smile. "But don't you know, Auntie dear, the sun is a dying star."

They try to mask their confusion but can't keep themselves from scanning my face.

"You are too smart for your own good," my aunt tells me. "I guess people with high IQs have always been eccentric, beyond the understanding of us ordinary folk . . ."

I laugh. A loud, clear laugh that bounces off the walls and rings around the room. Alien. Incorrigible.

∽

Meena is in the kitchen, putting away dishes. "Let's take a walk in the garden," she says. "I really need a cigarette, but I don't smoke in front of my family."

We walk past the men and their table of booze and *mazeh*.★ I grab what's left of the tequila. Men in hollow marriages follow us with their eyes. I swing my hips just to spite them. Past the large swimming pool, we disappear into the dark shadows at the far end of the garden.

The night is soft and balmy, a late summer night. The sky is clear, the moon full. We sit on the grass. A faint dampness seeps through our skin.

★ Snacks typically taken with alcohol.

"Don't your parents approve of Reza?" I ask her.

"They don't know."

"Why don't you tell them?"

"They won't approve."

"No money? No education?"

"He has some money, but no education."

"*Doctor shodan cheh asan, adam shodan cheh moshkel.*"★

Meena looks away. I lean back on the grass. It's peaceful here, far from the babble, the games and postures. Tom will be sitting on the roof, playing guitar under the full moon and waiting for me.

"Do you have a boyfriend?" Meena asks me.

"Yes."

"What does he do?"

"He's a musician."

"A musician? How interesting! Does he play in a chamber orchestra?"

"Are you going to marry Babak?"

"I don't know. At first I refused to meet him, but then all my friends told me to meet him at least once, it would do no harm and it would make my parents happy. I like him. He is nice and well established and my parents like him. But I can't imagine chopping herbs with him."

I look at her in surprise. She laughs. "With Reza I can see us slicing vegetables, chopping herbs and telling each other all the funny little details of our day. With Babak . . ."

"What will you do if Babak snores?"

It's her turn to look bemused.

"I mean, if you love them it's okay, but imagine lying next to someone who snores for the rest of your life! The bed rattles, the chandelier shakes, and the noise in your head—worse than a mosquito . . ."

We giggle and roll on the grass until green smears our dresses.

"Laila," she says suddenly, "why did you quit medical school?"

I sit up and watch the moonlight shimmer and dance on the pool's surface. I look again for that word, that first word that can lead to all the others.

★ A Persian proverb that translates as: "So easy to become a doctor, so hard to become human."

"Is it because of—you know, because of what happened?"

"Happened? You mean prison?"

"It must have been dreadful. How old were you? Sixteen? Only sixteen! My father thinks very highly of you, you know. He thinks we should all kiss your hands and feet. He thinks that if our nation had any decency, you would be treated like a national hero."

"A national hero?" I laugh and rest my head on my knees.

"Once, only once I thought I might die," I say. "It was midday and they called me. They called my name. They asked me to fetch my *chador* and come. They always called those who were to be executed at midday. My sentence was not death, but it happened sometimes. I was sure the time had come.

"The strangest thing was that I did not feel anything. No fear, no sorrow, nothing. The only thing I thought as I was being escorted down the hallway was that I had wanted to do many things . . ."

I lie back down on the grass. The stars are far away. So far away. And the moon is full.

"What happened?"

"Do you know that if you walk with your eye fixed on the moon you can walk forever without making any progress?"

Meena looks at me. Her face is pale and bewildered. In the moonlight her skin has a strange glow. I feel that if I touch her she will either burn me or melt. I am not sure which. I watch her grope for words she cannot catch.

"You are so brave and strong," she says finally. "I wish I was more like you."

"I'm not really brave at all," I say. "It wasn't half as bad as it sounds. See, I did not die." I grab the bottle.

"Another shot of tequila?" I ask. "And then we head back?"

En Route to Persepolis

❦

Amy Motlagh

We are lucky on Tuesday:
my father has found a man
to drive us there and back,
and wait in between.

There are good spirits today
and en route, my stepmother decides
that now is a good time for vocabulary
review. We re-trace what we've learned
as the parched fields glance by,
gypsy tents propped up among the wheat,
their women brilliant
in silks and the wealth of the tribes
stacked in *alangoo* up their arms.

Aren't they beautiful? my stepmother asks.
And mysterious? We nod.
In Farsi? *Gashang,* we answer.
Ziba. Good.

And now my back becomes a study
for the next lesson. She says, In Iran,
it is rude to show your back to someone.
If you do, you must say,
Bebaksheed; poshtam bay shomast.
I am sorry; my back faces you.
And the polite answer is

Gol posht va roo nadarad:
A flower has no back.

I face forward both ways,
to and from the ancient city.
On the way back, I am hotter,
I am told I have seen something
of great importance, but the fields
seem the same on both sides,
where the nomads pitch their tents
and their fires in the summer wheat
mark the air with sorrow.

Timing

SHEILA SHIRAZI

When did I make the journey?

At some point I traveled the arc
from unruly girl—
aching to feel
the fire of passion surge through her
—to solitary woman—
feeling the ache
of loss and self-denial.

Echoes of harsh voices and
shrill misunderstanding—
"What do you want him for?
        To fuck you?!"
—have faded into
silence
and thin smiles . . .
"Do you have a boyfriend?
        No? . . . That's okay."

Too young then, to be allowed sanctuary.
Too young now, to allow myself serenity.
The hands of a cultural clock
are closed 'round my throat.
My timing is off,
but I have an answer now—

"I don't want him.

I don't want anyone at all."

Are you happy now, Maman, Baba?

No more fucking.

Against the Kitchen White Wall

Michelle Koukhab

As we watch the slides he asks, "Didn't I look
so handsome then?" His face taut and thin,
black curly hair pressed like dried flowers.

In Iran, a young man in a cream wool sweater,
my father, sipped *chai* with my mother's
mother for the last time before they left

for America. The tea water in the cups fizzled
like a broken fountain. My mother watches
the slides too, anticipates the projection of herself

in a red bathing suit. (She never ate chocolates
or avocado before she got married.)
Against the white wall of my kitchen,

she waves, and poses with one leg in front
of the other, and thinks: I am so beautiful, so thin;
I am married to a handsome doctor

who will care for me, look at my sexy legs.
Perhaps she thinks none of this, really,
her thoughts, much simpler, about the photo-

graph being taken and all the times afterward
that she can remember herself this way.
We watch movies of my sisters and me

at our birthday parties eating mother's
spaghetti, holding our gifts up to the projector,
me in Wonder Woman Underoos jumping

off tables. Every year my parents look
thicker, a bit more poised, their eyes
tired of envisioning another life,

because there will not be enough room
for everything on the white wall.
When my father sees the Trevi, he thinks

how the builders celebrated with wine and
grapes, in the fountain. Their hands, like his hands
having felt the immense wait of success.

Road Trip

Shahrzad Zahedi

Not quite there yet,
Tehran, Shiraz, Esfahan—
blue arabesques dance on the polluted ceiling;
dark
black diamonds shine from the clamor
of the Nayeb Kababi.

Orange and white Paykans
honk deep
into my photo album.
Not quite gone yet—
in my Stockwell notebook,
listening to *Giovanni and Kim in the Morning,*
I press a Post-it on my life . . .
the passion, the people, the politics;
where the cab driver listens to Googoosh and Haydn
all day,
where the *farsh foroush* yells "Khanoum" in the background.
In this garden of cobwebs called
Tajrish,
pomegranates, cucumbers, and cherries fill
the prairie of the bazaar.
Is it the sound of a diva I hear
or just the shopkeeper yelling
"Gerdooh faghat divist toman."

Can't quite explain it—
the confusion, the color coordinations,

the shape of garments,
the symbols
engraved on the remains of *Persepolis* . . .
I sit in my condo—
I hear Snoop blasted on my street—
and I think
when will Bruce Willis land in Esfahan?
or the Persian supermodel become the James Bond girl?

Not quite full within:
been here, lived there,
traversed transitory crossroads,
set Baudelaire's wine
next to Hafiz's worship of the *Sarv ravan*.
Heard Leroy Jones lament the lost
bones
of African slaves,
and captured from my treasure
whispering laments of Rumi's broken
ney.

Why are they not broken yet?
The ties, the languages,
the Ghashghaii women
staring
from underneath their *chadors,*
holding a green-eyed baby in their arms.
Still . . .
the glitter on their orange dress
floats in my memory
right beside the navy jeans and the plain
white
t-shirt of the J. Crew boy.

The Break
(from *Saffron Sky*)

✑

GELAREH ASAYESH

Tuesday, 21st of Tir, 1356
(July 12th, 1977)

So we ARE going to America. We have plane tickets reserved for Mordad 22nd,
my father was on the phone to Morteza, my uncle, only last night; hotel reser-
vations in Paris. We have our visas and passports, Afsaneh and I. Homa and
Khalil don't yet. We've advertised in Keyhan International *for the house and*
have several answers. Khalil is under a lot of pressure arranging everything and
consequently irritable. I just sorted the books, storybooks I want to take. We're
to pack our cases since we're going to Mashad tomorrow . . .

When I left Iran for the second time, I said good-bye without a
backward glance.

I was fifteen years old. I was going to Amrika, which meant that
I no longer needed to envy my classmate Marjan, who ordered her
summer clothes from the Spiegel catalogue, my cousin Reza, who was
attending boarding school in England, or my friend Azadeh, who
would be going to school in Switzerland in the fall.

My only regret was leaving a boy I had fallen in love with that
summer of 1976. I met him during a vacation on the Caspian shore.
We had shared longing looks and one wordless walk on the beach. His
family had a villa on the sea; he told me he could predict its moods.
As we stood gazing across the tumbled green-gray water, the Soviet
Union an invisible landmass beyond, I wondered how that was pos-
sible. The night our families' cars went separate ways on the Chalus-
Tehran road we were both steeped in misery.

Sitting on the plane that would take me from Iran, I stared at the
dry horizon and arranged imaginary reunions with him. I was sanguine
about a future that would incorporate America without shifting my
center of gravity from Iran. Our last trip to America had ended with
a reunion in Iran and the resumption of the life I had always known.
I had no reason to believe that this trip would be any different.

If I had been an actress in a movie, the music would have signaled the significance of the moment. Somehow I would have known that I stood at the crossroads. Instead I turned away from my mother's tears, my father's tight expression. Even saying good-bye to my aunts did not seem to touch me.

That last day in Mashad, Khaleh Farah knelt in the midst of our belongings scattered through her guest room, wagged her finger at me, and said, "Don't you marry an American. If you marry an American, I won't be your *khaleh* anymore." Her eyes were bright with unshed tears, but I could not give her the reassurance she sought. On a shopping expedition before we left, Khaleh Mina was overcome by weeping. She stood sobbing at the side of the street we waited to cross and asked Afsaneh and me for a promise to remember, a promise to return. Sixteen-year-old Afsaneh consoled her. I searched for the first break in traffic and hurried across. Standing on the other side, I looked back at my aunt, feeling as if I was already far away.

I did not know how to cope with my family's emotions. I did not understand my own. I did not know, as they did, that this parting might last forever.

We stayed in Paris for a few days with my uncle Morteza, who was attending university there. There is a picture of us on the green grounds of Versailles, busy with summer tourists. My family looks morose and disconnected. The camera seems to have captured a heaviness of spirit among us that was in contrast to Dayi Morteza's smiling face. We were shell-shocked, and it showed.

The second plane ride, from Paris to New York, provided both physical and emotional distance from the trauma of leaving Iran. We were able to enter the bright lights of Raleigh-Durham Airport with a stir of excitement. We were returning to Chapel Hill after all, a place of memories, even if many were bad. Our closest friend there was Dr. Vakilzadeh, and he had come to greet us, his smiling face and dapper clothes comfortingly familiar. His sleek and shiny Oldsmobile was as big as a boat, swallowing us up without effort, bags and all.

It was an August night, and the smells and sounds I associated with America assailed me as soon as we left the airport: moisture hanging heavy in the air, the chirp of crickets, the scent of green growth. Homajoon told me to close the window—Dr. Vakilzadeh had the air-conditioning on. It took me a moment to figure out how to obey her, and Afsaneh and I watched with interest as the glass slid silently upward with the press of a button. I sat back against the chill leather, watching billboards flash by. The highway was brightly lit and smooth as silk. Soon road signs advertised the town of Chapel Hill, the university, the hospital. Before we could reach any of these familiar landmarks, the car left the highway for a wooded, affluent neighborhood at the edge of town. The Vakilzadehs' house was in Lake Forest, though not on the muddy brown lake itself. It stood on the slope of a small hill, surrounded by trees. The car pulled up under a streetlight, and we climbed out. Crossing the fragrant cedar walkway, waiting for the large wooden door to swing open, I felt suddenly hesitant and afraid.

A boy slightly older than I opened the door, welcoming us with a smile and polite greetings. His sister, Dr. Vakilzadeh's wife, Mina, was close behind him. We had last seen Mina-Khanoum during a visit to Tehran two years earlier. She greeted us in the foyer with warm embraces and the wide, vivid smile I remembered. Emerging from the perfumed folds of her caftan, Afsaneh and I looked around us with silent awe. The house was like the car, like America itself: shiny and wealthy and new. My eyes took in the mirror and glossy potted plants, smooth linoleum and gleaming appliances in the kitchen, a lime green carpet and banks of African violets in the greenhouse off the family room. In the high-ceilinged center of the house, a wall of glass revealed a redwood deck overlooking the woods. Nearby, a fountain was silent amid tropical plants. Later, I learned that Mina-Khanoum turned it on when she was entertaining. Muted light glowed softly on a big mural, painted in swirling oranges and browns, hanging over the sectional sofa. A baby, wrapped closely in blankets, slept on a burnt orange ottoman.

I felt dwarfed. My soul shrank within me, expanding a little only when I saw the baby. The Vakilzadehs' new son was the only thing in that room that did not seem alien to me. I gravitated immediately in his direction and sat, taking in the color scheme of my new life.

We found a house in Lake Forest on Honeysuckle Road, a long walk from the Vakilzadehs'. Mina-Khanoum took us shopping. We bought curved wooden chairs with orange and brown cushions to harmonize with the shag carpet in the family room, a canary yellow bedspread and matching mural for my parents' bedroom, a glass and chrome dining set for the kitchen. My sister and I had new sheets in bold floral patterns. Homajoon taught us to layer them under thin, fuzzy blankets made of some unnaturally soft synthetic fabric. We were to tuck them in at the base of our new beds. The sheets felt stiff against my skin, and the blankets never seemed to reach quite high enough. I quickly became accustomed to shimmying down in my bed so that I could stay warm. I never questioned that I had to make whatever adjustments were necessary to fit in this new life.

When September rolled around, Afsaneh was swallowed up on the verdant, teeming campus of the University of North Carolina. An orange bus peopled with strange, unfriendly faces took me to Chapel Hill High School. High school American-style was an endless series of shocks to my system. Used to standing up when the teacher walked into class, I marveled at the casual, dismissive attitude of my classmates. They chewed gum in class. They put their legs up on the desks. They seemed wholly unconstrained by the conventions familiar to me.

On the bus, I shuddered inwardly the first time a quiet, blond girl named Lisa, irritated over some minor issue, said the word "shit." I concluded that, contrary to appearances, she must not be a good girl. Profanity was a stranger to my vocabulary. In the cafeteria, I was shocked when I saw my classmate Samantha sit on a boy's lap. In the hallway I saw a boy and a girl entwined next to their lockers, kissing deeply, and felt rocked to my core.

It didn't matter that this second time in America I spoke English. If anything, my extensive vocabulary contributed to making me an outcast. I did not understand about fitting in, I did not know what it meant to be cool. I wore the wrong clothes—nylon knee-highs under my denim skirt, plain tops that revealed none of the fashion sense my classmates prized. I was earnest instead of nonchalant, jumping out of the bus to extinguish a smoking cigarette stub so that it wouldn't start a fire. My classmates drove cars on screeching tires and boasted of getting drunk on the weekends. As teenagers, they had done and seen things I would not have done and seen in a lifetime spent in Iran. I could not believe that in America children were allowed to drive, let alone partake of all those other unspeakables—sex and drugs and alcohol.

But in America childhood seemed to end early, to be replaced by a cultivated cynicism that masked both vulnerability and immaturity.

I was still a child, with a child's joy in simple pleasures and a secret delight in the safety of rules and restrictions. Going to high school in America felt like a violation of my childhood, an abrupt and painful loss of innocence.

I waited for the bus each day with anxiety knotting my stomach, resolving that today I would break through the wall that seemed to separate me from my classmates. I came home each afternoon, having failed, and sedated myself with endless episodes of *M*A*S*H* and *Gilligan's Island*. If I saw one of my classmates at the mall on the weekends, I walked the other way. The one Iranian I knew at school seemed to want nothing to do with me—he had been where I was not too long before, and he had no desire to go back. My closest friends were the characters on the television screen, Hawkeye and Radar and Gilligan. They were the only Americans I knew who seemed friendly and unthreatening.

My family fared no better. To this day, we do not talk of those first years in America. We do not acknowledge how they shaped us into what we are today. When a natural disaster hits, people talk for years about the height of the waves, the ferocity of the wind, the power of the earth tremor that remade the landscape of their lives. But the emotional disasters in our lives go largely unacknowledged, their repercussions unclaimed.

My family was wrenched from all that was loved and familiar, yet there were no rituals to mourn our loss, no baptism for the painful rebirth. Instead, we were driven to bury the evidence of our personal cataclysm. Our differentness was a taint that we carried. The consuming need to belong led us to purge ourselves of that which once made us who we were—our accents, our awkward clothes, our beliefs.

We were faced with an unspoken choice: to be alienated from the world around us or from our innermost selves.

☙

When we first moved to Chapel Hill, we saw America as an interlude in our Iranian lives. Homajoon and Baba planned to stay in North Carolina for a year, maybe two—just to see us settled, my father told us. Then they would return. After college—so the scenario went, although here my father's eyes showed fear and his words became overemphatic—we girls would return to Iran. We would get a Western education and put it to good use—in Iran.

We held on to that scenario long after we suspected in our hearts that there would be no return. We could not admit to ourselves that we had left it all behind for good—the house, the mountains, the people, the country we claimed as our own. Baba had been raised on the mantra of loving and serving Iran; he had tried to instill those values in us. As so often when one's choices diverge from one's beliefs, it was easier just to paper over the gap. So we continued to use the Iranian calendar. We ended long-distance phone conversations with the promise to visit—soon. We began sentences with the phrase: "When we go back."

At first we continuously juxtaposed our new life against the old. Iran was our primary frame of reference; America was full of oddities. In America, diners salted their watermelon instead of oranges. People wore torn clothes in the grocery store. Men tied their hair in pony-tails. Women smoked in public. The streetlight carried a deep yellow tint; so did the vanilla ice cream. The faces in the supermarket, the mall, the classrooms seemed pale and bland, somehow indistinguishable from one another.

Sometimes during the first year we were overcome by the futil-ity of holding onto the past. Iran was far away. My sister and I were misfits in school, my parents were heartsick and beleaguered and sud-denly a liability to their children, who longed to be absolved of the complexities of heritage. Piece by piece, we started letting go of the old and embracing the new. I bought a pair of rust-colored corduroys. My sister acquired, amid great family tension, a boyfriend. Homajoon started cultivating African violets. Baba unbent enough to venture out-doors in flipflops instead of proper shoes.

In time we became American in more substantial ways, in habits of thought and speech and expectation. By 1979, when I started col-lege, the feeling of being a foreigner, that churning nausea fed by fear and isolation, had begun to subside. The yellow tone of the streetlights, the taste of salted butter, the weekend trips to the mall, had become familiar. We kept our faces turned forward, and one day we crossed an invisible line so that when we looked back at the world we had left behind, it was across a widening gulf of space, time and culture.

For years I felt powerless to bridge this gulf. At my first newspaper job after college, friends told me with approval that I was "well adjusted," "Americanized." They could not see the Iranian in me. But with each year I became more aware of an inner schism. Deep inside, I could not forget that I began life as an Iranian.

In 1990, when I obtained the green card that cemented my foothold in the West and permitted travel to and from Iran, it was instinct that drove me to return. With that first trip back, I began the long, slow road toward resurrecting a buried self. And vowed I would never suffer that inner shriveling of an isolated core, the immigrant's small death, again.

Home

❧

SHADI ZIAEI

TAKE 1 — ½ WAY HOME

There's no place
Like home she says
Clicking her heels three times

In the dark
I click my heels
Rubber soul resists the hardwood
I lose my balance

TAKE 2 — ¼ WAY HOME

Home could be on Cherry Lane
On Camelback Road
On Manor Drive
Home is at the center
Home is at the heart of the matter
Arguments and all
Home is a four-letter word
Soft, scented, with a door
Home is an orange tree
A family of deer and a plastic dolphin
Home is love
Bus #11
Safeway and a stop sign
2% milk and Advil for pain

Home is not what was said
Home remains, perseveres, stays
Home   home   home
Love is a four-letter word
Home is a place where chairs and tables
And words
Don't stand in your way
Home is not physics
It's chemistry
Home is at the center
(I've said that)
Home is

TAKE 3—HOME

I say I'm renting a new home
Will you come and visit?
You'd love to you say
You really would
You'll bring the green tea ice cream you say

Me?
I can't wait to get home.

Persian Princess Insania

&

Leyla Momeny

*There are times when you want to be a
profusion of myths . . .*

—LALEH KHALILI, "IN EXILE"

I am america-girl:
britannica irania
persian princess insania
lavash skin, aquiline nose,
my heart emerged as a golden *oud,*
well-mannered and traveled,
have reached the skirts of esfahan
even arrived alongside my mother
where birthright yellow fish
swim in between my toes,
I was named after *bakhlava.*
born in iran
three years shy of the mighty *hijab*
my grandmother stole lust-filled glances
inside the emperor's gates.
two decades of shy smiling
have gotten me far—
my feet planted firmly
in waters of ambiguity
tell me you love me
without pomegranate-stained stones.
the men in my family
never learned how to cry

they built cities over their own dreams
engineers of a keener reason
rolex-wristed namesakes holding my hand,
nihilist-hedonist patriarchs taught me to fly!
my chastity, preserved.
twenty-two years
fermenting,
slow and depart
alongside this nile.
a secret spot under my spine
is targeted for assassinations,
shivering, deranged, hairs cocked,
caught in a world
of ancient goddesses,
I am limestone.
unveiled, arms wide,
a raven-haired pit
infected by trees.
I clung to tehrangeles
felt comfortable in leather,
even understood
the chinese, spanish, mexican faces
cemented on the silk roads.
and when the surrealists in my country
rejected the dead,
I watched their sons masturbate
with identity and isolation—
curious and detached,
I summoned a bloated airplane
to carry away their mothers . . .
and I, misplaced among arabs, latinas, *I-am-half* italians,
no longer believe in *us*.

Naderi

∞

AMY MOTLAGH

Only the café remains
as it was—the hotel, the garden
collapsed into decay, disuse.
Yet in that decay, outside windows
where old men sift
through leather cases for verse
scrawled on forgotten pages,
young pomegranates bud
still, water reflects
in the slim tiled pool
where my father plumbs
for a face, a younger face,
his own face of fifty years
past, the face the old Armenian waiter
inside remembers and awakens;
finds amidst the creases and flesh
the boy who favored café glace
and lingered, dreaming
of the trial by cobra.
Hedayat may have found the story here—
somewhere between the beaten wood
of the table and the bent light
refracted by uneven globes:
conceiving of the choices
men make, of the ways even
honorable men will betray
one another, those they love.

Where Does My Language Lie?

⤶

Zjaleh Hajibashi

pillow talk
muscled

swallows

the supple *s*
of
salaam

where I lie with which language
unspeakable
duplicity

                                         took me

draws me

twice
subdued

deep into my other tongue's mouth another tongue
mine

to   mute

not saying
this
not
saying

Inheritance

✂

Mitra Parineh

They are antique coins, strapped on, zigzag dancing in the street, fallen change from a pocket. They are bronze, slip-in-strap-around high heels I aim to balance in as I step quickly, hum the national anthem, mouth open, the smell of gin hot and sweet on my tongue. They take me away, lightning bolts flashing against pavement, leaving invisible slashes on the sidewalk where each foot strikes restless. They are exactly my age, gems from my mother, her footprints still outlined in the heel and toe of the shoes that slap like open palms on a table as the men bang, bang the dice against the *takhteh.* They are my inheritance, bought for one thousand francs in 1979 on the honeymoon when she fled, married, bred, and died in the same year. They are the only reason I have come, three weeks in this heat that has no breeze, no cool shade that relieves, no place for a woman to doff the scarf and pull her hair up high, away from the neck, the sweat on her back and face.

Khaleh, Auntie, gave me piles of things that were my mother's— but the shoes are all I take with me, all I will take home besides the sound, the laughter of men, everywhere, enjoying life as they play backgammon in the basement tea-houses, late into the night, sneak brandy under their coats, share stiff drags from the *ghalyoun,* and hesitate before passing the hookah to me.

Tehran. I can't even say it without sounding like a *kharejee,* a foreigner who can't do the rough *kh* in the back of her throat or the light *eh* (T*eh*ran) pushed like a sigh from the sides of her mouth. My mother was born here, and pretty much, she died here. At least I know she wanted to die here. But Daddy talked her out of it, in Spain and France and Italy and Portugal; he said, "you will love it." She told him about her bad feeling, kept lighting incense, insisted that, despite the revolt, home was where she needed to be. But he brought her to Washington, D.C., instead, and I was dragged out of her womb, crushed up between the metal, ripped open by surgical sheers, encompassed by hands waiting to pull me out where the pump had stopped working. Everything was covered in blood: seat, skirt, stockings, and the bronze-beige high-heel shoes. Khaleh tried to clean them, but couldn't erase the toe and heel marks where the blood had stained to show the exact size and shape of her feet. So she took them back with her, to Iran, to where my mother had so wanted to go. Of course, my mother couldn't know that the place she begged to go, home, had died around the same time the blue Honda missed the red light and sped into the passenger's side of their car, causing her to scream out *Laleh*.

Or at least Daddy says that is how it all happened. And how I was named.

They are a little loose around my ankles, a little narrow at the toes. But I wear them anyway. I like the feeling of history tied to my feet. Nothing like the expensive vintage we buy back home, where the history is never your own. Nothing like the cheap secondhand stuff that we (my friends and I) wouldn't dare buy. This is my mother, strapped to my feet for my last night in her city where it is so damn hot.

Instead of smoking *ghalyoun* tonight, listening to the smash of the dice against the broad board, waiting for the laughter to ripple on each man's lips, I am going to a party. There will be parties at nearly every other house in the whole city, as there are each night, with tea, liquor, watermelon, children sleeping on laps, teenagers watching MTV on illegal satellite, discussing American politics, putting aside their studies for one (but just one) night. The parks will be filled with picnicking families until one, two, three in the morning, even though it is a Tuesday (it means nothing here to be a weekday, a weekend).

And the tea-houses, built below ground to keep the customers cool, will be filled with the regular company that I usually join several times a week, watching as they play their games, drink, smoke, smile, and occasionally invite me to play a round. I always lose, without a chance that I will bring even one of my pieces home in time. And the conversation is always a hushed buzz, as I ask about the same stuff: their wives, daughters, and women's politics. They nod, somberly, you are right, are right, and suck the sweet-flavored tobacco from the hookah. Nothing ever goes anywhere and I never win a game.

That's why I've decided that a party, for the last night, is the thing to do. Ease out quietly, before anyone notices I was here. Watch MTV as if I am almost home. Help the women pour tea.

So I am surprised when I find myself drunk on gin and running from a tea-house at five A.M. I expected to go back to Khaleh's early, sleep, and leave for the airport in the morning. But now I've done it, what she begged me not to do since the day I set foot in the crowded, smelly city, determined to walk the three miles from the airport to home in the midday heat, refusing to board the back of the bus. (We couldn't get a cab.)

—Khaleh! I tried to explain. We did this with black people, in our country, a long time ago! How can you be serious? I will not ride that fucking bus!

I went on like this, shouting, crying a little, so hot I didn't know what to do with my swollen fingers and red face. Khaleh grabbed my wrist and spun me towards her.

—Stop it. This is not your country. This is not your people.

She said it in English, the best she knew how. Her eyes begged me: behave, try. So I rode the bus, sat behind the bar that divided men from women, crying the short trip home as other passengers stared— a full-grown girl, tear-streaked and sobbing into the shrouded neck of her old auntie. For shame, they whispered in the ears of their children who sat in their laps like little angels, still and quiet.

After that day, I did try. Mostly. So how I ended up at the tea-house tonight and then drunk on the street was accidental, and only a little purposeful. Accidental, because we didn't mean to run into the girls intentionally, and purposeful, because I did follow them after the run-in. I was with Shohreh, a girl my aunt had introduced to me as the Shah's niece (no one seemed to know or care about royalty anymore). Shohreh is round and beautiful with ivory skin that looks thick and smooth as butter and eyes so big and expressive and sexy, they make me blush just to look at them (the eyes everywhere here are like that, so I am blushing a lot). In the past three weeks, she has taken me out (restaurants, parties, parks, pizza shops), listened to me cry (I hate this fucking place and the heat), answered my questions (How do you live here? Like this?), and pretended Mexican food sounded appealing when I described it (God, for one burrito, I would just about die, die, die).

She made a special request to her black-market delivery man who rang the bell weekly with offerings of liquor, American videos, banned magazines, and books. She ordered and paid extra for gin, an American favorite, right? When I arrived at her house tonight, she told me her parents were in Shomal, the north of Iran, for the weekend. So there would be no tea pouring; it was just us young people.

❦

There are ten of us, all in our late teens or early twenties, watching *American Pie*. At every scene, someone laughs but doesn't get the joke, so they ask me, is it a really like that? Then they laugh when I explain, even if the joke still doesn't make sense, because it can't all be translated. We drink gin, eat the horrible pizza Shohreh's bought (no one else thinks it's horrible, but Iranians really can't make pizza), and then we dance. We have to keep the music low, of course, but no one minds. When Green Day comes on, I start to cry and explain how in the States, everyone our age, and younger and older, knows every word to the song that is playing. I sing it loudly, as if it will start to mean for them what it does for me. Then I realize it is mostly just memories, not meaning in the lyrics, and then I can let it go and dry my face and dance some more.

We put on Persian music and shake our hips and hands and the other girls are so beautiful that instead of dancing I can only stare stare stare. Then it is two A.M., and all us girls tie the scarves over our heads and, despite the heat, pull the mandatory ponchos or light wraps about our frames and hug and laugh and say good-bye. The boys wait cordially at the door and we all kiss cheek-to-cheek, before departing.

When everyone turns to leave, Shohreh tugs at my hand, telling me to stay. We talk and clean together (though she doesn't really let me clean) and she pours the remaining gin into a small flask that she sneaks into my coat pocket. For your trip back to America, she says, and then offers to walk me home.

—I will walk you.

—Don't be silly. It is only a few blocks.

—I insist.

—Shohreh, no, you don't have to.

—*Ta'rof nakon!*

—*Ta'rof nakon!*

We carry on like this for five minutes. (I have mastered the *ta'rof*:

I can insist on being cordial and resist being a burden as well as any of them. Would you like some tea? Oh, nono, thank you. Would you like some sweets? Oh, nono, nono! And after the third or fourth or sixth time, a polite, very timid, if you insist, my pleasure, oh my, and hand-made cookies, aren't they? And where do you buy your tea leaves? So good, I can't believe it! This must be *chai sonati*—authentic, traditional tea—from a special store?)

Finally, Shohreh wins, and walks me the three blocks to Khaleh's house. On the corner of her street, we see them. A gang of girls, smooth like water, seemingly chilly in the evening that is still burning hot. The heat doesn't seem to affect them, cause a single one to ripple a hand out of place to smooth back a sweaty strand of hair that might have escaped its holdings and landed on her face. They stand tall in their high heels, hold their painted fingernails to their mouths, and wear bright blouses and jeans. They look just ordinary to me. Shohreh has to point it out.

Their hair falls in long waves down their backs, not peeking out from the edge of the *hijab,* a defiant and unabashed challenge to the *pasdars* who sit holding their guns in their boy arms, waiting—it isn't just a few inches, highlighted strands teasing passersby, testing the morality of men, who are too weak to control their desires. It is free in all its villainy, the hair, luscious, sexual, raw, begging for rape, begging for the immorality of men, burning desires into their otherwise chaste heads. These girls stand scarf-free, laughing like men on the streets of Tehran. Of course, I have to follow them.

∽

Shohreh wants to leave immediately, as soon as she catches sight of them. She refuses to follow the girls who linger, already unveiled as if they are indoors, safe.

—They are really bad news, Laleh. Please go to your *khaleh's* house. Don't be ridiculous, you are almost home. Just go.

I tell her I can't do that, this is what I have come for (or suddenly, it seems like what I have come for). So we hug, a quick hug, two kisses, and a final look that says "be safe." Then she leaves me on the street corner where I have no fear of being mugged or murdered, but perhaps dragged to prison for indecency (the shoes are sandals, after all). Looking at these girls, however, I doubt the *pasdars* would come for me first.

I want to say hello, but I can't. So I wait, staring, and then I realize I do know one of them, a tall girl with orangish hair. At the same time, she recognizes me, and embarrassed, I turn to leave. But she calls to me, says she remembers meeting me at her grandmother's house, and do I want to come with them? They're going to have fun. My palms sweat a little when I say yes.

We walk just around the corner, opposite Khaleh's house. It is obvious now that they've removed their wraps because they are almost at their destination (I presume a house, because otherwise, what are they undressing for?). So they don't really walk the streets bareheaded; I am a little disappointed. But once inside, our destination more than makes up for my dismay: it is not a home. One of the girls smiles and winks at a man who opens the door, and we step into a tea-house. It is more traditional looking than the others, with cushions on the floors that are covered, corner to corner, with Persian rugs. Smaller rugs and tapestries hang on the walls, old paintings wither in the corners, the *ghalyoun* a customer smokes from looks antique. This is their secret, a place where their wraps can come off though they are technically in "public."

There are four of us: Shayna, Layla, Mana, and me. The one I know is Shayna: tan, tall, smells like strong perfume, shakes her orange head when she laughs. She has dyed her hair in an effort to match her eyes which are a color we don't have at home. Something between gold and fire. She likes to smoke cigarettes. Layla, short, plump, and very pale, asks the questions.

—So you are American, right?

—Yes.

—And your parents are both Iranian?

—Yes. But I don't know my mom. She died. My dad raised me.

The small pendant of a man-bird hanging from my necklace catches her attention.

—You are wearing a Faravahar—fashion?

—No, I really am Zoroastrian.

—Oh, are you? How cool!

There is a pause, so I ask a question in return.

—Are you girls Muslim?

They all laugh. Layla plays with her frizzy, syrup-colored hair.

—Your name is Laleh, right? Laleh *joon,* my dear. No one is really Muslim.

And this is how the evening goes. Mana is the smartest, constantly sarcastic. She is milky-skinned, black-haired, serious looking. She talks only sometimes, offers me hashish, laughs when I refuse. She is impressed when I pull the gin from my pocket and we girls share. Shayna is the pretty one, Mana the smart one, Layla the social one. That's how I figure them in my head. That's all I have time for.

Then the boys come. Cyrus and Moussa, both short, dark, one very handsome, one not. Both greet me with a handshake, and settle onto the cushions beside us. In this tea-house, the manager does not stare when Moussa takes Shayna's hand, or Cyrus tickles Mana, who slaps him away. The only other customers appear to be regulars as well, private clients in this pseudo-public place.

They don't ask many questions about America. It seems they've all been there before. Instead we talk about fashion, movies, music. They ask if I am having a good time. They tell me my Farsi is very good and then they speak many words in English. I am practicing the word *khanoum,* lady, when the *pasdars* arrive.

When the *pasdars* come, it is confusing, because I can't tell in what order it all happens. The gin makes it this way, but also I lose track when the small tea table that reaches just up to our knees is kicked in by one of the officers until it breaks. And I do not know if he grabs for Mana's hair and she screams or if he fires a warning shot against the wall that splatters Moussa's shoulder and makes him fall soft and quiet against my legs—which comes first, I mean, I'm not sure. But now they leave with the money they have come for—apparently the tea-house is behind on its payments to the *pasdars* (or else they aren't and the *pasdars* are just being greedy, who can tell?)—and the people in the room come rushing like rain down a pipe, sitting Moussa up against my feet and shins, cooling his face with a cloth, applying a towel and steady pressure to the wound as they force minty tea and rosewater cookies into his mouth. He needs sugar in his blood to keep him going, they all say. He needs a hospital, Shayna murmurs. The short, balding owner of the tea-house runs for his car keys, yells at us to keep pressure on the towel and the boy will be fine. Sometime soon after, I begin to run.

My feet press hard against them, dark, dirty coins, passed from hand to hand. The bronze edges are brown, mud-caked, bloodied. Khaleh catches me as I am on my way out. She can only guess what has happened as she looks me up and down, eyes pausing at my toes that are rosy and blistered from the running. She says nothing, but kisses my cheeks and pushes me through the door, towards the cab that waits in the street.

—I'm sorry, Khaleh, I begin to tell her. She shakes her head. Either there is no time or no need; I'm not sure which.

—Ay, Khaleh, she says to me and sighs big. I am listening carefully, hoping she'll say something, and it occurs to me for the first time: why we do this in Farsi? I call her Khaleh, Auntie, and she calls me Khaleh back. I think of my father. Baba, Daddy. Baba *joon*, he calls me, Daddy dear. They reverse the casual term of endearment and it becomes that—endearing, affectionate.

I smell the incense from inside; she's been praying over it to ward off the evil eye, and scare away bad feelings. Khaleh's hands flutter only a little at my shoulders as she ushers me out, back to my people.

❧

She screamed out *Laleh*. My name. It means Tulip. All the beauty and freshness in the world was what she wanted for me with a name like that. Or that's what my auntie says when I call her on a perfect day to say hello from California.

Revolution 1979

❧

TARA BAHRAMPOUR

"Iran has become heaven,"
the schoolteacher wrote
to her older son in America.

During the night
people left their doors unlocked
so wounded students could find shelter.
In the end
the soldiers simply shot into the air.
The country hugged them.

But then the arrests and killings began.
"Allah-o-Akbar" still echoed from the rooftops
but now it had an ominous tone.
When the schoolteacher's younger son climbed up to the roof
she screamed at him to get down—
the war started; he left for Los Angeles.

"Before the revolution,"
she writes to him now
"a kilo of rice went for 6 toumans.
Now it is 900."

Portland, Oregon 1979

∽

TARA BAHRAMPOUR

After the revolution
we stopped our car in a cul-de-sac.
Our neighbors were the Davisons,
the Pattinsons, and the Magnusons.
I babysat Lindsay and Courtney,
and Debbie and Dave's baby Daniel,
blond, blond, blond
babies came in twos and fours
each with a hand to hold.

Even the dogs lived the good life,
taking off in a pack across the sloping park
stealing a chicken off Mrs. Lee's counter
sleeping on asphalt.
When I crested the hill after school
their heads rose—
black Hedwig, long ears perked
unable to believe it
leaped up each day to embrace me.

My father had no job
My father had too many jobs
draftsman, carpenter, draftsman again.
But often he was home all day
the paper spread open, a pen in his hand.

The Magnusons' father
went every morning to Magnuson's, the Men's Shop.

The Davisons' father was gone all day too.
The mothers made pies and casseroles
while we, watched over by the dogs,
played kick-the-can and hide-and-seek until dark.

That was how it was
raspberries in the yard, blackberries in the park.
Hedwig came home once with her nails painted pink,
the little girls up the street giggling.
One winter an ice storm froze us in
the trees crystalline
the dads tried to get their cars up the hill,
starting all the way back, revving their engines
only to slide back down to us
zipped into our coats
shaking diamonds off the branches.

Back in our old neighborhood, uncles were being arrested.
Cousins dressed as sheep
escaped on hands and knees over the Pakistan border
to avoid the war.
Here in America, in states that started with I or O,
students were beaten, insulted,
put on planes back to Iran.

But I worried most about my father
not going to work
and my mother
not making pies
or cleaning house much.

Years after Hedwig died (fenced up in a California backyard)
I went back to Portland for a reading.

People at the bookstore lined up
I heard giggles—and then,
"She looks the same!"

It was the Magnusons, or half of them—
Lindsay and her mom
still blond and shining
grinning like conspirators.
I asked about Courtney (who was in college)
and Mr. Magnuson—they rolled their eyes—
he'd left years ago.

"You know I always envied you guys," Lindsay said.
"I loved to go to your house.
It was so bohemian and interesting
and free."

She'd envied us,
who'd moved out of the cul-de-sac
after only three years.
We'd run out of money
and none of my sobbing or vows to stay
could stop us.

Lindsay said, "Oh, you know we moved soon after you did."
The Magnusons had gone a few streets over
and then, soon after,
left the neighborhood forever.

Blue house
Ghost of a briefcase
Raspberry pies

With a Little Help from My Friends
(from *Funny in Farsi*)

✆

FIROOZEH DUMAS

I was lucky to have come to America years before the upheaval in Iran. The Americans we encountered were kind and curious, unafraid to ask questions and willing to listen. As soon as I spoke enough English to communicate, I found myself being interviewed nonstop by children and adults alike. My life became one long-running *Oprah* show, minus the free luxury accommodations in Chicago, and Oprah.

On the topic of Iran, American minds were tabulae rasae. Judging from the questions asked, it was clear that most Americans in 1972 had never heard of Iran. We did our best to educate. "You know Asia? Well, you go south at the Soviet Union and there we are." Or we'd try to be more bucolic, mentioning being south of the beautiful Caspian Sea, "where the famous caviar comes from." Most people in Whittier did not know about the famous caviar and once we explained what it was, they'd scrunch up their faces. "Fish eggs?" they would say. "Gross." We tried mentioning our proximity to Afghanistan or Iraq, but it was no use. Having exhausted our geographical clues, we would say, "You've heard of India, Japan, or China? We're on the same continent."

We had always known that ours is a small country and that America is very big. But even as a seven-year-old, I was surprised that so many Americans had never noticed us on the map. Perhaps it's like driving a Yugo and realizing that the eighteen-wheeler can't see you.

In Iran, geography is a requirement in every grade. Since the government issues textbooks, every student studies the same material in the same grade. In first-grade geography, I had to learn the shape of Iran and the location of its capital, Tehran. I had to memorize that we shared borders with Turkey, Afghanistan, Pakistan, Iraq, and the USSR. I also knew that I lived on the continent of Asia.

None of the kids in Whittier, a city an hour outside of Los Angeles, ever asked me about geography. They wanted to know about more important things, such as camels. How many did we have back home? What did we feed them? Was it a bumpy ride? I always disappointed them by admitting that I had never seen a camel in my entire life. And as far as a ride goes, our Chevrolet was rather smooth. They reacted as if I had told them that there really was a person in the Mickey Mouse costume.

We were also asked about electricity, tents, and the Sahara. Once again, we disappointed, admitting that we had electricity, that we did not own a tent, and that the Sahara was on another continent. Intent to remedy the image of our homeland as backward, my father took it upon himself to enlighten Americans whenever possible. Any unsuspecting American who asked my father a question received, as a bonus, a lecture on the successful history of the petroleum industry in Iran. As my father droned on, I watched the faces of these kind Americans, who were undoubtedly making mental notes never to talk to a foreigner again.

My family and I wondered why Americans had such a mistaken image of Iran. We were offered a clue one day by a neighbor, who told us that he knew about Iran because he had seen *Lawrence of Arabia*. Whoever Lawrence was, we had never heard of him, we said. My father then explained that Iranians are an Indo-European people; we are not Arabs. We do, however, have things in common with Saudi Arabia, he continued: "Islam and petroleum." "Now, I won't bore you with religion," he said, "but let me tell you about the petroleum industry."

∞

Another neighbor, a kindly old lady who taught me how to take care of indoor plants, asked whether we had many cats back home. My father, with his uncanny ability to forge friendships, said, "We don't keep pets in our homes. They are dirty." "But your cats are so beautiful!" our neighbor said. We had no idea what she was talking about. Seeing our puzzled expressions, she showed us a picture of a beautiful long-haired cat. "It's a Persian cat," she said. That was news to us; the only cats we had ever seen back home were the mangy strays that ate scraps behind people's houses. From that day, when I told people I was from Iran, I added, "where Persian cats come from." That impressed them.

I tried my best to be a worthy representative of my homeland, but, like a Hollywood celebrity relentlessly pursued by paparazzi, I sometimes got tired of the questions. I, however, never punched anybody with my fists; I used words. One boy at school had a habit of asking me particularly stupid questions. One day he inquired about camels, again. This time, perhaps foreshadowing a vocation in storytelling, I told him that, yes, we had camels, a one-hump and a two-hump. The one-hump belonged to my parents and the two-humps was our family station wagon. His eyes widened.

"Where do you keep them?" he asked.

"In the garage, of course," I told him.

Having heard what he wanted to hear, he ran off to share his knowledge with the rest of the kids on the playground. He was very angry once he realized that I had fooled him, but at least he never asked me another question.

Often kids tried to be funny by chanting, "I ran to I-ran, I ran to I-ran." The correct pronunciation, I always informed them, is "Ee-rahn." "I ran" is a sentence, I told them, as in "I ran away from my geography lesson."

Older boys often asked me to teach them "some bad words in your language." At first, I politely refused. My refusal merely increased their determination, so I solved the problem by teaching them phrases like *man kharam,* which means "I'm an idiot." I told them that what I was teaching them was so nasty that they would have to promise never to repeat it to anyone. They would then spend all of recess running around yelling, "I'm an idiot! I'm an idiot!" I never told them the truth. I figured that someday, somebody would.

But almost every person who asked us a question asked with kindness. Questions were often followed by suggestions to visit in California. At school, the same children who inquired about camels also shared their food with me. "I bet you've never tried an Oreo! Have one," or "My mom just baked these peanut butter cookies and she sent you one." Kids invited me to their houses to show me what their rooms looked like. On Halloween, one family brought over a costume, knowing that I would surely be the only kid in the Halloween parade without one. If someone had been able to encapsulate the kindness of these second-graders in pill form, the pills would undoubtedly put many war correspondents out of business.

After almost two years in Whittier, my father's assignment was completed and we had to return home. The last month of our stay, I attended one slumber party after another, all thrown in my honor. This avalanche of kindness did not make our impending departure any easier. Everyone wanted to know when we would come back to America. We had no answer, but we invited them all to visit us in Iran. I knew no one would ever take us up on our offer, because Iran was off the radar screen for most people. My friends considered visiting their grandmothers in Oregon to be a long trip, so visiting me in Iran was like taking a left turn at the next moon. It wasn't going to happen. I didn't know then that I would be returning to America about two years later.

Between frenzied shopping trips to Sears to buy presents for our relatives back home, my mother spent her last few weeks giving gifts to our American friends. I had wondered why my mother had brought so many Persian handicrafts with her; now I knew. Everyone, from my teachers to the crossing guard to the Brownie leader to the neighbors, received something. "Dees eez from my countay-ree. Es-pay-shay-ley for you," she would explain. These handicrafts, which probably turned up in garage sales the following year, were received with tears and promises to write.

My mother was particularly sad to return to Iran. I had always assumed that she would be relieved to return to her family and to a land where she spoke the language and didn't need me to act as her interpreter. But I realized later that even though my mother could not understand anything the crossing guard, Mrs. Popkin, said, she understood that this woman looked out for me. And she understood her smiles. Even though my mother never attended a Brownie meeting, she knew that the leader, Carrie's mom, opened up her home to us every week and led us through all kinds of projects. No one paid her for this. And my mother knew that when it had been my turn to bring snacks for the class, one of the moms had stepped in and baked cupcakes. My best friend Connie's older sister, Michele, had tried to teach me to ride a bike, and Heather's mom, although single with two daughters, had hosted me overnight more times than I can remember. Even though I had been the beneficiary of all the attention, my mother, watching silently from a distance, had also felt the warmth of generosity and kindness. It was hard to leave.

∽

When my parents and I get together today, we often talk about our first year in America. Even though thirty years have passed, our memories have not faded. We remember the kindness more than ever, knowing that our relatives who immigrated to this country after the Iranian revolution did not encounter the same America. They saw Americans who had bumper stickers on their cars that read "Iranians: Go Home" or "We Play Cowboys and Iranians." The Americans they met rarely invited them to their houses. These Americans felt that they knew all about Iran and its people, and they had no questions, just opinions. My relatives did not think Americans were very kind.

Another Quiet New Year
(Tehran, January 2004)

⁜

Nika Khanjani

It's 10:01 P.M. and everyone in the house is already asleep. This will be my second New Year's that has slipped by without fanfare and for which I'll probably be asleep when the clock strikes.

The streets, though, were bustling. After dinner I decided to save money and walk home—the weather was nice and the young hipsters paraded around in the latest styles. A cab drove up and offered to take me the whole way for a very good price. I made the ceremonial "that's too expensive!" face and said I didn't need a ride. But it *was* getting late and I had a stack of work to finish. Then he lowered the price.

He drove an old Peykon, the Iranian national car, white like most of the others. Unlike the others, though, his was spotless and the upholstery was intact. He offered to roll up the window if I was cold. I'm okay, thanks. I figured he'd light a cigarette so I preferred the window down. He said something about the streets being unusually busy tonight. It hadn't occurred to him that New Year's energy in much of the world had seeped through Iran's semi-permeable membrane and driven the restless to the streets.

He drove like a Canadian—signaling before switching lanes, stopping completely at red lights and to let pedestrians cross. He didn't cut anyone off, didn't come to any grinding halts, and he didn't scream insults. I don't think he even honked his horn. I was relieved that he wasn't peering at me through the rearview mirror but kept his eyes steady on the road ahead, occasionally turning his gray head to the left or right to check for oncoming cars. It was a few minutes into the ride before it occurred to me that I wasn't digging my nails into the palm of my hand, my typical reflex when I'm in a cab in Tehran. This, I said to myself, was a first.

To my surprise, he didn't even assault me with weird questions except to ask if my destination was, in fact, the amusement park—the landmark by our house that I usually tell cab drivers.

"Actually, I'm going a little ways into Evin, just up the hill."

"Very well."

What? No haggling for a higher fee? My driver was a cross between Gandhi and Yoda.

My car experiences in Iran often result in near-to-fully-realized freak-outs. Something is always going wrong, or feels like it will any second. Either I'm wedged between two huge, burly men, with one of them asking me if I'm "available" while the other inches his fingers closer to my leg, or the driver is gripped in a screaming match with a car that just cut him off while his cigarette loosens ashes and smoke directly into my face. In especially uncomfortable moments, I make a mental list of the contents in my bag—I think through what I have that could possibly be used to identify my disfigured body. Or I check to see that I have enough money to catch another cab because I'm planning my escape from the one I'm in. This time, though, I was practicing what to say because I wanted to give him a generous tip and thank him for such a pleasant ride. I had to practice saying this in my head because, after all these years of not speaking Farsi, my mother tongue felt more like my second cousin's half sister.

A while back, I learned that if I want to point out something positive—like a subtle gesture that would normally be overlooked—it's best to be *very* specific. To say, "That was nice!" or "Thanks for being so sweet" is not as effective a technique for reinforcing good behavior as something like, "Gosh, it was a very tactful how you pointed out that her skirt was tucked into her pantyhose" or "What a well-crafted and concise message you left on my voicemail . . ." To encourage good behavior, we have to train ourselves to spot it and articulate it immediately to the person caught in the act. That way, maybe they'll repeat it.

So there I sat, thinking of how to say, "I really appreciate how well you maintained your car," "I wanted to thank you for being such a conscientious driver," "Your high professional standards are commendable!" But, unfortunately, in most languages I learn the bad words first. I can spew rapid-fire complaints and insults, surprising myself as much as the unsuspecting offender. "Look, you unshaven baboon, if you can't drive a goddamn car without steamrolling two cats and grazing an old lady, getting us lost *and* making me an hour late, then be prepared to foot my hairdresser's bill for what it's going to cost me to cover the grays I got riding in your diesel-spitting heap of shit." As it was, I was searching my mind for the Persian translation of *conscientious, commendable,* and *appreciate.*

Instead, I thought of only my usual gratitudes: "Thank you for not asking if I'm married" and "I'm so happy that I'm not dead." We were getting closer to my stop and I could see the top of the Ferris wheel of Shahreh Bazi, suspended in motion for the winter.

He drove without my guidance and soon we arrived at the top of my street. I pointed to the pizza shop where I would get out. I fumbled through my wallet for two touman, instead of the one-fifty we had agreed on, and when I handed it over to him I said, "Don't need any change, thanks."

"*Khodah barekat bedeh,*" he replied. "May God shower you with blessings."

And as I opened the door, I took a deep breath, collected myself, and did the best I could at that moment.

"Tonight was the first time that my nerves were not wrecked in a cab—thank you for driving like a Canadian and have a happy New Year."

My Brother at the Canadian Border

❧

SHOLEH WOLPÉ

For Omid

On their way to Canada in a red Mazda, my brother and his friend, Ph.D.'s and little sense, stopped at the border and the guard leaned forward, asked: *Where you boys heading?* My brother, *Welcome to Canada* poster in his eyes, replied: *Mexico.* The guard blinked, stepped back then forward, said: *Sir, this is the Canadian border.* My brother turned to his friend, grabbed the map from his hands, slammed it on his shaved head. *You stupid idiot,* he yelled, *you've been holding the map upside down.*

In the interrogation room full of metal desks and chairs with wheels that squeaked and fluorescent light humming, bombarded with questions, and finally: *Race?* Stymied, my brother confessed: *I really don't know, my parents never said,* and the woman behind the desk widened her blue eyes to take in my brother's olive skin, hazel eyes, the blond fur that covered his arms and legs. Disappearing behind a plastic partition, she returned with a dusty book, thick as *War and Peace,* said: *This will tell us your race. Where was your father born?* she asked, putting on her horn-rimmed glasses. *Persia,* he said. *Do you mean I-ran?*

I ran, you ran, we all ran, he smiled. *Where's your mother from?* Voice cold as a gun. *Russia,* he replied. She put one finger on a word above a chart in the book, the other on a word at the bottom of the page, brought them together looking like a mad mathematician bent on solving the crime of zero times zero divided by one. Her fingers stopped on a word. Declared: *You are white.*

My brother stumbled back, a hand on his chest, eyes wide, mouth in an O as in *O my God! All these years and I did not know.* Then to the room, to the woman and the guards: *I am white I can go anywhere Do anything I can go to Canada and pretend it's Mexico At last, I am white and you have no reason to keep me here.*

1979

❧

PAZ

Nineteen seventy-nine was the year that was the beginning of the end and the beginning of a new beginning. The Democrats were about to lose their hold on the White House and Reaganomics would soon become an unavoidable reality. *Nightline* was born that year. It was created as a means to keep the American public glued to their TV sets as daily countdowns were broadcast of the Iranian hostage crisis: day 10, day 55, day 126! Ratings skyrocketed as repeating images of the wild-eyed, flag-burning natives of Iran with their barbaric black beards and their black-veiled, machine-gun-toting women became a common, almost expected sight on the nightly news. It was the year my parents had to make a painful decision: return to Iran, return to their families, return to the upper-class wealth and property that was rightly theirs, or stay in the United States, give up all their wealth, give up their families, but avoid the war with Iraq, avoid the political upheaval, avoid Khomeini. This was also the year that the golden age of my childhood was tarnished, the year I lost my innocence on many levels, the year I experienced hatred for the first time, and the year that my blossoming queer sexuality was effectively extinguished for a very long time.

I was seven going on thirty when my world shifted dramatically. I had worked hard to establish myself socially and academically within the microcosm of my little world in Arizona. Earlier that year, I had victoriously won the award for being the top student in reading/writing and subsequently won the love and respect (not to mention a box of chocolates) of my sweet, redheaded teacher, Mrs. Cope. Not a bad feat for an immigrant child who had just three years prior rolled into the dusty town of Phoenix, Arizona, squashed in the back of her parents' rust orange Camaro. I didn't have a clue that my life was about to change. After my first traumatic day in kindergarten, I was determined to conquer my surroundings and take control of my murky destiny. I spent what felt like eternity that first day, looking in horror at all the pale, fair-haired aliens surrounding me, muttering gibberish and eating what looked like dry cardboard squares dipped in milk. I wasn't sure if *they* were the freaks or if *I* was . . . but I wasn't going to take any chances. Immediately, I began assimilating to my new surroundings. With an almost obsessive frenzy, I read everything around me: shampoo bottles, Pennysavers, cracker boxes, junk mail, my mother's secret hair-dye containers (that none of us were supposed to know about), anything at all.

Subsequently, I became the eyes and ears of my parents. Even though I was only five or six years old, it was I who would go up to store clerks to ask where the frozen lima beans were kept; I who would be the interpreter in the emergency room when my baby brother's appendix burst; I who would order everyone's meals at McDonald's. My parents had not yet accepted the fact that fate had landed them indefinitely in a country where they did not speak the language, understand the culture, or abide by the Christian laws of the land. This denial of the fact that they might never again return to or live in their beautiful homeland bore deep into their psyches and crippled their ability to adjust and acclimate to their new surroundings. It also, unfortunately, spilled over into how they chose to raise me. They were blind to the fact that I was desperately trying to belong, assimilate, and become one with the new world they had thrust me into. But despite the obstacles that their old world values and rules created for me, I was determined to thrive in the rich land of opportunity that had been opened up in front of me.

My parents had set up what would be one of a series of temporary housing situations for us in low-income, predominately white neighborhoods. Within weeks of our frequent moves, I would have generally made my rounds of the community playgrounds and would have established myself as the wild-eyed gypsy-child who got everyone to pull down their pants in the sandbox to compare notes, so to speak. I always tried to hide my "foreignness" by attempting to mask it, though sometimes the English language would foil my plans. Like the day I returned to school after being sick only to find out that a makeup test did not mean I was going to get graded on how well I could apply lipstick to my tiny mouth. Or when I eagerly volunteered to go into a "booby trap" that my pals had set up in an alleyway only to find out that this had absolutely nothing to do with tits, which is what I was hoping to find waiting for me on the other side of the fence.

It was not only my academic world that had begun to thrive by the time I was in second grade, circa 1979. My social life outside of school was becoming more and more intriguing as well, as I explored uncharted territories in the innocent yet forbidden realms of human sexuality. This was a time in my life when I had no concept of shame, guilt, or fear about anything. I started to have "special" girlfriends. Looking back, we had no idea how taboo our relationships with each other were. We just knew that we had some need, desire to touch, explore, play. We would congregate behind the sour orange trees with the whitewashed trunks that lined the perimeter of our apartment complex. I always imagined the white tree trunks as proper ladies wearing long, white gloves—prim, chaste, and quite unapproachable. We were constantly being warned by the old ladies in the neighborhood not to eat the fruit—that we would get sick if we sank our teeth into the sourly bitter flesh of the "ornamental" orange trees, as they were called. So naturally, we found the shade and pungent smell of rotting oranges a welcome haven for our fumbling explorations.

Oblivious to how taboo and forbidden our explorations were, one very knowledgeable older friend, who was in fourth grade, suggested we take our experimentations to my unlocked bedroom. We would casually enter my apartment from the back patio, pass my parents who were glued to the TV set, tears running down from their eyes as the daily news of tragedy from Iran ignited new grief in them. In the privacy of my small bedroom, Becky opened my eyes to things I had never imagined. One of my favorite memories is of the time when Becky showed me how to use a red, plastic Barbie golf club to get myself off, and then subsequently to get her off as well. After we were done playing in the lazy, sun-strewn desert afternoons, we would then slip away to Becky's apartment to eat an early American supper. I was always especially excited when her mom served us pork chops with applesauce, or boiled sausages and sauerkraut. I viewed these meals as not only exotic but also forbidden, which only made me want to eat them with a more voracious appetite.

I may have been completely unaware of how inappropriate my sexual relationships would seem to my parents, but I was completely aware that I was breaking the rules big-time by eating pork! Pigs were *haram,* or forbidden, in Islamic law and even the idea of petting a pig, much less eating one, was considered completely repulsive. Later in life, I would find out that my desire for women was even more *haram* than eating a hot dog. But for now, I thrilled in my secret dining experiences with the American girls in my neighborhood. Since Iranians generally didn't eat dinner till much later in the evening, I was always able to muster up an appetite for my mother's savory Persian stews and fragrant basmati rice, thus avoiding being caught in the act of sneaking *haram* meals at American families' homes.

It was the year 1979 when things started to fall apart in my world. I started to have a nagging feeling that I was somehow to blame for whatever was on the television set. How else could I explain the series of events that started to tear my world apart shortly after *Nightline* started airing its broadcast of the crisis in Iran? First, my mother told me not to tell people I was Iranian. I didn't understand. This coming from a woman who was fiercely proud of her country? Who defiantly refused to serve us frozen Swansons dinners, reminding us that we were Iranian and that no food on earth was as delicious as Iranian food? This same woman was now whispering in my ear as I stepped onto the school bus to be silent about my heritage. Soon, the silence would turn into lies. Soon it wasn't enough to not be Iranian, I needed to be Christian also. Soon I became Greek. It was easy to be Greek. In the eyes of my provincial Southwestern classmates and teachers, anything not blond and blue-eyed was clearly Mexican. And if you claimed to be something other than Mexican, then they wouldn't be able to tell the difference anyway. It was easy to be Greek. I could still take my pita sandwiches and *bakhlava* to school and no one would know the difference.

I started third grade a few months before Reagan was elected president, shortly before the hostage crisis came to an end. I was startled to return to the school cafeteria after the long summer break only to find the words "Iranians Go To Hell" scribbled in black permanent marker across the white-tiled walls. I looked around me, at the crowds of students and teachers milling about the long lines of plastic tables and chairs, waiting for someone else to be as mortified as I was by what I read. But no one else seemed to feel the sting of the words like I did. I started to wonder if these words were only visible to me, since weeks would pass and the janitor would not wipe away a single letter. I started to wonder if I, myself, was invisible to my teachers, as I would catch them condemning all Iranians, Arabs, Muslims in heated breaths as I would pass them in the hallways.

My ability to excel in reading and writing, math and science was no longer extolled by my teachers, but treated with an icy glare of suspicion. It was not good, not good at all that the wild-eyed, uni-browed foreign child of questionable origin was grasping the American language better than the native children were. My classmates didn't find my somewhat precocious and confident attitude towards school very charming either. Recess went from being a time of chasing cute girls around the playground and collecting Garbage Pail Kid stickers to a half hour of fear. I would hide myself in the dark corners of the library, to be out of the reach of the strong boys who would inevitably try to pull my hair and bang me up against the lockers and then pretend to pierce my body from head to toe with imaginary machine guns, complete with sound effects: "Th-th-th-t-t-t-t-t. Bang bang. We're gonna blow you up damn I-raynian." I hated when they pronounced the word *Iran* like they were from Texas. I-ran. "I-ran so far away . . . and I-raaaan, I-raaaan so far away." Then some wiseguy came up with a brilliant version of the Beach Boys song: "Bomb, bomb, bomb . . . bomb, bomb Iran. Bomb, bomb, bomb . . . bomb, bomb Iran." You get the picture. I could see my days of social integration quickly coming to an end.

Becky's family stopped inviting me over for pork dinners. The Wright sisters, who were my favorite orange tree pals, were no longer allowed to come over in the afternoons to play. Their father, who was a minister at the Presbyterian church around the corner, stopped dropping by to have enlightened religious conversations with my father. And someone—to this day I don't know who—blew the cover on my sexual adventures.

❧

Shortly after my game was revealed, I started getting little bedtime sermons from my father. The main sermon I got from him as he tucked me into bed was about the golden castle that was being built for me in heaven. God's angels were busily building a castle for me in heaven out of gold bricks. Every time I had good thoughts or did good deeds, they would add a golden brick to my future home in the sky. But every time I had bad thoughts or did bad deeds, they would take five bricks away. I was no dummy. I did the math and realized that I had better get my act "straight" or I would be homeless by the time I died and went to heaven. I started to ask my dad what was "good" and what was "bad." My eyes were opened to the fact that a lot of who I was and what I was doing was "bad." I was shocked. Who knew? Panic swept over me as I started to calculate in my head whether all the good I had done was enough to make up for all the bad I was clearly capable of. It became clear, as my calculations began to add up, that I probably didn't have more than a few bricks standing between me and homelessness when I died. I knew it was time to change my ways and become a "good girl" so that my parents, my teachers, my classmates would all love me again.

It was 1979 and I realized that my whole world had shifted. I was going to have to reinvent myself so I could belong in America, belong to my Muslim Iranian family, belong to a world which didn't like me as I was. I had a long, hard road ahead of me.

Captions

∝

Layli Arbab Shirani

For Manijeh . . .

> *Qu'y puis-je*
>
> *Il faut bien commencer.*
>
> *Commencer quoi?*
>
> *La seule chose au monde qui vaille*
> *la peine de commencer:*
> *La Fin du monde parbleu.*

—AIMÉ CESAIRE,
*NOTEBOOK OF A RETURN
TO THE NATIVE LAND*

SOMEWHERE TO BEGIN:

I know it was the rain, a conversation with a friend, a downward glance, and—with this alignment—the possibility that I would have, at long last, something of *myself* to pour. These were my beginnings for this, a less reproachful way of examining my chronology of escape, paralysis, and pleasure.

[PARENTHETICALLY:]

[I was born here. And with that I can say that as jarring an experience as "birth" can be, it doesn't seem to matter where you're born. Trying to identify my identity, where do I begin? Perhaps where I switched passports when boarding a flight to Tehran, and became "Iranian," or maybe later still, when I draped a scarf across my head, wore a manteau, and became "Iranian Woman." Maybe I'm pressing the obvious—we all know that nationality and identity are not one and the same—but doesn't one question the other? Am I not writing in English, and to an audience whose facility with this language is probably greater? Why am I writing at all—what in me necessitates such an exploration?

This is how I begin. These are the questions most available to me as I begin, and as I do so I am excited that I don't know what will follow, what I'll find. I only know that I cannot approach these questions directly, and that in searching, as it were, for my identity, I cannot look for "it," but for those places where I might find it.]

DISTILLATE HOPE: PRELUDE?

I appropriate my imagination. From that I fantasize a prism that refracts, from all distortion, light.

LUGGAGE—OR "STILL-LIFE WITH SUITCASE":

In a room with Maman. She kneels before an object too big to be a suitcase and too unfirm to be a trunk. She is removing, examining, refolding, replacing. As she does this she is remembering, sometimes aloud, where they come from.

Looking for my identity. Am I looking or overcome? Overcome by the new memory that is forming of the hands that have moved across eighty years of life, reaching back perhaps a hundred more, retrieving, collecting, assembling a history. Overcome, even more, by the care of the hands that placed them, the hands that brought them here, and the hands, now, that unearth them for me. I am burdened by these objects, moved by these hands, overcome by my responsibility. It has always been this way, for me, with hands.

Why is it that when I begin to probe and prod my memory, to examine those scenes in which I locate myself, I am left with this? When did this stop being exciting, stop symbolizing as much *return* as it did *separation*? What overcomes me, and what does it mean to say that I am "overcome"? It is the act and the diligence with which it is committed; it is the conversation of those hands with history, their communion with me. It is during these silent observations that I think

I will do anything, become anything to measure up to this act, be worthy of this. But it is also in another way that this feeling overcomes me. I am burdened by my attachment to the memories in that trunk. I am burdened by my vulnerability to and responsibility for them. These old stamps, these faded photographs I don't recognize, old report cards, a broken watch, and equal to my grandfather's *taar*—the cloth that wraps it: I am the keeper of the creases in that cloth.

PLACE:

I think I am the last of something. As though my parents stood in this place, and with their feet planted firmly *elsewhere,* released me. My daughter, not yet conceived, thinks *she* is the last of something. My language, for her, a delectable buffet. My history, with its stories adorned and exoticized by memory and distance, for her an intimate stranger, a distant friend, conjured at whim. I am her very own colony.

Will her ties to her heritage be as faded, as watered down by flight, tragedy, and hope as the ties of those who pour their past into a measuring cup and say: "I am one-quarter Irish, one-quarter Lebanese, one-eighth Sioux . . ."? Will she say, "I am half-Iranian, half- . . ."?

[Half what? I am still working on *my* half—I'm not ready to divide just yet.]

A TRICKLE:

On good days, bright, orange days, I revel in my difference, approach myself as a Sunday crossword, then etch, erase, and discard myself.

[Look at me: I can only sketch, digress, I can't finish anything, at least not in the way it's understood. Completion. Me, I am replete with fragments, and digression is my mode of travel.]

THE BODY CORPOREAL:

The notion of embarking . . . a funny one, curiously linear—is it? I am lying on my back, all to the ground. Beginning with the outer rounds of my ankles, to the curves in my calves, not the backs of my knees, all my thighs (alas!), leading to hips . . . an arch upward and then my back—its troubled vertebrae. A warm glance up through my neck and we are at the back of my head, cushioned with hair. And that is only the middle; we have said nothing of the shoulders, pressed down, and the upper arms, pressed down, with what's in them flowing downward, thinning, ending in fingers cupping a tiny hollow of air. Am I embarking or being launched?

COMPOUNDS:

"Cross" this, *"post"* that, *"dis"* everything, *"trans"* blah, *"inter"* what? These are not my positions, my lacunae, my periscopes, my chronographs, compasses, chronicles. I shut my eyes, descend into myself, and retrieve a worn suitcase. Opening it, I unpack shame first, push confusion into a corner, lay aside time. Sifting, my hands unearth a pair of glasses, perched precariously on my younger face. Through those lenses I glimpse snapshots of wild hair, sneakered feet, and soccer balls amid a blur of yellow brick, yellowing grass, asphalt and oleander. This is the foreground of my life, and in the background is revolution, and I am reading *Gone With the Wind* and I am flying down the street on my skateboard, and just before reaching my driveway I am slowing down, turning to Amir and asking: "Who is this Khomeini guy anyway?" Then I am in my father's study, and he is telling me what he has long held back from me, and that night I have nightmares about the Shah, only in these ones he is tied to a chair—a chair in the study— and from then on—and this is where the image blurs the most—brews the most discord: I am in shorts and a tank-top, I am atop a building, I am chanting at the top of my pre-adolescent lungs "Long live Khomeini!" or *"Marg bar Amrika!"* (figure it out), or some rhymed variation on that theme . . . or I am straining my eyes at the moon, because, I am told, it is possible to discern Khomeini's image, if you *believe* hard enough. I put the glasses down.

APOSIOPESIS—OR "A BIG WORD":

"A sudden breaking off in the midst of a sentence, as if from inability or unwillingness to proceed" (*Random House Dictionary*).

COURAGE:

What I have written (all that I've left unsaid) has been about having, lacking, desiring, awaiting, imagining, fabricating, producing, simulating . . . courage. Everything, it seems to me, stands in some kind of relation to courage, and even now as I review these . . . etchings . . . I am at once pained by their lack of completion, and wary of an audacity that supposed they *could,* somehow, be complete. That I, having, in a sense, submerged myself, would emerge with wet hair and a fresh perspective. That I, rather than being "launched," would march forth from here: embark. That I could find a way of holding the contents of my suitcase, and Maman's too. There is much more that I know now. For instance this, which sounds like the end, is really the middle; and I know that now, having confronted my frustration, I may continue, by making, of this middling end: a new beginning.

A FISSURE—OR "STILL-LIFE OF LANGUAGE":

I am female, twenty-eight, and far from "innocence." For a married me, these are the dull facts. I am single, and so they are my confession.

("When tradition becomes too flexible, irony enters the voice" [Don DeLillo, *White Noise*]).

DOUBT DE-STILLED:

A man approaches me, sits closer. What about the sincere one—the one in the bar? And what about the voice at the other end of the line? What about the nameless, the faceless, and what about the faithless—what about *me*?

A man approaches me, sits closer. Memory flows upstream, bearing desire, guilt, poetry, play, shame, language, wine, and forgetfulness . . . and the pleasure in all. Memory flows upstream bearing pleasure: intellect dilutes. Desire flows upstream bearing shame: intellect diverts.

To the men who approached me:

I am the cultural stereotype, inverted. I am the one who grew freely, wildly, shamelessly. Not the shy, the embarrassed one, I am the one with the foul mouth. No tale of woe, no patriarchal father, I grew up with only my immunity to proclaim. I grew up an Iranian, among Iranians, eating Iranian food, swallowing Iranian germs, but feeding a Western intellect that has no memory, no history, no knowledge of my suitcase. I had to overcome my shame, because it was never there, and I had to heap my suspicion on you, *your* motives—because I knew myself, because I was guilty—as we are in the West—of draping my freedom around me like a warm blanket (like a *chador?*), and incubating my ignorance.

A man approaches me, sits closer. His ration: my rationale.

She sits at a big white desk, an anchor in a spacious room that has the appearance of one only recently occupied or about to become vacant. Her gaze, though intent, should also carry the requisite blankness of someone who stares at a computer's screen for inspiration, as though its imposing flatness will send her deeper into herself. She is thinking about the struggle toward conclusion, one that makes its presence known by form, and so she struggles through these sketches—their loose strands—for something that, simply by virtue of being at the end, will not be conclusive. She is thinking about the wrinkles in her shirt. She is thinking a secret thought . . . pass the torch, Forugh . . .
Pass it to me.

Arrivals and Departures

❦

Sharon L. Parker

My flight landed at Mehrabad Airport on a cold January night in 2001. This was the first time I had been back to Iran since 1977 and I was nervous. I fiddled with my headscarf, worried that it would be seen as inadequate by the person who had the authority to stamp my passport allowing me entry into the country. People standing in line ahead of and behind me were quietly waiting to have their passports and paperwork scrutinized. No one pushed ahead of anyone else. They simply waited. In front of the long line of men, women and children, a young man and a young woman sat in adjoining booths which blocked the way into the rest of the building. As I watched them look carefully at the documents of those in front of me, I wondered if I should admit to understanding Farsi when it was my turn to give them my passport. Or should I remain silent unless they asked me questions in English? What would I learn if they did not know that I spoke the language? Finally it was my turn. I gave my passport to the woman in front of me. "*Amrika-i,*" she said to the man in the next booth. "Why is she here?" he asked. "To study," I answered in Persian. "*Farsi sobat mekonid*—You speak Farsi," he said. "Yes," I replied. They both waited. "I lived here a long time ago," I volunteered. I waited. They conferred and my passport was stamped. I had made it into the country.

Maybe it was the lateness of the hour or the cold winter evening that made everything seem muted. Or perhaps it was just me. But entering Iran in 2001 was very different from what I remember of my first arrival in Tehran with my parents and sisters. Our flight landed at the airport on a warm April evening in 1958. The night sky was filled with more stars than I had ever seen. I felt as if I could reach up and grasp them in my hands. Inside the airport terminal, crowded with people talking, shouting and pushing against one another, the scent of roses and jasmine mingled with the smell of urine and sweat. My mother, sisters and I stood to one side while my father looked for our suitcases and boxes. Months later we realized that we did not have everything we had packed in San Francisco to take to Tehran; many containers were missing. This would often happen: we spent much time looking for something only to eventually realize that the container it had been packed in was lost. Since my father and another pilot had flown the plane we traveled in as far as Beirut, where it was picked up by an Air Jordan crew, and we had also stopped in Damascus en route to Tehran, there was no telling where these things had gone. But the loss of belongings became less and less important over time.

While I cannot recall the ride from the airport to the pension near Maidan-e-Ferdowsi where we stayed for several weeks, or the Iran Air pilot who met us and took us there, I well remember awakening the next morning to the sounds of traffic, carts and donkeys, street venders, women talking and children playing in the courtyard below the room I shared with my sisters. After our first breakfast of tea, cheese, jam and Barbari and other Iranian breads, I was hooked. I still prefer Iranian bread to any other kind.

The importance of learning what to eat and how it had to be prepared was brought to our attention shortly after we moved to Tehran. In the late 1950s, Iranian vegetables were often washed in a purple solution guaranteed to kill off any type of problem bug. Sometimes laundry soap would be used instead. We were told that if it could not be peeled or boiled it should not be eaten. Drinking boiled water was necessary because effective water treatment was not yet generally available. Initially it was difficult to remember what could or could not be consumed. However, it did not take long for us to understand why we had been told to be careful about the food we ate. Mother became ill first, followed shortly thereafter by my sisters and me. We succumbed to what was called "Tehran Tummy." But my father, who had had two extended stays in Iran prior to our move there, remained healthy and began working right away. Mornings and evenings were marked by the sound of the crew car coming to take my father to the airport and bringing him home again after a day of flying. In contrast, our days of misery were interspersed with visits from our doctor and get-well messages from our new acquaintances. We were given yogurt, rice, fruit salts and some sort of tonic that Dr. Homayoun was particularly fond of dispensing. Over the course of the next several years I consumed all the various tonics that Dr. Homayoun felt were necessary for my health and well-being. Each had its own peculiar taste and smell. Many were dark reddish brown in color and some tasted like burnt liver. These were supposed to be particularly effective in treating "bad blood" and, since I often tested positive for anemia, I was given them on a regular basis. Tonics were made to our doctor's specification at the pharmacy near his office. I disliked all of them equally. But I did grow to like yogurt.

Dr. Homayoun was a striking man with thick gray hair and piercing blue eyes. He was from the southern part of Iran and his wife was English. Their house and clinic were in a small street near the British Embassy. Our doctor had treated my father for an illness when he was in Iran a few years before, and so he became our physician once we moved to Tehran. Dr. Homayoun was firm and to the point about the necessity of adhering to the correct treatment, and never turned away anyone from his clinic door, regardless of the patient's ability to pay. I can still recall sitting in the small reception area waiting to be seen while beside me might be a man with a small basket of eggs brought for payment, or a woman wrapped in a *chador* holding a small doll on which she would indicate the specific region of her body needing treatment because it would have been unseemly for her to submit to an examination by a male doctor. Several years later, when my parents moved from Iran and I stayed behind, this doctor and his wife were part of my extended family network, providing care and comfort whenever this was necessitated by my various life circumstances.

In 1950s America, the body was a taboo subject not to be discussed in public, and illness was seen as something peculiar to particular individuals. Cancer was an embarrassing illness. So too was depression. Surgeries, as well as pregnancies, were talked about in hushed voices. My mother's multiple surgeries, and bouts of depression, in the two years prior to moving to Iran were never discussed inside or outside our household. On the days when the house was dark and our mother stayed in her room my sisters and I moved about very quietly. Mother's depression came and went during her pregnancies with my brothers, both of whom were born in Tehran. But this was not discussed—even inside our family. In contrast, the mood swings and severe depression of the mother of my best friend in Iran were a matter of general knowledge. Family and friends suffered with her during her bouts of illness, with periods of severe depression exacerbated by the birth of her last child.

Bodily functions are particularly embarrassing for young adolescent girls and I was no exception. During my first few weeks in Tehran I was mortified when asked about my "tummy" by well-meaning people. Since I did not yet speak Farsi, and some of the people asking did not speak English, much of their questioning consisted of tummy patting and other gestures, along with various facial expressions. I did not want anyone to know what or how my "tummy" was doing but I had no way of politely changing the subject. Eventually I was on the mend and the topic of my "tummy" was fortunately left behind!

Unlike late 1950s America, where the body could not be mentioned (but could be revealed in clothing specifically designed to titillate), in Iran the body, which had to be discreetly covered but not necessarily veiled in the case of women, could be discussed at great length. I quickly learned that couching things in terms of the body was normal, particularly in interactions with friends and family members; that love could be expressed through the liver, a curse could be placed on a head, and that if someone sneezed when preparing to leave the house, it was necessary for everyone to sit down and wait for some time before leaving. I was not sure exactly why the latter was necessary but did it anyway. Asking about someone's health was serious business requiring close listening, careful consideration of the descriptions of symptoms, and an offering up of possible remedies. In time, the discussion of the body, as both an abstract and a concrete entity, became so much a part of what I was accustomed to that I no longer remembered that although many Americans felt compelled to ask, "How are you?" they really did not want to know the answer. This was brought home to me most clearly when, having moved to Tucson to enter a graduate program at the university, a faculty member asked how I was doing. Her eyes glazed over as I proceeded to tell her, and she walked away before I had finished speaking.

In addition to my father's attachment to Dr. Homayoun, he was also particularly fond of several of the physicians at the Nemazee Hospital in Shiraz. As we approached our second month in Tehran, my mother, sisters and I flew to Shiraz for a complete physical. While there, we were poked, prodded and peered at by various medical personnel at the hospital. Rebecca, Janice and I stayed with one of the doctors and his family. Our mother stayed in the hospital. In between X-rays and blood and other tests, my sisters and I were taken to Persepolis and the tomb of Hafez. Finally given a clean bill of health, we returned to Tehran and took up residence in a house off Old Shimron Road near Golhak.

Our house sat in the middle of a small street bounded by a neighborhood mosque at one end and a row of small shops at the other, including a greengrocer, a pharmacy, and a small store that carried various types of rice and other dry goods. It had a small pool in the garden that was surrounded by high walls covered with climbing roses in one area and jasmine in another. Pots filled with geraniums covered much of the terrace. Because of the height of the wall we could hear, but not see, people, carts and animals just outside.

Across a narrow alleyway lived an Iranian family with whom we spent many afternoons and evenings. My sisters and I often were invited over for large meals that were followed by a ride in an overly crowded car to Tajrish for ice cream. We were sometimes packed three deep in each seat, except the one occupied by the chauffeur, who had one all to himself. I suspect he needed it in order to drive.

My developing facility in Farsi led to many different levels of responsibility. Any time anything official had to be accomplished, I accompanied my father to the appropriate office to make sure that what was communicated to him was what was actually being said. As a result of this I went to many meetings at the Iran Air headquarters, where contracts were being discussed and negotiated. I sat quietly in a large office and listened to the discussions between some of the pilots and the administrators. Later I would tell my father what I had heard. I am not sure what the chief pilot thought of me being in the room but no one remarked on my presence.

My mother traveled frequently with my father on the short flights between Tehran and Shiraz, Esfahan, Hamadan, Mashad, Abadan and other cities, so she knew the Persian name of practically every tool needed to do quick repairs on an aircraft. But she knew very few words for foods. So I either did the shopping alone, or went with her in order to translate. Because the first supermarket would not be built for several more years, and it was necessary to haggle over the price of each item, shopping was an all-day affair. We did some of it at the small markets in our neighborhood; the rest of our shopping took place near the center of the city. Eggs, which were bought at the small shop on the corner of our street, were particularly mysterious to me. I knew I had to hold each of them up to a light bulb and peer at it, but I was never sure why. I just hoped not to look too stupid so that I would not be offered bad ones to buy. I think that the process of purchasing eggs was an even more mysterious activity for my mother. After going to our corner store for eggs the first time, she just sent me down to buy the eggs by myself. Eventually I learned that holding an egg to the light had something to do with checking to see if it was fertilized. But I still could not quite understand what made a particular egg the best one of the lot to buy.

As I adjusted to life, in Iran I moved between my American family at home and my Iranian friends and their families outside. I only knew a handful of other American adolescents, none of whom were close friends. Because we were living within the Iranian community and not amongst the diplomatic or military personnel, I did not meet many other American teenagers. Most Fridays I went to girlfriends' houses for a large lunch. After eating we napped on the beautifully colored Persian carpets covering the floor. After sleeping for awhile we would drink Turkish coffee and one aunt or another would read our fortunes through the grounds left in the cups. Holding the small cups in their hands, one after another would examine the leftover grounds very closely and tell us about the wonderful things in our futures. Occasionally one of the women might frown and hold the cup for another to examine. At those times we would just be told not to worry, which would only increase our curiosity and concern. Nevertheless, we were always assured that things would turn out well for us in the end.

After returning to Tehran in 2001, one day I had lunch at a restaurant with two friends. Later we went to their cousin's house for a nap before going to an evening event. As I lay on a mat on the richly patterned Persian carpet that covered the floor, with cushions under my head, and with my friends nearby, I really knew I had come home again. When we awoke we ate fruit and sweets, drank Turkish coffee and checked the grounds for information.

Iran was the first place my family lived for an extended period of time. In the United States, because of my father's job as an airline pilot without much seniority, we were nomads traveling back and forth across the continent several times a year. Airline transfers took us from the East

Coast to the West Coast, with stops in Dallas in between. I often changed schools two or three times per year. However, once we moved to Tehran I was able to put down roots. My attachment to this city was such that it was very difficult for me to leave the country, even to go on vacation—unless it was inside the country. In fact, I felt a physical pain whenever we left Tehran for Europe. On the outbound flight I always sat in the window seat so I could see Mount Damavand for as long as possible. The ache in my body remained until we returned and I could see this mountain again.

Following their already established nomadic tradition, my parents moved several times while they lived in Tehran, always staying in the northern sector of the city. My favorite house was in the area of Zafaranieh and had twelve cherry trees in the garden. They were beautiful when in bloom, and the fruit they produced was wonderful to eat. The small pool at the bottom of the garden was just right for wading, and the large one close to the house was good for everything from swimming to washing Persian rugs. But I think my sister Rebecca preferred another house that was on a migration route. When the large groups of people, camels, donkeys and sheep camped beside our garden wall she was delighted. She played, had her hands decorated with henna, danced, ate, rode camels and just generally had a good time. To this day she likes camels. I don't, as I have personal experience as to how accurately these beasts can spit and hit their designated targets! Unlike Rebecca, whose dark hair often led to her being mistaken for Iranian, our sister Janice was very fair. She often had her cheeks affectionately pinched by women who were quite taken by this little four-year-old. Neighbors referred to her as "that blond Iranian girl" since she had virtually no accent in Persian. As time passed, my siblings and I spoke a mixture of English and Persian with each other as well as with our friends, making it difficult for our parents to understand our conversations. Needless to say, we often used this to our advantage. My Iranian-born brothers spoke Farsi before they spoke English. But it is difficult to know if this was because they also found it advantageous or because Farsi just came more easily to them.

In the hot summer days and the cooler evenings, before air-conditioning or water coolers were fairly common, we slept on mattresses placed on the flat roof of our house. The sun always woke us very early in the morning and I would then go back to my bedroom to sleep for another hour or so. As we neared the end of August the smell of fall permeated the air. When winter approached, bringing the first hint of snow, beets roasting on charcoal braziers placed on street corners filled my senses. During our Friday visits my friends' aunts pulled out little cast-iron containers that held live coals. As the days grew colder we would sit inside the house on cushions, with our feet pointing towards the coals underneath a table that was covered by quilts big enough to envelop us. We sipped tea, ate sweets, played backgammon, read cards and Turkish coffee grounds and talked. Our houses were warmed by small kerosene heaters. We were only warm when we were either seated under the quilts, or in danger of being burned by being too close to the heater.

On our first Christmas Eve in Iran, a tradition was created which continued for as long as my parents and siblings lived in Iran. My best friend, her parents and all of her brothers and sisters came for dinner and hot chocolate and then decorated the Christmas tree that her father, who was also an Iran Air pilot, and mine had chosen during one of their lay-overs in Germany. Previously, we had been accustomed to the tree taking all evening to decorate. But suddenly, with the combined effort of both families, the tree was completely covered with decorations in the space of fifteen minutes. My mother was astounded. And forever thereafter, the tree was decorated in the same amount of time each year.

Whereas preparation for the Christmas holiday was over in a flash, the Iranian New Year celebration required days of cleaning and preparation. As our network of friends expanded, my siblings and I happily participated in Muslim, Jewish and Christian holiday celebrations. Tehran was the best of all possible places for children and adolescents to live. Our grandparents, who could not understand why we had moved so far away, felt much better once they came for an extended visit and saw the network of friends that we had made.

I left Iran in 1967 and did not return until 1976. The intervening years had brought many changes to Tehran, including new roads and buildings, and an increased tension, which was palpable. I had not spoken Farsi in the years I had been gone and thought I no longer remembered it. But suddenly it again was the language of my dreams. This time I only stayed a year and then moved back to a country I had not lived in since I was a young adolescent.

In 1979 I was living in Portland, Oregon. After the Iranian revolution and during the U.S. Embassy hostage crisis, most nights I dreamed of trying to get back into Iran. I attempted to fly into Tehran, drive in from Turkey, cross over from the Gulf. Regardless of the particular route I tried to take in my dreams, I could not get across the barriers. For some time my dreams were in both English and Farsi. Gradually I stopped dreaming about Iran altogether, until just before my last trip. Then it began in earnest. I saw myself in the old familiar neighborhoods of my adolescence, but the people I had known there were gone.

In January 2001, the hotel I stayed in for a few days after returning to Iran was very different from the pension I had been in with my family in 1958. It was not as warm or inviting, and there were no sounds of children laughing or playing in the courtyard below. Corner shops sold a variety of foodstuffs, and there was a restaurant or two in the area. As far as I could tell, I was the only person in the hotel on the floor where I was located. Although everyone was kind, I felt very isolated. The windows in my room faced a tall building with heavily draped windows. It was a singularly uninviting view. But within a couple of weeks my situation changed completely. I gratefully accepted an invitation to stay with friends of a friend of mine. After I moved into my room in their apartment, I felt as if I had been transported back to an earlier time. I could see the mountains from their window. There was color inside the apartment, and although it was winter, the plants on the enclosed balcony flourished. Nevertheless, the city had been transformed. Gone were the sounds of donkeys and carts, street vendors and children playing. This city had become more serious.

Some Iranians living in the United States identify themselves as Iranian American; others call themselves Iranian exiles. Recently I was told by one of them that I am an American Iranian. That felt correct. Perhaps if I had lived in one place in the United States before moving to Iran, I would have experienced my stay there differently. But that is not the way it happened.

From *To See and See Again: A Life in Iran and America*

୬

TARA BARAMPOUR

That night in bed I watch the clouds race like horses over the moon. I think of Baba as a boy, galloping up into those hills to hunt, secure in the life his father has built for him. Agha Jan's house sheltered his siblings, his wives and their relatives, and his children and servants. By the time Baba was born, Agha Jan's hairline had receded and his stomach was round and all the villagers for miles around came to him for their needs. His dynasty had become part of the landscape, a dominion that could no longer be downed by a single bullet, or a greedy prince—or, in the end, by the Shah's land reforms. Even today, some of the older villagers still come to Dadash, asking him to "please accept this portion of our earnings and give your sisters and brothers their shares so that our profits will be *halal*"—clean and pure. And even today, a man barely old enough to remember Agha Jan remembers that he was once the lord, and that his father, Haj Abdollah-khan, was the man whose name went with that empty castle of aqueducts.

I look up at the high corners of the ceiling. Dadash built this yellow brick farmhouse thirty-five years ago, but it feels older, and not just because of the old-style colored glass windows and curved archways. The white plaster walls are hung with the dried wildflowers that Leila-khanoum gathers in the mountains and the solid wood furniture was made by local woodcarvers. The décor is elegant and calm, as I imagine Iranian houses were before gilt-edged European chairs and lacquered end tables made their appearance.

On the mantelpiece above my head, a young Agha Jan looks down from a wood-framed photograph. Dashing in a black Qajar fez and frock coat, he stands on a Persian carpet, his arm resting upon a false Grecian column, with a vague Parthenon sketched onto the backdrop. I look at his dark eyes, his brows curved like sabers, and I imagine him standing silently as his father's assassin was hanged; I picture him curling around his wife to warm her, and I see him watching his three sons die despite the doctors and the prayers. When only one son was left, Wife-of-Agha Jan begged God not to let him die of smallpox too; he died of whooping cough instead. By the time Agha Jan had reached his thirties, he knew it was fruitless to try to rearrange the stars of fate. It was what God wanted, he said when his wife became barren, and he said it again when Khosrow died, and again when the lands were taken away.

In imagining Iranians to all be terrorists and fanatics, Westerners do not always notice their submissiveness, although it is elemental to Shi'ism. Within the "fanaticism," within the willingness to be martyred and bend to the will of God, lies a simple desire to get from one day to the next without interference from the evil eye. It is not prudent to protest, to ask too many questions, to delve too deeply into the past or future. Ammejun waited fifty years to be driven down the road to her old home. Homa-khanoum refuses to look at the date on her airplane tickets. Niki warns me not to marry outside the family. Ask for too many details, look too far off, and surely you will reel in some misfortune. Better to leave things to God.

And yet, once in a while, these same practicers of submission suddenly take to the streets, turn into Hossein in the desert, risk their lives to give voice to their passions. Only fifteen years ago, there was a revolution here. But sometimes it is hard to see where it came from.

❧

Omid, the younger Kurdish boy, is small and skinny, even for a twelve-year-old. When he carries my bag out the door, his arm strains under the weight.

"That suitcase has wheels," I tell him. "You can roll it."

He shakes his head manfully and we walk out toward the car where Mohammad is filling the trunk with apples for Dadash to sell in town.

Omid heaves my bag up with one thrust. "Lucky you," he says. "I wish I were going to America." He grins and rubs his hand against the fuzz of his shaved head. "Can I come with you? In your suitcase?"

"Well, I guess you're not too heavy," I say, reaching for the zipper. "Get in."

"No, really," he says. "Do you think I could find work in America?"

"Yeah, probably, when you're a little older. But what if you didn't like it there?"

"Oh, well, then I'd come back here," he says. "I just want to see what it's like."

"How about you, Mohammad?" I say. "You want to come?"

"Nah," the taller boy says, tipping his head up. "What would I do in America? The most beautiful place in the world is Kurdistan. As soon as I have enough money, I'm going back there. I'm going to open up a shop."

"You don't want to stay here and open a shop?" I ask. "To be near your parents?"

"Nah." He looks at the trees along the sunbaked wall and wrinkles his nose.

"He doesn't like working for other people," Omid says.

Mohammad's face reddens, and he casts a quick glance at me. "I just want my own shop," he mumbles.

"So next time I'll have to visit you in Kurdistan. What kind of shop are you going to have?"

"Oh, a store that sells everything," he says, brightening. "Anything you want, I'll have."

"How about you, Arezou?" I say. "Will you come to America with me?"

Arezou gives a slight tip of her head—no—but I can't see her face under her scarf. She just started wearing it a few days ago, on her own, and her father keeps walking by and yanking it down to tease her.

"Kurdistan, then?" I say. "Or Tehran?"

She shakes her head. "My father and mother are here. Everyone I know is here."

"Well, what if your father and mother moved back to Kurdistan?" I ask. "Would you go with them then?"

She thinks for a few seconds, then shakes her head again. "I mean, I am Kurdish. But I'm from here now."

As I walk out of the house, Leila-khanoum hurries over with a tray. "Kiss the Qu'ran," she says and, murmuring a prayer, she holds the tray up for me to walk under three times. Then she lowers the tray, and I close my eyes and kiss the old copy of the Qu'ran that is sitting next to a bowl of water with a rose in it. As I walk out to the car I hear the splattering of water on the gravel—a good-luck ritual to ensure my safe return.

We do this all the time in America now. Neither Baba nor Mama nor any of us kids will go on a long trip without walking under the Qu'ran. We, who back in Iran never believed in religion or bad luck, are now willing to miss an airplane in order to run back and kiss an old leather book. Mama says if we didn't do it she would not be able to sleep; and even after we left home and moved to Berkeley, Ali and I would faithfully go to each other's houses before an early-morning flight to put up a sprig of a houseplant next to a Qu'ran and toss a cup of water down the stairs.

The bus pulls away from the town depot and my stomach lurches. I can still feel Ami's vigorous kisses on my cheeks and my forehead, and Abu-bakr's warm calloused hand, hard as stone, shaking mine in farewell. I can hear the catch in Leila-khanoum's voice when she said good-bye and I can see Dadash in the parking lot, standing straight and alone in a silent gesture of communion as my bus passed through the gates. I want to jump off and run back to them. I want to assert my presence in this place that seems in danger of collapsing under so much abandonment. The village, once the center of life for so many, is now a vista of eroding fortresses. The children who grew up here are scattered all over the world; they might someday bring their own children from America or Canada to visit the farm, but they won't move back. Dadash and Leila-khanoum are the last members of our family still here, and no one is set to carry on after them. It is unbearable to think that their house could be sold to strangers or left to crumble after they are gone.

The bus trundles along through the narrow, quiet streets of the town, still cool and shadowy, with only a few blades of sunlight piercing between the low brick buildings. Yesterday at this time, I woke up early and wandered over the dewy fields to the next village. Like Dadash's village, it had no roads or cars or signs to announce it. Thinking myself alone, I stooped to collect a handful of the blue flowers growing along the cow path.

"Who are you?"

Three wrinkled faces peered down at me. Under their loose *chadors* and frizzy hennaed hair, six lizard eyes, bright and unblinking, fixed upon me.

"I am the older daughter of the youngest brother of Abdollah-khan," I said, pointing back toward the trees.

Three wavering voices repeated this to each other.

"Who is your father?" asked the middle one.

I said his name.

They turned to each other, grimacing, frowning, muttering Baba's name.

Suddenly one of the faces lit up. "Esfandiar-khan? The son of Haj Morad-Ali-khan?" The old woman put her hand on an imaginary child's head. "Esfandiar-khan," she said to the others. "From over the mountain." She pointed to the purple-gray peak to my left, the direction of Ammejun's fort. Three toothless mouths broke into smiles. "Ah, yes, the brother of Abdollah-khan, Haj Mora-Ali-khan's son, Esfandiar-khan— what a sweet little boy." The middle woman clasped my hand and pulled me in as if to kiss me, then pushed my hand back and put her own hand to her heart, smiling and nodding, her eyes moist with ancient memory.

What was it she remembered? Some distant day when Baba was driven through here; some village wedding where this woman noticed a little laughing-eyed boy and held onto the image for fifty years? Walking back along the river, I thought of that boy with his round shaved head and the mole on his cheek, and of the village women who used to stop him in the road to plant kisses on his head. It must have felt good to him to know that they knew him; to be seven years old and already have a place in the world. I knew it must, because it felt good to me. These women had never seen me before, but hearing the name of my father had brought tears of recognition to their eyes.

I bent down and trailed my hand in the cold river, letting my fingers sway like the roots of trees along the bank. This was the river I had walked along as a child, the river Baba had fished in, the river Agha Jan's first wife had crossed on the Qajar-jeweled horse that carried her over the hill to her new life. Our own new lives—Baba's and my own— strayed far from this river; but for those who stayed, life retained a continuity that cannot be found anywhere else. I can see it in their faces—in the wonder-struck eyes of Ammejun when she finds the son of her childhood playmate; in the pleased recognition in Ami's eyes when she pins her Kurdish clothes on me; in Leila's appreciative smile when she runs her hand up my thigh and tells me to marry Mehdi. All this touching between women bothered Mama when she was in Iran; she hated the way that after lunch the women would all go off and take naps together, massaging each other's sore legs, braiding each other's hair, plucking each other's eyebrows and smoothing ointment on afterward.

She found these rituals intrusive—especially when coupled with the sexual jokes and insinuations that passed between giggling married women, jokes designed to be tantalizingly inscrutable to unmarried girls who might be listening. But none of this bothers me. I like the slightly bawdy banter among women in my family; I like the touching. It reminds me of the way I used to touch my friends and cousins before a sixth-grader in America warned me not to. Once in America, I forgot the pleasure of casually entwined fingers, or arms linked together in friendship. I strictly followed the rules of American adolescence and made it clear to my family that kissing me was no longer acceptable. Physicality became confined to romance, and it was many years before I began to remember the comfort that comes with owning, and being owned by, a large, affectionate clan.

Now, back in it again, I have the sense that it is not just me they are touching. Running her hand up my thigh, Leila-khanoum is also touching her own, remembered self, and that is part of her pleasure. Every girl is a version of the woman, every woman a model for what the girl will someday be; and at the end of the day, when the sun has set and everyone has helped with the apple harvesting and the baking of bread and the cooking of dinner, the candlelight flickers over the faces, and the differences are smoothed away.

If I were to stay here I would probably be only partly satisfied. I would always feel I belonged; I would always feel glad to run into those old ladies who remembered the child my father was. But being away from America, I might also start to feel more American, more trapped. I might become impatient with the old ladies' talk of marriage and deaths and old property squabbles, and start missing the other kind of old lady—the book-reading, hiking and swimming old lady that I imagine my mother will be and that I want to be too. An old lady who might live far from Iran but would bring her grandchildren back here to discover the places from their past that don't change no matter who comes or goes. Fifty years from now, they would find the same cool river and the same smell of mountain grass. They would find a row of white poplars glowing in the sunset; and a husband and wife who laughed as they grabbed at each other under the cows; and, inside the house, a fire in the grate, a table laden with fresh cutlets and yogurt, and a basketful of mint from a rained-on garden.

For
Tradition

For Tradition

❦

Susan Atefat-Peckham

I struggled with my grandmother's rosebush,
pinching and bending branches, picking
each red and yellow petal from tender
stems. I pushed them into a glass of water
set on the cement ledge and waited patiently
in her lap, lacing my inked fingers around
her neck, stroking the flushed skin, watching
the callouses on a soldier's hands
through a space in the gate and wondered
if his twitching fingers could reach the glass.

I now see the deep lines in her forehead,
and a whispered prayer plays on her wrinkled
lips. She holds the Qu'ran to my swelling mouth
waiting for me, a woman now, to kiss the ruffled
pages and pass under its broken spine. I hear
her, full with care, spill the water at the gate
and drop warm petals, For tradition, she says,
for my quick return, as if the trail smeared
in the mortar behind the car made a difference,
as if a kiss on the holy book would keep us safe.

Sister

∞

FARNAZ FATEMI

Mehrabad Airport, Tehran
outside the terminal doors
we are a crushing pre-dawn crowd,
we swarm out between the glass exits
and the taxi stands:
on one side, my grandmother,
the other, my mother.
My first visit
since my grandfather's death
years earlier.
The sister disembarks,
trails us by meters,
is round, middle-aged,
draped in black veils and skirts.
She begins to scream in anguish
sags with the folds of cloth, downward,
drops to her knees
arcs her arms upward,
over her head
then down, like two axes, down,
while she cries,
as if to pray and thresh the ground
in punishment,
pray and punish
pray and punish.

She is wailing:

My brother—
my brother,
the only one I had.
I only had one brother
my brother
He was the only one I had.
Strangers, a dozen deep,
surround her, drawn by the keening
of her loss.
Her pitch rises as her body falls
sideways, she leans there.
The only one I had.
A ring of women,
now wailing,
reach her.
The sky above us swells
with their sounds.

We hover near the sister,
my grandmother's face opens wide
cheeks flush, eyes pooling,
my mother's face an answer
lips trembling, parted.
And my aunt's, my sister's, my heart
all flail open
toward this crooning
while my grandfather's memory takes shape
between us, sprung loose
as if by incantation:
He was the only one I had.

Twin

&

FARNAZ FATEMI

When I am a little girl
I learn to feel the space between
me and my twin sister
as if it is an atomic bond
and we are ions—
the relative connection only shifts
by push and pull. A peel apart
is a chemical surprise. Each split
is innocent, she is never mean
by leaving, but she is easily bored
by the games I spend hours with—
jigsaw puzzles and every variation
on the dictionary game I can think of—
I fall gracefully into the trap of believing
I can keep her here.
I feel unreal when her energy
lessens, when the gleam
of her laughter
casts distracted off our table.
Every time my lover's attention
drifts, I reach for my sister's arm
to keep her here, to clutch the wish
of my reflection in a mirror,
sit it down next to me and
feel the space between us
strangle into the kind of bond
that retains its innocence

and wards off change.
She looks away
and shines her light on the mirror
of our sameness, refracts back
the deviations. When I am five
I don't know that atomic bonds
are composed of charged particles.
Her body doesn't leave my side
but she was the first to learn
how to leave, instructing me
on the solitude of loving,
shocking me now that
seeing my own body
next to another is what makes me
feel so alone.

The Persian Bath

❧

MICHELLE KOUKHAB

When the sumac berries are as ripe as sunrise
we bathe at the Hammam-e umumy, a purple dome,

skylit, where ladies talk of marriage and a suitor's wishes
to engage. My mother brings romaine lettuce

and vinegar syrup—*sekanjebin*—to eat with pomegranate
seeds and salt. In the Sarbineh, we change our clothes,

stretch, massage, scrub our legs with *kiseh,*
the wool rough like sandpaper against our skin.

Sisters wrap my mother's waist with egg yolk
and chick-pea paste. In the bath, more hands spread

powder paste and oil. We celebrate the healthy
birth and drink rosewater with basil.

In America, we shower babies with presents, celebrate
in anticipation. Blue for boys, girls wear pink.

I can have children, but no healing ceremony.
In my healing of parts below the navel, I can only spread

glue with tongue depressors. This gap opens sometimes
between the places we are born, and the places that we live.

A Love Song

PARINAZ ELEISH

Peninsula, peninsula,
a word blue, green, gold.
My father collecting pink seashells.
A student of natural sciences,
he fed me seaweed and bread.
Smoke coiling out of the old chimney
into the dusk that lingered.

A peninsula,
and everything I tell you is true.
The old man that fished
a fish as large and pink as our house,
the little boy who spoke the seagull-tongue,
and you in my eyes.
My eyes full of your face.

Pomegranates

❧

PERSIS M. KARIM

In loving memory of my Baba

To root themselves in their new home
Mother and Baba planted native trees: madrone, oak
and the manzanita at the end of the drive.
To remind them of their foreignness
they planted olive, almond, quince, pomegranate.

The first time my mother packed one in my lunch
I shrank in embarrassment, quickly returning
the leathery bulb to the brown bag.
How to eat a pomegranate without being conspicuous?
It is a slow and exacting endeavor,
an act of worship.

You never slice them with a knife, my father would say
when the September heat made the trees
sag with the ornaments of autumn.
In his world, men sold them on the streets
for a few toumans, shouting, "*Anar-e Khoshmazeh!*"
"Delicious pomegranates!" rolling the sun-flushed
hides between two palms.
Customers at the corner of a cart,
kneaded, coaxed the last of the blood-red juice
from a hole, allowing it to touch only their lips.

Our American sensibility refused this technique.
We never took their exotic form for granted.

"Throw them in the air, let them crack open!"
my brothers yelled, waiting for the quiet
thud and then, the invisible seam
that split them open like an unhealed wound.
We liked the splatter of color on face and hands,
evidence of pomegranate carnage.

In my twenties, I finally understood the fecund symbol.
A magazine in the chiropractor's office
advised women wanting to conceive:
Eat estrogen-rich foods—shrimp, scallops,
pomegranates. Like the larvae of some magical butterfly
the red ovules offered a cure for barren women.

There are two kinds of people in the world:
those who pluck the seeds from the waxy yellow
membrane, tossing them into their mouths—
and those who hoard the ruby jewels,
jealously guarding the pile until the last
crimson kernel is extracted.

Once in a child's game of war,
my brother plucked a pomegranate,
tore its feathery crown, and with a heave
mimicked the sound of a grenade
exploding with his mouth full of saliva.
"Bury it!" I said, looking at its inedible remains.
Baba would not tolerate such sacrilege.

When I learned a Sephardic version of the fall—
that it was a pomegranate and not an apple—
I felt a kind of secret pride.
It's too cold for apples in the Garden of Eden,

I told a friend, knowing with certainty
they wouldn't be wearing fig leaves.

This fall, my two-year-old son,
undaunted, eats his first pomegranate.
His tiny, probing fingers harvest the seeds
one by one. With hands stained
by this baptism, he offers them to me
like the remnants of an untold story
inherited in the womb.

Passover

∞

AMY MOTLAGH

In the market, no gift is suitable for your parents.
The waxen green limbs of the lilies bend outward, beseeching,
but they are not the thing that's wanted. At dinner, two
    holidays collide
in my stomach and I feel it as bitter herb and egg and brisket
    swim together, uncertain
of how to be digested with the candied fruit of buns crossed
    in icing.
On the contrary, you are a quick study for Easter, ready to
    sacrifice your diet
to its hollow chocolate hares and the buttercream eggs my
    mother remembers
to mail ahead of time, frosted with pastel petals in a California
    confectionery
then hardened for travel. She and I know how far I am
from egg hunt and Sunday brunch and the small gold cross
that hung from my fervent adolescent neck, and that in the
    same season
in which we would fast together, abstaining sometimes
from meat, sometimes from sugar, I now make-believe
in another observance, closing my mouth against the leavened
    bread
and candy bunnies Jesus died, then rose, to free me for.
The lilies lift their heads as I pass, gripping
your arm in the doorway of the second-night Seder.

ajun

Mahru Elahi

one.
her smooth skin
exhales cardamom
the sweet sharp
musky
green smell
that lurks in the back of kitchen cupboards
she
throws them whole
like candy
into *sholeh-zard*

two.
rosewater her *chador*
a long veil unfurling in her wake
slowly
she moves down a dark hallway
her
daughter's home
slippers tapping
shutters drawn against the light

three.
her hands hold mine
the sound of tides retreating wearily
through her nose
tickling my palms she

begins to lightly trace
the fine lines
anxiously awaiting her touch
telling me
my life will be long
and happy

four.
baba
tells me this
while i know the intonations the
curving lilt that strains itself
elongates pulls to a fine point before
releasing
long stroke of a calligrapher's brush
i do not understand her
nemifahman
solitary words emerge from the arch of sound
though i strain
as if hearing hard enough
will make me comprehend

i am losing something i never had
her stories
like flowers
curling back in on themselves

five.
broken speech
falls
once it leaves our mouths
doesn't float

ethereal
instead clatters to the floor between us
with such force
leaves a dent in the linoleum
we stoop to pick it up
"how is your mommy grandma?"
"say hi your mommy grandma"
"i love you"
i say: *khayli khoobeh*
i say: *baleh, baleh*
i say: I love you too

six.
she is lonely
she asks
for warm arms
soft faces
voices that cluck and coo
serve her
memory
hot tea in small glasses
rooms lined with the heavy moist scent of rugs

seven.
however
she is tired
dismisses
baba's offers to convey her
hands demurely clasped atop the
frayed plastic purse on her lap
sitting patiently throughout the journey

eight.
instead
she shuts her door
amid handmade lace
rustling bowls of fragrant
petals
photographs glowing behind inlaid frames
listens
to the radio station
broadcasting
24 hours in farsi
listens
as baba's car moves down the hill
joins the rush of others
speeding past her window

nine.
after pressing *adas pollo kuku sabzi*
on guests
she sits heavily
elbow resting on the kitchen table
eyes that look large and tragic
behind thick lenses
are fixed on their plates
once empty
filling them again
quickly and expertly
amid polite protests

ten.
she does not
drive

this is not tehran
where friends live close
where an army of extended family
could deliver her to those
who do not
where soldiers
pushed her down
knees skinning the pavement
her hair peeking out beneath divine law

eleven.
she took one look at me
said
she must pray in a house
of God
protect me from the evil eye
because
no mosque was nearby
a local lutheran church
would do

twelve.
she is forgetting
lucy says
on the phone
through crackling static
lucy will stay with her
this weekend
her
daughter's home
quiet and empty
lucy has been reading

about thoughts traveling far
irretrievable
from weathered minds that used to
reminisce
about how
the reason those stricken continually ask
where they are
who you are
is because
they want to know they're safe

i am losing something i never had
her stories
like flowers
curling back in on themselves

Next Year in Cyprus

∝

Tarssa Yazdani

My mother was never the typical Southern beauty. Dry and win-some as a Texas sunset, she wore her long blond hair down and loose throughout the pincurled fifties, read Dostoevsky and Unamuno, lis-tened to Lightnin' Hopkins and jazz, and dreamed of becoming a lawyer. A settlement from a car wreck paid for college. She was the first in her family to go. One night while riding her bike across the North Texas State campus with a bottle of wine in her basket, she came upon my father, a radical, a foreigner, the only man on campus with a beard. He was a Marxist and a revolutionary. She must have liked that about him, although she's never said. In the nearly forty years since, she has never once admitted to me that she loved him. The most she's ever shared is that she wanted two things from life: adventure and children.

My mother married in black, head to toe, with a little black pill-box hat. Afterwards she tossed her wedding ring into the river in Reno, filled, according to tradition, with the rings of the newly divorced. Soon after, with my brother still a baby and my mother pregnant with me, my family moved to Iran, first to the Tehran mansion of my grand-father, then to the oil company compounds of Abadan. She realized her mistake almost immediately.

The epiphany came in a movie theater, when the audience was required to rise and salute the Shah's portrait. Mom refused, true to her principles, contemptuous of the despot. My father yanked her up by the arm, forcing her to comply, and for the first time she realized both the stakes of real revolution in a foreign land and her utterly vulnerable sta-tus as a woman and wife. Through that one gesture, she grasped the enor-mity of her action. No longer considered an American citizen, she had naively put herself into a situation in which she had forfeited absolutely every civil, political, and human right afforded an American. Almost as soon as she arrived in Iran she began plotting her escape.

I don't know the whole truth, only the family mythology, the few stories codified by time and faithful retellings which never elaborated on but only embedded the same incomplete information. Mom was beaten, threatened with divorce and automatic loss of her children. Jars of acid were waved in her face; insults were hurled at her heritage. Years later she would acerbically recount my father's favorite line: "You and your goddamn American tanks!" She tried to get help from the U.S. consulate, but was told that while she and her son stood a slim chance, her daughter, born on Iranian soil, was beyond help. So she declined further assistance from official channels. Finally, eight months pregnant with my younger brother, she convinced my father to allow her to come back to the States to give birth. Once home, she said, she would arrange for his visa. We left Iran with one suitcase, packed for a short stay.

Mom had my father's visa permanently revoked, divorced him, changed our last names, and moved us all to California. When my older brother, at two and a half, realized we were not going back, he stopped speaking Persian and soon forgot it entirely. We never saw our father again, and that's nearly everything I know about it. Our history, the story of my parents, was like an ancient poem with most of the parchment missing, stanzas left untranslated, the result of my half-hearted scholarship. Mom refused to talk about it, and we learned not to pry. All the charming, harrowing, and thrilling anecdotes that she would ever tell were already in circulation. The stories never changed, no new nuances, no late revelations saved until adolescence, adulthood. My brothers and I lost interest over the years.

We never envisioned a reckoning, never imagined we would ever be found, knew we shouldn't be, and lived with a distant fear of kidnapping, distant only because we never thought of our father as real, therefore never a real threat. I grew up fascinated by world culture, anthropology, geography, and languages. But I never sought out information about Iranian culture in particular beyond the surface level at which I studied the world at large. The taboos were so internalized I hardly realized they were there.

When my older brother turned sixteen and needed a Social Security card and driver's license, my family finally faced a small reckoning. The last name we had chosen for ourselves had never been legalized. So my mother arranged for us all to go to court together, but in a rebellious gesture, I refused. I no longer wanted to be the daughter of an offhand invention, a fictitious name. For me, it was less about claiming my father and his heritage and more about accepting my own mysterious, dramatic, and unique identity. I thought that the beautiful name of my ancestors, a name I have never pronounced correctly, could be made my own, a one-of-a-kind name for an original me. I don't remember any strong family dissent about it. We were years removed from the early kidnapping fears that had justified the first name change. I enrolled at the same university my parents had attended, in the fall of 1980, during the full-blown hostage crisis, under my obviously Iranian name. I had never met an Iranian in my life.

At college I witnessed *hijab,* the Islamic dress code for females, in its early and harshest form. It made me cringe. It reinforced for me that which I was not, in vivid "there but for the grace of God go I" terms. I did eventually meet many Iranians, mostly assimilated students who had no intention of returning in the revolution's aftermath. Most of them were very kind to me, but I think I disappointed quite a few over the years with my steadfast refusal to dabble in my father's heritage, to learn his language, memorize his holidays and traditions. It took me years to articulate the reason why I never sought to claim even marginal membership as a half Iranian. Beyond all the political and cultural suspicions, what I am at heart is a fatherless child. What lies between my personal identity and my father's culture is a deep crater that denotes his absence, a distance too far to leap. He could have been Bosnian or Brazilian, and I still would have felt as American, and as fatherless.

Then last July, the phone rang. By the way he pronounced my name when he asked for me, I knew he was Iranian. I thought he was a telemarketer, and I waited for the pitch. He said, "My name is Babak, and I think I'm your cousin." I said, "What?" I think I recall him asking, "Does that make sense to you?" I kept repeating, "What?" He said, "You're thirty-six years old, aren't you?" And right then I knew it was true. I was astonished at my own delight, and I couldn't think fast enough to ask him any questions. He said that a large number of our family had lived in Los Angeles for the past twenty years, and then he mentioned that he hadn't seen my father since 1986. That sent a sudden deep jolt through my spine, like the shiver you get when you hear someone has died. I said, "You mean he's alive?" Babak said, Of course.

Until that moment, I had never thought or spoken of my father in the present tense. The fact that someone had seen him as recently as fifteen years prior was simply stunning. For the first time in my life, I actually pictured him as someone who had lived on without us, someone with real experiences, unconnected to me, unknown to me, but alive. It made me cry. Babak understood. He explained that while sitting around with some of the older aunts and uncles in Los Angeles, they had begun discussing family genealogy, mentioning the lost American children. Babak had casually offered to do a Web search on our names. He found me within minutes under my father's name, the name I was born with but had not taken as my own until the age of seventeen, the name I retained when I married a decade ago.

I still wonder if Babak knew what he was getting into that first day he called. He teases me whenever I ask him. He likens me to a child who wants to hear the same marvelous story over and over again. But I can't help it. I want to know everything that went through his mind when he thought about me and my brothers. I want to know how we are connected, if we are. I want to know who I would have been had I known him all my life. And that's an impossible request. So he teases me gently, too gracious to mention that the experience of our meeting was not spectacularly momentous for him, only for me.

I have a sister whose name means Fairy Tale. Ten years younger than I, she is the daughter of my father and his second wife. She has lived in Tehran all her life, beautiful and cultured, a brilliant statistician and textbook author. She said, in our first email exchange, that she has always known and wondered about me. She had studied our baby pictures with the same intensity that we had gazed at those few black-and-whites of our twenty-five-year-old father. She is the mirror of me, and I adore her. I want to see her world through her eyes. I want to know where we begin and end and overlap. We email each other several times a week. Once a month or so, my father writes a long note by hand, and Afsaneh types it into the computer, but there is still so much we don't discuss.

In this delicate exchange of identities and memories, we are all careful to point our conversations toward the future and not eulogize the past. All my questions, all my suspended-in-time incompletes, I have tried to let go of, for the sake of both my parents. Neither wants to display old scars. For my mother, there will be no reckoning; she wants no part of this reunion, and we have tried to respect her privacy while opening our lives to the first people we have ever known who belonged to us only, who were our family, but not hers.

I have never for a moment doubted the wisdom of my mother's courageous decision to leave my father and forge a tough but rewarding life for herself and her children. The first choice my brothers and I had to make, before we could send the first email, was whether to forgive him. We had to confront long-buried, childish but still potent feelings of anger, helplessness, and loss. We found that after thirty-five years, the fundamental matters that concerned us were less about accounting for past transgressions and more about the possibility of redemption, for him, ourselves, and our family. What we have discovered through emails and phone calls is that he is enormously interesting, flawed, funny, sincere in his love for us and humble in his gratitude to fate for bringing back his missing children. His name is Sirous, two syllables I sounded silently as a child, like a mantra. Now that those sounds connect with a living person, a voice that talks back, I feel a little embarrassed whenever I say it, Sirous, once a secret word I kept to myself.

I still find it amusing that through all the complications of time and random movement, what reunited us was a simple combination of spur-of-the-moment curiosity and fingertip technology. We barely even tried, no exhaustive searches, detectives hired, or money spent. It turned out all we needed was the instantaneous precision of a Web crawler trolling for an unusual name, then later only a blip full of the heart's gifts shooting instantly through networks across the ocean and vast cultural divide with a zip and a flash. It still makes me laugh. But the Internet isn't enough.

That's why I dream of next year in Cyprus. I can see us all on a beach at the edge of the Mediterranean, sipping tea, my fairy tale sister, long-lost father, faithful brothers, and me, one side of our family on a neutral, beautiful island, crafting the beginnings of a shared identity. We still speak of it in dream terms, in wouldn't-it-be-wonderful terms, but I see it happening, this year or the next. I have made a promise more than once in my life that I will never go to Iran. My father cannot come here. Cyprus is one of only two countries in the world where Iranians may visit without a visa. And I've heard it's very beautiful at certain times of year. Imagine that.

Recovery

✷

NASRIN RAHIMIEH

For my sister, Nahid

The days leading up to Aunt Ezzat's wedding were filled with activity. Carpets were turned upside-down to prevent them from being stained by the throng of guests expected on the second story of our house where the wedding was to be held, extra chairs and china sets stacked throughout the living room and the parlor. I remember only the frantic pace of preparations and my own annoyance at the excitement engulfing our house. I was angry about losing my aunt, or *ammeh*—the term designating her relation to me as my father's sister—to a low-class *bazaari* living in Rasht, some forty kilometers away from our hometown of Anzali.

Being a teenager, I disguised my anger as disdain for traditional Iranian marriage negotiations between the prospective husband and a male guardian, in my aunt's case my father, several years her junior. When Hajji Golmarvi had first approached my father, asking for Ezzat Ammeh's hand in marriage, the extended family had been amused by this big-nosed Rashti, whose nasalized voice accentuated the very feature of his physiognomy that made him into the prototypical resident of Rasht, the capital of the province of Gilan.

Those of us who had the good fortune to be born in Anzali, on the coast of the Caspian, never tired of ridiculing Rasht for its muddy streets and its misfortune of being landlocked. It did not help that the word *rasht* was reputed to mean "garbage." The Rashtis, we liked to believe, were the butt of the interminable jokes about Gilanis. Rashti men were particularly targeted for their gullibility, especially vis-à-vis their womenfolk, with a keen appetite for extramarital affairs. The differences we exaggerated between Rashtis and other inhabitants of Gilan mattered little to other Iranians, who did not understand our dialect, Gilaki, and considered us all cut from the same cloth. When I was older, I would hear fellow Gilanis dismiss the jokes as rooted in fear of our liberal ways. Gilani women worked alongside their men, perhaps worked harder than the men, and did not kowtow to male authority. It followed that Gilani men were seen as putty in the hands of their wives. In those heady times of transition in the early years of the seventies, Gilanis could gloat about having been ahead of their compatriots who had only just recently converted to progressive ways.

During the summers of my youth, the white sandy beaches of our hometown teemed with vacationers from all over the country, some awkward and self-conscious in their designer bathing suits. In those days, our town bore the name of the royal family, Pahlavi, and reveled in its history of having been Iran's first gateway to Europe. The Qajar kings, immediately preceding the Pahlavis, had boarded ships in Anzali to travel to Europe.

The first Pahlavi monarch, Reza Shah, renamed the town after himself and engaged an Austrian architect to design a park, known even today as "the boulevard," and government buildings that would rival those of Europe. The boulevard, nestled on the sea and protected by two breakwaters built around the same time, looks across to the port. The breakwaters, protecting the harbor, were also symbolic fortifications against the cascade of Bolshevik ideas that had spilled over from across the border and incited Gilan to declare itself, albeit briefly, an independent socialist republic. The Pahlavi monarch acted quickly, but Gilanis continued to flirt with communism even after the uprising was subdued and the residents of Gilan brought back into the nation's fold.

Despite its recent shabbiness the boulevard has remained the town's favorite spot for evening strolls. When Anzali was being transformed into Pahlavi, appearances mattered. The boulevard's flowerbeds were meticulously groomed, as were the strollers dressed in the new fashions dictated by a king anxious to make Iranians equal to Europeans. The Shah ordered women to cast off their *chadors*, uncover their heads, and, if modesty got the better of them, don European-style hats. Any other form of head-cover for women became unlawful. Men had new sartorial ordinances of their own. The Pahlavi hat, resembling a French field marshal's, and European suits were their lot. In the thirties, Pahlavi, like the rest of the country, was legislated into modernity.

Generations later, the town would revert to its old name, Anzali, briefly having run the risk of being called Khomeini. Having withstood this particular onslaught of a new orthodoxy, the town did suc-cumb to other changes. As if responding to the new zeal sweeping the country, the Caspian rose by several meters and buried the sandy beaches where scantily clad men and women had once cavorted. New makeshift breakwaters had to be erected once the rising water sub-merged beachfront villas. Summertime vacationers, conforming to a new dress code, now perch on the new beachfront breakwater, expos-ing only their faces to the cool Caspian breeze.

Back in the days when Hajji Golmarvi entered our lives, the town was still called Pahlavi and we, especially the self-assured younger gen-eration, scoffed at tradition. Hajji Golmarvi's social status, as a shop owner in the Rasht bazaar with rudimentary education, speaking a heavily accented Persian, did little to help his overall standing in our eyes. Concealing our Gilani accent when we spoke Persian marked us as citizens of a unified and progressive nation. Our mother's career as a teacher had convinced her that my sister and I would speak Persian at home. She herself was fluent in Gilaki and Turkish, or Azari, the lan-guage of her émigré father from Baku. Switching among Persian, Azari, and Gilaki came to her naturally, but she did not want the bur-den of her past to stand in her daughters' way. We grew up knowing what needed to be discarded for us to become full-fledged Iranians.

The fact that Hajji Golmarvi had made a pilgrimage to Mecca rendered him even more suspect. Clearly he clung to old values an edu-cated family like ours, preoccupied with raising levels of literacy and basic health care, did not endorse. His wealth would have been better spent on the needy people around him rather than on a trip to Mecca, so we thought along with the intellectuals of the time. Never mind that some members of our family had made the same pilgrimage as a sign of their devotion. But being a *hajji* in Mr. Golmarvi's case stood as another sign of his backwardness.

The night Hajji Golmarvi was invited to dinner at our home to welcome him to the family became the stuff of family legend. My father, my mother, and aunts and uncles did their best to keep the event on an even keel, but at the end of the lavish dinner prepared by my mother, Hajji Golmarvi showed his appreciation by filling a moment of silence with a loud belch that quickly dissolved young and old into peals of laughter. Ezzat Ammeh led the way with a furtive glance at my sister and me, who had to be excused from the table after attempts to stop our fit of giggles failed. Our father, himself prone to unstoppable laughter, shepherded us out of the dining room, using the momentary absence as a means of composing himself.

Ezzat Ammeh's complicit look and her sharing in the collective mirth at her future husband's expense convinced me that she was abandoning us. I believed firmly that she had agreed to the marriage only to save her younger brother the financial burden of supporting her. Maybe she even thought she was providing the family with a source of amusement. Surely she could not respect Hajji Golmarvi.

On the day of the wedding, I became convinced that it was not too late to stop the marriage. I found a co-conspirator in my cousin Alyeh, who joined me in railing against our *ammeh* being sacrificed at the altar of tradition. Ridiculing Hajji Golmarvi, we wondered whether he would belch at the crucial moment during the ceremony. We retired to my room, far away from the hubbub of guests, to solidify our plans for rescuing Ezzat Ammeh. Elders impatient with our barrage of invectives were only too happy to shoo us out of the way, reassuring us that they would let us know when the ceremony was about to begin. Lost in our impassioned discussions, far away from those who had promised to come and get us, Alyeh and I missed the marriage ceremony. We emerged from my room to discover that Ezzat Ammeh had been married to Hajji Golmarvi.

Ezzat Ammeh left her luxurious paternal home and moved into Hajji's modest house in Rasht, where she has lived since that day and where I am told she is about to die.

As on the day she was married, I am once again far away from her—this time continents apart—regretting that neither of us is in that house we loved so much. Lately, in my dreams, I have been traveling back to our house, where I find Ezzat Ammeh downstairs busy with one chore or another. She is always the young woman of my childhood, bustling about and laughing at my antics.

Worlds apart, Ezzat Ammeh and I are dreaming the same impossible dream of returning to the house built by her father and my grandfather. In her rare moments of lucidity, my mother tells me, Ezzat Ammeh asks to be taken home. But she is at home, doctors reassure her, not understanding that the home she seeks exists now in our collective imagination only.

Our house sits empty, having been sold by my mother when she could no longer maintain it after my father's death. Every time I passed by it during my last visit home, I felt a little pinch in my heart. Some of the windowpanes are broken; other windows swing open, making me think back to all those years ago when at the sign of any downpour I would become anxious about windows that might have been left open, worrying that the torrential rains of Anzali would rot the carved wood of the panes no workman could replicate.

I wished I had the key to the house and I could let myself in, shut the windows, repair the damage, and make it ours again. I did visit the house during the trip before last, when it was being used as a girls' school. I took pictures of every room and hallway to which I was permitted access by the new owners. But the pictures are disappointing. They do not capture the spirit of the home once teeming with life.

My grandfather, a well-to-do merchant, a *hajji* of a different era, had the house built in the second decade of the twentieth century, the year of my father's birth. In fact, my father was born in that house where he would live almost all of his life with the exception of the years he spent at Tehran University, studying to become a dentist, and his year of military service in the southeastern province of Baluchistan. Unlike many of his peers who set up practices in Tehran and apparently made fortunes, my father returned home. I knew my father was destined to live out his years in his paternal home when, one day playing in the yard, I discovered his nickname, Askar, written in a clumsy hand, emerging from beneath a freshly painted wall. Coats of paint could not hide the fateful inscription, perhaps executed by my own father, who was inseparable from that soulful house.

The two-story U-shaped house was designed with an inner room on each floor with five doors opening onto three rooms and a hallway along the western side, used mostly as storage space. Two additional rooms, on the two northern corners of the house, facing the Caspian, were connected through doors to the remaining rooms, converging on the central one.

My mother was fond of mocking the architecture of our house which reminded her of a passage she had read in a Russian novel depicting a similar design and pondering its futility. This house of many doors leading to the inner core reminded her of circumambulating a shrine. The nearby mosque, with its regular reminders of the call to prayer, only reinforced the image. When the mosque acquired a loudspeaker, pointed north toward our house, at prayer times we retreated to that inner sanctum, shutting doors against the noise and the gaze of the curious onlookers from the mosque's second-story women's quarters. My father once threatened to borrow a hunting rifle and disable the loudspeaker. The threat was relayed to the religious leaders, who retaliated by spreading word that my father had become a Baha'i. Lengthy negotiations, through the intervention of influential relatives, resulted in the loudspeaker being directed southward to the center of town.

When my father became the sole owner of the paternal home after his father's death, having reimbursed his siblings for their share of the inherited property, he renovated it periodically. Upstairs a wall connecting the south-facing room, our parlor, to the dining room was removed to create a better sense of space. Eventually the elaborate wood-burning central heating system, whose inner structure no one knew how to repair, was dismantled. Out went some of the original furniture. Our old heavy wooden dining table with carved curvy legs was replaced with a plain modern one. The result of growing local mass production, our new dining set was prone to squeaking and occasionally coming unglued. The chairs were particularly precarious and could sometimes bring the house down when one of their occupants tottered onto the floor.

One evening my sister, my father, a cousin who had moved in with us to attend teachers' college in our town, and I were watching on television the arrival of the dignitaries for the extravagant celebrations marking twenty-five hundred years of monarchic rule in Iran. My cousin, Shokufeh, daughter of one of my father's older brothers, who had married into the family of our town's Friday prayer leader, had been raised in a traditional environment and seemed ill at ease with our irreverent ways. Shokufeh wore long, modest dresses while my sister and I had been raised in shorts and miniskirts. She knew her prayers and was diffident toward elders.

My parents, disinclined to give in to Shokufeh's sense of modesty, insisted that she join us in everything. That evening she sat rigidly at the dining table watching television. My father suggested a game of counting the number of visitors from each country as they descended from planes and were greeted by the Shah on the tarmac of the Tehran airport. Just as we began keeping count, planeloads of guests arrived from neighboring Arab countries, dressed in their robes and headgear. Unlike visitors from other corners of the globe, the Arab delegations traveled with large entourages. My sister and I took up the count, with our father acting as backup, keeping an eye on the new arrivals lining up to shake hands with the Shah. Sometimes our father would lean his chair back, relaxing his vigilance. Moments later he would anchor the chair legs on the floor, lean forward, and say, "Get set, go, here comes another troupe." Before long we were laughing too hard to keep count, tears streaming down our faces. In the middle of one of these bouts of laughter, our father leaned his chair back a little too far, and the chair fell backwards, coming apart and landing him on his back end. My sister and I rushed to him to see if he was all right, interrupting our laughter only briefly to assess the damage. The commotion, like the earlier fits of laughter, had produced no apparent effect on Shokufeh, whose gaze was unnaturally fixed on the television screen. Suddenly conscious of her stillness, we turned our attention to her and noticed the enormous effort to suppress laughter contorting her face. "Look, Papa, Shokufeh is trying not to laugh," one of us said, catapulting a snorting Shokufeh from her seat, running for cover.

The chair was set aside to be later reglued, and Shokufeh was coaxed back into the dining room, where she received an avuncular lecture on the need to be less guarded with us. I do not know how the time Shokufeh spent with us affected her, but I like to believe that something of the expansive spirit of that rambling house stayed with her.

The house's southern exposure, the inside of the U, was wrapped by a veranda on both floors overlooking a courtyard and, in the old days, a shallow goldfish pool that is a traditional fixture of Iranian houses. When an earthquake left a large crack on one side of the pool, my father had it removed. In its place was installed a swing set I treasured. The swings faced the garden, away from the two low apertures to the crawl space under the house, inhabited in the spring by mama cats and their litters.

My sister and I used to feed the mamas and wait with bated breath for the time they would emerge with their playful kittens. Some of the cats adopted our house as their permanent abode. At one point we had fourteen cats living with us. My aunts and parents did not like the feline overpopulation, and now and then my father would take some of the cats to the hospital grounds, where he assured us they would be fed the kitchen leftovers. But even he did not have the heart to rob us of our most cherished cats, on whom we bestowed royal names and honorifics. Kamran Mirza, one of our most beloved pets, had his infections treated with antibiotics mixed with caviar to disguise the taste. He was exempted from the condition that cats stay in the yard. Years after Kamran Mirza's disappearance two doors were installed at each end of the first-floor veranda to prevent other cats from roaming through the house.

The enclosed veranda's countless windows extended to the tall ceilings and reached down to waist-high solid wood banisters, carved in the same design as the window frames and shutters. The rooms facing north and east all had bay windows where I spent many hours sitting and eavesdropping on the conversations of passersby. Diagonally set, crisscrossed wrought-iron bars protected the first-floor windows facing the streets. Wrought-iron banisters also ran along the side of the stairs leading up to the second floor.

The upstairs windows did not have bars and served the useful function of allowing us to survey people ringing the front doorbell. For a brief period a section of the second story was devoted to my father's practice. His patients used the back door located in the northwest corner of the house, which led up to the hallway along the western wall. Apparently our habit of leaning out upstairs windows to see who was at the door developed in the years my father's office was at home, when desperate patients thought nothing of dropping by to see their dentist at all hours of the night. By the time I was a teenager we had an intercom installed, which with our old-style visual aid saved us from descending the twenty or so steps to let visitors in.

My grandparents and their ten offspring used mostly the first story of the house, reserving the upstairs for guests. I never saw the house when aunts, uncles, their spouses and their children inhabited it. Even when my mother arrived on the scene the house was far less populated. By the time of my birth, both grandparents had died; all but three of the ten offspring were married and had moved to other cities or homes of their own. My parents and my sisters and I lived upstairs, the three unmarried aunts downstairs. The house seemed to be able to expand and shrink, depending on the needs of the extended family.

More than that, it was a repository for all family stories, even those that had taken place beyond its walls.

My father's family seems to have an amusing tale for any period of history. When the authoritarian Reza Shah banned all public displays of religiosity associated with the martyrdom of Imam Hussein, a pivotal figure in the history of Shi'ism, my devout grandparents hired a mullah, a clergyman, to come to the house and recite from the Qu'ran, commemorating the traditional period of religious mourning. To ensure that the prohibited prayers would not be heard outside the house, my grandmother placed the clergyman in the innermost room and ordered all the doors shut. When the clergyman was left alone for a brief period to continue his recitation, my youngest uncle, then a child of six or seven years, took it into his head to disrobe in front of the clergyman and dance to the tune of his incantations. The offended clergyman was handsomely rewarded for his services, but not before delivering a lecture on the importance of raising children with proper respect for religion.

My grandmother, Belqu'ais, was too amused by her son's shenanigans to take the lecture to heart. *She* knew best how to raise her children. My grandmother was a strong-willed woman who controlled the finances of the house and the fate of all members of the household. My oldest uncle's wife told me once that if, at the time my grandmother was alive, women were allowed to serve in public office, my grandmother would have been the country's prime minister. It was Grandmother Belqu'ais who orchestrated the rescue of two of her nephews, pursued by the police for their membership in the communist Tudeh party. When the nephews got word that the police had gone to their home with arrest warrants they took refuge in their aunt's house. It did not take the police long to trace the two fugitives' steps and arrive at my grandparents' house. My grandmother herself greeted the policemen at the front door, denying that her nephews were hiding under her roof. The policemen insisted on searching the house, and my grandmother consented grudgingly but ordered them to begin upstairs where she knew her nephews were indeed hiding. Stunned by their mother's apparent error in judgment, her children remained silent. My grandmother accompanied the policemen up the flights of stairs, announcing in a loud voice which room they were about to enter. She weaved a path through the interconnected rooms, giving her nephews time to slink from room to room just ahead of the policemen and eventually out of the back door of the house. The search having produced no results, she dispatched the policemen, reminding them of the sanctity of the family home.

My grandmother was also known for her haughtiness—the reason often cited for three of her daughters having remained unmarried. Ezzat Ammeh told my mother that when she was young, she had many suitors, but her mother rejected them all for what she perceived as their inappropriate status to marry into our family. She, not her husband, held the right of veto in their household. She could also be cruel, my mother tells me. She refused to provide for the family of one of her married daughters when they were in need because she did not like her daughter's husband. Rather than sell her share of the inherited paternal home to her brother, she made an ostentatious show of transferring her share to her youngest son and erecting a fence around it.

Maybe Grandmother Belqu'ais was meant for a different life, one entitling her to public prominence. She traveled alone to Baluchistan, where my father was posted during his military service, to ensure that he had reasonable living conditions and, while there, adopted the role of his assistant. If patients suffering from toothaches came by and my father happened to be away, she would dispense home remedies of her own, described in Gilaki to the mystified Baluchis, who would return later to ask her son for a translation. Barriers of language and custom never fazed her. She returned home to tell stories about substandard Baluchi living conditions and know-how.

Her husband, my grandfather, was a quiet man of unswerving routine. He had a reputation for always taking the same route from his house to his shop in the city's bazaar. One of my older cousins mocks our grandfather for his routine and dismisses it as a sign of unimaginativeness. Mules and donkeys too always travel the same path, he is keen to point out. This cousin tells me our grandfather was cranky and tightfisted, but others speak of his compassion and generosity. When family names became a legal requirement under Reza Shah, our grandfather acquired a name echoing one of God's sacred names, compassionate. My cousin thinks this detail irrelevant and warns me against delving too deeply into our family's history, certain that I will find a host of nobodies and ne'er-do-wells.

The only pictures I have of my grandfather capture him as an austere man. One is a professional photograph of him in a Pahlavi hat, scowling at the camera and giving nothing away. The other photograph was taken by my father and shows his father resting at home with his hookah. His downcast eyes make him look tired. My father knew this man as a loving father who spent nights awake at his children's side when they were sick. I will never be able to reconcile these two opposing images of my grandfather. Something of a similar paradox plagued my own father throughout his life.

Outside our home, he was known as a reticent and serious man. My mother's friends and colleagues frequently asked her how she coped with his lack of humor and paucity of words. Little did they know that he reserved his sense of humor and playfulness for his private life. He was deadly serious about preserving the home front for the innermost circles of relatives and friends. He never tired of the continuous arrival of vacationing relatives in the summer. They would spend the days on the beach and return to us at night. When they insisted that we spend Friday lunches with them on the beach, my father would respond: "If I want to spice my food with sand, I'll go down to the yard and grab a handful." He did always give in reluctantly, but his preference was for large family gatherings at our home. Now and then when he returned home at night to the unannounced arrival of a group of visitors, he would ask teasingly, "Didn't the management tell you the hotel is full tonight?"

One Friday, long after my sister and I had left home, my parents hosted a lunch for a number of out-of-town relatives. Other aunts, uncles, nieces and nephews, who knew where the visitors were staying, kept arriving, swelling the numbers and sending my mother back to the freezer where she always had food ready for just such an occasion. My father was off entertaining the children when word came that another of his nieces was at the door with her husband. He abandoned his young charges, rushed to one of the bay windows overlooking the street, where he leaned out from his seated position and shouted: "I am sorry, but we are filled to capacity. Don't you see that the host himself has nowhere to sit but this window?" At a time when joking about the revolution and the Iran-Iraq War was to court disaster, he asked his niece if on her way she had noticed families of martyrs also being directed to his house for lunch. At last he descended the stairs, let the visitors in, latched the long iron bar across the front door, and turned back to the onlookers from the upper veranda, announcing that he was barring the door for their own good, otherwise there would not be enough food to go around.

My happiest memories of our home are of evenings I would accompany my mother downstairs and sit around with the *ammehs*. I can still smell the traditional Gilani straw mats that covered their floors. Sitting cross-legged on the floor with them, my mother would become their confidant and social advisor. If they felt jilted by one of their friends or acquaintances, my mother would advise them to be forgiving and generous. In turn she would tell them about the goings-on in her school, filling them with awe at her ability to manage difficult people.

Recently, my mother heard Ezzat Ammeh ask to be taken home to die in peace. Ezzat Ammeh's request worked itself into my mother's dreams. She too began to dream of our house, and then she knew exactly what to do. She went to visit Ezzat Ammeh and told her that she and I had both been dreaming of our old home. One of my mother's sisters sent along word that she would give up her plot in the Anzali cemetery so that Ezzat Ammeh could be buried next to my father and his oldest sister. As my mother relayed this to Ezzat Ammeh, adding that I had begun writing about our home, feeding her spoonfuls of her homemade broth, Ezzat Ammeh began showing signs of improvement. My mother tells me she is recovering well. We are all being nourished now by the memories and dreams of our cherished home. I can almost smell the straw mats.

Baba's Passing — February 2005

PERSIS M. KARIM

In the snow-covered streets,
alleys of Tehran, people
hail taxis they cannot see.
It is the largest snowfall since 1971,
the twenty-sixth anniversary of the revolution.

Red and green lights strung up
celebrate, not Christmas,
but the holiday for those gathered
in heavy coats, shouting, "*Marg bar Amrika!*"
"Death to America!"

Here in America, death
has arrived at my house.
My father, who left that place
more than fifty years ago
has faded into the white
light of winter.
The week-long vigil
at his bedside, waiting
for a sign is over.

Death arrived and we,
we welcomed it for him.
The fight he gave after the stroke,

the squeeze of his hand,
the twitch of feet and palms
made me pray for a sign.

The answer rang in my ear.

Through the crackling telephone
my broken (heart)
Persian feels weighted
by the grief of my uncle.
Del-be-Del Rah Dareh.
I say it, with certainty, exactly
as I heard Baba say it:
Our Hearts Travel the Same Road.

Joys of a Simple Meal

❧

Esther Kamkar

Bring me
A loaf of rough bread
A ladle of olives
A handful of figs

A token of feta cheese that
Comes from the sheep of Kefalonia
A bunch of muscadine grape that
Grows wild and

Half a pomegranate
I will eat
Be filled and satisfied
No hunger for even

One morsel
Of fancy foods
Or for love
If you bring me

Raw Walnuts

∽

NEGIN NEGHABAT

To my mother
and to her mother

Crack the hard shell of walnuts, throw the shell away and place the walnuts in a jar of water. Change the water every few hours, and repeat this for several days. Eventually, the thin brown skin gets soft and can be peeled off easily. With only the bare, white part of the walnut remaining, add some salt, and try tasting the "raw walnut." For me, this taste brings back memories of a time when I still had a nation and the sense of belonging.

∽

The bad odor of city smog and exhaust fumes from congested cars filled the air. My grandmother was irritated by the strength of my grip as she was leading me, my hand in hers, through narrow alleys, across busy roads, and past overcrowded shops. Then, I started crying because she didn't hold my hand back with the same strength I held hers. She finally did. Maybe I was feeling the frailty of my life in Iran as it was coming to an end, and it was this feeling that pushed me to hold on as well as I could. Maybe this was why I fixated on vigorously holding Mami's hand. Or maybe I was, in fact, just an unusually difficult child, as I was led to believe.

We crossed large streets, lingering our way through the masses of cars that seemed to be standing still in the typical traffic of Tehran. The incessant honking of cars, their drivers' cursing, and the constant complaining of people standing by are the sounds I hear after all these years, like the sound of the ocean captured in a seashell.

We got trapped in the traffic, our way across the street blocked by the side of a large, gray van with a horizontal, metal door handle exactly at my height. I was urged to hold on to the metal handle with the same vigor as I held on to Mami's hand; and I did. Suddenly, the van started moving; I still refused to let go until I was pulled back by Mami's hand. Her loud shriek was followed by a worried, angry lecture over the danger I had put myself in.

We walked almost daily to the bazaar, where she bought vegetables, fruits, and the like. People's smiles and compliments there, in my first country, stood in such massive contrast to the cold, harsh treatment I received in the country that eventually became my second home—Germany.

At the bazaar, we enjoyed the attention of merchants and other customers. I remember Mami's bargaining skills, still, as if it were only a few days ago. Now, her behavior strikes me as deeply confident when I think back to those days or, really, any days I spent with her. Mami was a remarkably beautiful woman, not just then, but at every age. I remember the attention we would receive as a compliment to her beauty and confidence, but also to her wit and eloquent language. It was normal that I was thought to be her daughter rather than granddaughter, and she didn't make efforts to clarify this misconception. I also became used to receiving compliments, and it spoiled me to the point of feeling insulted for the rest of my life whenever I did not receive my due attention.

The walnuts from the markets of Tehran did not come in a jar of water, but in their original green shell, the shell that later turns brown. They were real "raw" walnuts that were kept fresh by the merchants, typically wrapped in large amounts into wet cloths. Peeling off the brown skin was difficult for me then because I was less than five years old. But someone always helped me. We usually bought small plastic bags full of these nuts—of course, only during the season for raw walnuts.

Mami was always very attentive to weight issues. She and my mother didn't want me to eat a lot of nuts. They are very calorie-rich, and I had always been a little fat. "Walnuts and Nutella are the reason she's chubby," Mami would tell my mother, and while raw walnuts were only seasonal, Nutella—a European chocolate paste—was available to me all year long because my mother worked for an Austrian company.

⁂

Raw walnuts cannot be carried into other countries because it is not possible to constantly keep them wet in pieces of cloth when traveling for a long time. Moreover, agricultural foods are not allowed to cross national borders. Like so many of my family's belongings, they have been left behind a line drawn on a map which constitutes the border, or rather, the frontier for many of us. But there was no restriction on carrying with me the most important of my belongings—my memories. Now, the closest I can get to having "raw" walnuts is these memories, or settling for the substitute, not-at-all raw walnuts that are re-"rawed" in water.

I was thirteen years old when I had real "raw" walnuts again after not having them for eight years. That was in the markets of Tehran again, this time with my mother, both of us wrapped in long coats, our hair hidden under dark veils. Our one-month vacation there happened to fall right in the walnut season, which was the only good thing about the trip.

Eating walnuts in the streets of Tehran, after so many years of an unhappy childhood in a strange country, I felt at home again. It was brief, but the feeling of being home was momentarily nurturing and comforting. I craved more and more walnuts during that summer in Iran.

I still crave them.

The Camel and the Cantaloupe

MICHELLE KOUKHAB

As high as the humps on its back,
as thick as the hair that warms it,
and as difficult as it is to see
in the middle of the night,
my grandfather's camel is moving,
quickly, its feet spreading the sand
for distance, escape, without knowledge
of morning's beginnings and travel's
endings. The camel carries my grandfather
past boundaries, stops only when papers
are requested, guides changed, or
for his sudden desire to hold on
to what he is leaving. Iran's mountains
becoming low hills in the distance.

As smooth as the skin on the surface,
as bright as the sun that makes it,
a light orange, sweet to taste,
the cantaloupe captures my grandfather's
country. He meets a roadside man,
and shares the fruits of his homeland
on a *sofreh* in the desert. Slicing
the cold skin of the melon in half,
they forget about leaving. For the last time
he gathers in the Kavir desert until dusk,
and the cut of the cantaloupe is bursting
like the sunrise. Even when it's dark,

he will remember this *sofreh* spread out
against the market of a fading light.

In another place, at another time,
I stumble into a store of jewels,
photographs of woven carpets,
miniature women with hair of gold,
turquoise finger-bands, and camel
hair. I sit for amber tea and cookies
and speak Farsi, slightly broken
and weightless with forgotten words.
The owner knows my grandfather.
I open the window to change the air.
They shared an October afternoon
in the desert, as the sun evaporated
and the mountains disappeared,
two camels and a cantaloupe.

Ode to the Eggplant

PERSIS M. KARIM

A much misunderstood creature,
the eggplant is like an exile.
The tongue of its deep purple
mouth, trapped in the bitterness
of those who cannot speak.

Poor eggplant—even your name
compromises your beauty.
Like a wayward traveler
arriving at Ellis Island,
someone took one look at you
and declared: "Eggplant!"

If only they'd spoken French,
and written down "aubergine" instead.
Your American name belies your mystery—
you are an egg, yes, but also the curve
of a human calf, a shiny black phallus
in the starkness of day.
You are the waxy underbelly of a bird,
the slope of a mountain,
smooth stones from the bottom of a river.

How could anyone have missed
your taste in the appellation?
You are neither animal nor vegetable,
but your flavor is requited love—

the thing that makes all others complete:
garlic, tomato, lentil, lamb, rice.
Olive oil would simply be lost without you.

And the heat from which you are born
is the heat you unleash
in the slow simmer of sauce and stew
that gathers people to an intimate table.

Torches

SUSAN ATEFAT-PECKHAM

Three days and the flames gleamed
up the south wall stairs onto Esmat's
roof, forty flaming heads lifting
the night then pulling back along
each concrete edge. Tables lined
one end of the flat tarred roof. I
remember only swinging
from clothes lines—a small, frail
child. The noon sun beat
the top of the house,
honeysuckle, evenings when Nina
hummed downstairs in her room
at the open window, her voice rising
air ducts jutting rectangular chimneys
from the tar. I am not there to see
this new roof, lit like this, a funeral
pyre of kabob and rice.

This fire is not the flame of luck,
the pyres they jump over in streets
at Noruz. These are the lights
of those who wait, burning 'til
embers of forgetting, as they fill
the tables, while Grandfather hovers
in the fluid space between flame
and sky. He is this shining, shimmering

space, this hot halo, this whispered
hat held over the house, tipped
with forgiveness, the fire held
close, scalding the sky.

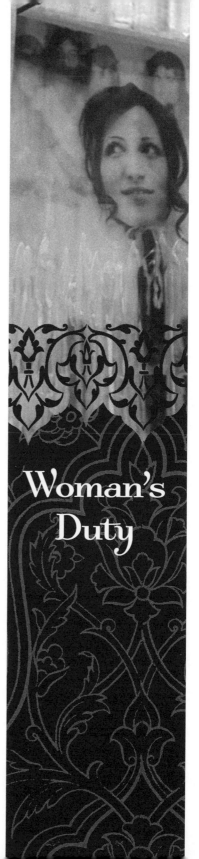

Woman's
Duty

Avenue Vali Asr

⌀

SUSAN ATEFAT-PECKHAM

For Kholeh Lili

We need another Rosa Parks
to pin herself to that front seat
and say, I am too old for later.

Smoke folded edges in city air.
Buses littered streets, dented, worn,
old tin cans crushed at the station.

I unstuck the front doors, pushed
the edges forward and apart to meet
the fat thumb pointing backward.

Boro Ounja! he said. Over there!
And I turned to see my place
among the colored scarves behind.

My breasts warmed steel rounds
at my ribs. I was half-sick of standing
there, breathing in wet wool
of hair, breathing in their breaths.
We are not sheep, I said, We are not
sheep. A woman turned. I tugged

at clinging cloth. Someone shushed
me quiet. Do not speak, she said,
It is good this way, without voice.

She dabbed her head and sweat pressed
through colored silk. She pushed
and shoved the heat for space.

I saw her hand grip at the window.
I heard the bustle of a large woman
behind me telling the others to hear

and peasants lolled in their chairs
up front, sunned their hairy hands
under the smoke of windows, kicked

their feet up on empty chairs, leering
into the small noises we made.
I know that words can't help them here.

Hot breath hovers in old wind.
A folded sky spreads in Tehran.

Woman's Duty

TARA FATEMI

button sewing: my only seamstress skill
one torn hem and it's off to the tailor.

were my hands possessed for one hour?
with needle and thread I sewed my lips together

no word could fly out and hum bee-stings
into our tender ears, darling. stitches

so even and fine they were invisible.
months later I got too close

to the mirror, jumped back from
dangling lipthreads and screamed

to ears whose drums had closed
from lack of use.

The Next Day Is Always So Still
(New York, October 2001)

NIKA KHANJANI

Tell me—how long did it last?
The final bump, the closing line
Well into the A.M. the sun rise
the day
break

Alone again
With the tick
talking in my head

Flashbacks of the scene
Soaking it all in
to let it all hang
Out to drip
And, girl, did you ever

"My heart will burst" I tell them
"And your feet will hurt in the morning"
they reply

They watch as
I lean in when I step back
My constant motion
My cock-tease devotion

My demolition and my hiding
Sometimes ties are most dividing

Just, please, one more thing
Let me sink, let me sway
Watch me from above
And tell me in the morning
That it's okay

Waiting for Ulysses

∝⃜

LALEH KHALILI

Penelope in darkness
unraveled

awaiting the end of all exile

groves of tangerine and *naranj* rotten on the branches
and the algaed imperturbability of lonely reflecting pools
in forgotten courtyards

Penelope
cooking endless feasts
for endless suitors

her fresh taut from abstinence
her breath sweet
and her temples throbbing from the banquet of fear

all the while her beloved
scoundrel, pilgrim, and exile
measuring the breadth of the
beds of sirens
queens
and consorts

Penelope
unraveling perpetually

tender calloused fingers
in darkened bleak rooms of her loneliness

The woman has veto power

HALEH HATAMI

that her sisters of other species
do not, and, of course, this has evolved
over millennia of death
by childbirth due to the enormity
of the human head that houses
the human brain and the difficulties
of passing that cranial anomaly
through the sorry hole of the pelvic
bone and a woman's bone memory
—quite an innovation, really—
that penetration is somehow linked
to conception and therefore pain
and self-sacrifice for new life,
and the question becomes one
of veto and the subsequent frustration
on the part of the male species
on the other end of moratorium,
and so it is said that the rise
of patriarchy is directly tied
to male frustration with veto
when they see all around them
other species joining in the female
season, that is, when she is in heat
and she has to have it and doesn't
think about the birth pain
because her animal pain is less fatal
on average, or such as statistics
and physiology will lead us

to believe, and really, if you understand
that man standing bipedal upright
puts tremendous pressure on internal
organs as they rest directly on the frail
pelvic bone, as opposed to swinging
in the muscle membrane of the quadra-
pedal mammal who enjoys a more
flexible birth channel, you begin to see
that the human female can only decree
her own comfort and say no.

On the Rooftop

∝

Farnoosh Moshiri

Under her black veil, in the darkest fold, where the sharp odor of rosewater mixes with the scent of earth and dust of many holy shrines, in a hidden corner, under her long, thick *chador,* death sits silently, brooding.

She knows he is here, but she ignores him and busies herself with the routines of her evening prayer. Not praying for him to go, because if he is here, living under her *chador,* it's meant by God, it's His will and who is she to confront the Almighty? If he is here, sitting with that narrow body of his, with knees folded into his chest, breathing quietly, brooding, waiting for her to finish her day's chores, let him be. If her time has come, it has come.

So she doesn't pray for him to leave, she prays for her children, who are not with her anymore. The boy is down there, for the past ten years, in the courtyard, buried under the persimmon tree, where he used to play as a child, and the girl is somewhere on the other side of the ocean, in a dark, faraway place, damper and lonelier than where her brother lives. She prays for the girl more—who is alive—than the buried boy, because she thinks that the boy, who was killed and his corpse was brought home one rainy day, is now in the sunny courtyard of his own house, but the girl, who left one sunny day, is now somewhere rainy, lonely and dark. She needs God's attention, she deserves a prayer more than her brother does, who lies in peace.

This way, thinking about them, seeing their faces in her mind, imagining them in their dark places, measuring their comfort and discomfort, as she has done all through her life, she spreads her cashmere cloth on the carpet, faces the diamond-shaped window and slowly unfolds her embroidered prayer kerchief, as if the sacred stone and the carnelian rosary are made of ether and will evaporate. She kisses the Sura that is carved on the stone and lays the smooth rock gently on the kerchief next to the rosary. After arranging everything meticulously she pulls the black *chador* off her head and folds it in four. She does this slowly and gently as if a butterfly is trapped inside the folds of the veil and she doesn't want to chase it away.

When she lays the folded fabric on the carpet a faint odor of camphor rises and this startles her. He's here waiting, she thinks, with that peculiar smell of his, but he's a patient boy, he won't rush. Now she picks up her white, transparent prayer veil and arranges it on her head, then looks out the diamond of the window, which has framed the courtyard. Under the heavy persimmon, now leafless but shining with glowing orange fruits, there is a rectangular flowerbed, covered with purple pansies. That's where her son sleeps. She murmurs the words of the prayer absentmindedly and listens to the neighbor's children playing in the next yard. For a second she confuses time and place and feels the presence of her own children and thinks that they are chasing each other around the pool, shouting with excitement. When she comes to, she murmurs the words whose meaning she's never learned, the words of the language of God, which are not hers but are sacred and she has memorized them and repeated them like a parrot since she was a child.

The real prayer for her is when the foreign words end and it's her turn to talk. And she talks with God the way she talks with her sister, Poori. God is her absent friend, her invisible companion, an intimate roommate, closer than her husband used to be the first years of their marriage, closer than even her sister; God is her own self.

She talks to God as if she talks to her image in the mirror and gazes outside until dusk descends. She stares at the darkening courtyard and says: "Well, God, you've sent for me and he's sitting here under my veil, waiting patiently. This must be my last talk to you, so I'm telling you that I'm ready to go. The boy is under the tree, inside your earth, and I'll tell my sister to keep decorating his little flowerbed with pansies in the spring and autumn, marigolds in the summer and lilies in the freezing winter. I know that he is not up there with you, he's right here where he belongs and is resting in peace at last.

"But do you remember his restlessness? His riotous spirit? His sharp tongue? Remember how he wanted to change the world and fight with demons and restore justice, as he kept saying? What happened then? The devil took him, put him against the wall, your wall, God, and pierced him with hot bullets—your bullets. Because if you had not willed him to die, he wouldn't have died the way he did. You could at least have let him live a few more years, get married, and bring me a grandchild. Then this uninvited guest wouldn't crawl under my *chador* like a hissing snake, waiting for me to finish my chores. He'd know that there is another child to raise, he'd wait twenty more years. But it's all your will, God, and it's too late anyway; so I submit as I've always done and obey your orders.

"And the girl is in that remote land, which is dark most of the time, and it rains all day in spring and summer and snows the rest of the year. How can she be happy without the sun, God? Could you be happy without sunshine?

"You remember that after the guards brought her brother and we buried him together under this persimmon, the girl didn't stop sobbing for a long time. I heard her every night in her room, pressing her face to the pillow to muffle her cries. I sent her to this class and that class, because they wouldn't let her inside their universities, and she learned and half-learned a bit of this and a bit of that—language, drawing, sewing and typing. But her night sobs wouldn't stop. One day, you're my witness, I called her and told her, 'Your uncle's daughter is going abroad to study; do you want to go with her? Your share of the inheritance, what your father left for you, is untouched, your brother's money is yours too. Take it and go. The house is good enough for me. I can always let the two rooms, take tenants in and manage my life. And you know that I like to be alone. Your auntie Poori visits me every Friday like a clock and spends the whole weekend with me, so I won't be that lonely and the neighbors are nice too. I've lived here for thirty years, for God's sake—people know me and care for me. Go girl, go with your cousin and take that scarf off your pretty head. Let your hair breathe, dear, let the wind blow your sorrows away. Don't you know that I can hear you every night, your head in the pillow, weeping and shaking like a willow?'

"So she leaves. I send her off and I'm relieved. And that's your will, God. If you hadn't put those words in my head, I could never have convinced the girl to go. She insisted for months. She said she should stay with me and take care of me. But I could see that now a pair of candles burned in her eyes. Her eyes had a glow they didn't have before, and you know what that glow was.

"So she insisted for a while but didn't weep in her bed anymore.

I called her uncle and talked to him and gave him the money and the money bought her freedom. Her uncle bribed whomever he needed to bribe, bought the girls' visas and passports and they left.

"Now why am I telling you all this? Didn't you arrange it yourself? Weren't you behind everything?"

⚬⚬

This way she murmurs and whispers and tells and retells stories that her God has already heard. Now she stops and collects her prayer stone and rosary, wraps them in the kerchief and wraps the kerchief in the square cashmere cloth and puts the bundle on the table. She takes the white prayer veil off and folds it in four, but she doesn't put on the black veil yet; she leaves it in the corner of the room in its dark folds, watching it for a second, noticing that it's throbbing faintly, as if a ghost breathes underneath.

There is a wooden box she keeps under her bed; she carries it to the living room and sets it next to the prayer bundle. She unlocks the box with a small golden key and opens it gently as if there are ashes of burned memories there and they'll blow off with a faint breeze. But inside the box there are smaller boxes, something of the past hiding in them. The smallest of all is a tiny tin box containing three little teeth. The teeth belonged to her son, when he was six, and lost them to grow the new ones. The slightly bigger box contains her daughter's hair. When she was fourteen she cut her long hair for the first time to become fashionable. Now lifeless and dry, the dark braid coils like the fossil of a boa in the box. The third box contains her late husband's wedding band, cufflinks and tiepin. The large gold band still shines, but the silver cufflinks and the pin are tarnished. In the larger box there are a few letters. Her son sent them from prison, twice a year maybe, whenever they allowed him to write. She doesn't want to open them and read them again. The phrases are dry formulas, obvious lies about how well he is and how the jail food is good. He kept sending these letters just to say that he was alive, until the day that there was no letter and she knew that they had put him against the wall.

Underneath these boxes dry petals of jasmine, rosebuds, gladiolas and all the flowers of her son's funeral give out a sharp scent. She stares at all these boxes, rearranges the contents and closes their lids and the lid of the big one. She leaves a brief note for her sister next to the prayer bundle and the wooden box, picks up the folded black veil, steps outside and locks the door.

On the porch, with the folded veil over her left arm, she stands facing the late summer evening. The air is light and thin and she breathes it in deeply, keeping it in her lungs as if wanting to hold it there forever. Now she smells the wood smoke of the vendors, who grill ears of corn in the nearby market, and she remembers that she has not eaten all day. She decides not to eat tonight and sits on the stone step looking at the darkening flowerbed and the orange persimmons hanging like lanterns.

The next-door neighbor, a young woman who likes her, opens her window and calls, "I know you're meditating again, Sima Jaan, but I've cooked some vermicelli soup for my kids, do you want a bowl?"

"I'm not hungry, dear, thank you. Enjoy it."

"I've left a bowl for you, anyway, maybe you'll need it tomorrow when your sister comes by."

"Yes, tomorrow, tomorrow—" she says quickly to dismiss her.

The evening gets chilly and she needs to wear something. But she doesn't want to go inside again. The black veil is still hanging on her arm, ceremoniously, like a silk jacket, a piece of formal clothing that might get wrinkled if she lays it down. Should she unfold it and put it on to get warm? She decides not to wear it now. She is not ready yet. She lays the veil on the step next to her and looks at it in the dark. She pats it as if patting the soft back of a house pet and hears something whizzing inside. It's him, she thinks. He's not getting much air in the folds of the veil; he's suffocating.

What else does she need to do? Nothing. What else does she need to say? Nothing.

"I said whatever I needed to say to God, and I'm done. So I better go up on the roof and sleep there tonight. I know it's cold, but I'm not going back into that house again and here the neighbors will see me. The wooden bed is still on the roof. The mosquito net is there too; I'll sleep on the roof tonight."

Excited about sleeping on the roof she smiles and remembers the many summer nights when the kids were little and the house was warm and they all slept on the roof. The children giggled and played until late and she gazed at the stars, tracing them, naming them. Her husband snored, the children fell asleep, and she lay flat on her back, looking up at the sky. She didn't believe in God then. Not like now. She didn't even think about God. When she was young she didn't wear a veil, either, not even a scarf. She drank beer with her husband many times, and once or twice she had vodka. God came in when they left one by one. No, God came in when she began going to the holy shrines to pray for her son. No. God came earlier, when they arrested her son. Yes, He came to her one night in a dream, as a voice, and said, "You'll need me now. Get up, cover your hair and go to the holy shrine of Ghasem and pray and feed the poor. Go on foot if you want your son to get released." And she did. She woke up early in the morning and packed some bread and cheese and took a thermos of water and wore the black veil, which was folded for years at the bottom of a trunk. Her daughter asked, Why the veil? She said she was going to wear it from now on. Her daughter asked, Where are you going? She said, To the shrine of Ghasem. Her daughter said, Mother, you don't even remember how to pray—. I'll remember soon, she said.

She walked all day at the edge of a long road and she found other women, mothers of prisoners, walking to the shrine, and she didn't feel alone. They walked and walked until the sun set and they lodged in a caravansary at night and walked again the next day. Their shoes tore; they bought new ones in remote bazaars and walked more, until they reached the shrine of the son of the Imam, Ghasem. They prayed in the cool courtyard of the shrine and drank rosewater sherbet. They tied a piece of cloth to the post and gave alms to the beggars and walked back. All the while the mothers of the prisoners told stories of their sons and daughters; she listened, but didn't tell any story. What was there to tell? The boy was stubborn, wanted to change the world and the devil took him. That was all. How could one change the world of God, the world that God had designed?

So these pilgrimages happened three times. Three times God came to her dreams as a deep voice and commanded her to go to a holy shrine and she listened. She went to the shrines of Ghasem, Hassan and Abdullah. She learned chants and prayers she'd never known before. She even went to fortune-tellers with the other mothers, and her coffee cup was always as dark as the day of doom.

But all this began with her son's arrest. Before that she danced at birthday parties, wore nylon stockings and painted her nails red. When she was younger her husband paid attention to her nails.

"Don't cut your nails like men. Let them grow. Paint them red! I'll bring some nail polish for you from the store."

She laughed and said, "Then who'll wash the dishes?"

He bought a dishwasher for her, a luxury in those times, just because he loved long red nails. He was an eccentric in some ways; for example, before they went to bed, he liked to watch her changing her clothes. She felt shy and hid behind the closet door, but he craned his neck to see her, or caught her image in the mirror. But in bed he never touched her or even stroked her hair. He just crawled over her like a wet seal, found his way inside her and did his job and crawled back.

⚭

Now she caresses the slippery surface of the *chador,* as if it's a black cat purring next to her. "Be patient, be patient," she whispers. "In a minute."

"So that's when you came," she tells God. "When I went to three shrines on foot with the women and cooked sacred rice pudding and prayed five times a day, you came and stayed and that was when they all left me alone. But didn't I really want them to go? Didn't I feel relieved when they left? I can't lie to you, God. I wanted them to go and I was relieved when they did."

It began with her husband. The kids were in high school when he died. One day he closed his accessory store and as usual bought a watermelon and held it in one arm and carried his business bag in the other hand and walked toward home. The neighbors who saw him that evening say that he collapsed right at the corner of the cul-de-sac, where the blind dervish sat with his brass bowl. The watermelon fell and split open. The children who were playing on the sidewalk thought it was the man's brain and blood; they screamed and ran away. Some men brought him home, but it was too late.

That first night his body was on the bed. The family had to wait until the next day to take him to a morgue. Her son and daughter told her not to sleep in that room, but she didn't listen to them. Poori, who was staying with her, cried and begged her not to go into the bedroom.

But when she insisted, they let her alone. They thought it was because of love, grief and loss. They thought she wanted to lie down next to her husband for the last time. But this was not true. She wanted to undress in the middle of the room, with all the lights on, without him watching her. She wanted to stand there, alone and free, and take all her clothes off with no man peeping or craning his neck to look at her nakedness. She was sad, immensely sad, but so relieved.

∞

Her son gave her trouble. Since the time he began to read in his room all night, since the time he went to meetings with his friends and stayed out late, since the time he hid stacks of leaflets under his mattress, he was a trouble. He argued with her and gave her a hard time. He said she didn't understand. There were things she didn't know and she would never know, because she was not out in the world. He said the world was rotten and he wanted to change it and make it livable. But he picked the wrong time to change the rotten world, because that was exactly when others were planning to do the same thing in their own ways and the conflict began.

In his first letter from prison he wrote, "Mother, don't blame me for your suffering. It's a war, one wins, one loses. We lost."

So she prayed and fasted and walked to the three shrines, and cooked sacred pudding, and gave alms, but nothing worked. The devil pierced the boy with hot bullets against the Wall of the Almighty and since he was an atheist the guards didn't bury him, but brought his corpse home.

Only after digging the flowerbed with her daughter and washing him and wrapping him in a white shroud and laying him at the bottom of the cold hole and covering the grave and planting pansies on it, did she feel relief. That night when the smell of freshly dug earth came in the room with the September breeze, she took her tea to the bedroom, opened the window, sat there with her tea on the sill and gave out a long sigh. The boy was dead, lying silently under the earth. No one in this house was going to change the rotten world anymore. She was relieved.

Then she sent her daughter away.

"On purpose, God, on purpose! I sent her away to be alone. I didn't want to hear her crying in her pillow every night. I didn't want her going to typing class hunched under that long, navy uniform. I wanted her to go away and take that scarf off her head and let her hair breathe. But, no, it wasn't just that, it was for me too. I wanted to be by myself."

She murmurs these things, nods sometimes and shakes her head. She pats the black veil once in a while and the scent of camphor rises. She whispers, "In a minute, a minute—"

Night becomes deep and dark; silence falls on the neighborhood. She thinks that now it's time for her to go up to the roof and sleep. What if she leaves the veil here? What if she tricks the small, narrow thing that is now hissing in a dark corner? But it's cold up there, she doesn't have a jacket with her and she is not going back inside that house again. She needs the *chador* to keep her warm.

On the roof, she sits on the damp, wooden cot that has been there since old times, when they didn't have the air-conditioner and they slept on the roof. The bed is dusty and smells of mildew. She sits on the edge and puts the folded *chador* next to her. She imagines unfolding the veil, lying down and covering her body. She imagines closing her eyes and letting the small creature do whatever he's come to do.

Will her sister check the roof tomorrow? Will anyone check the rooftop?

She sits on the edge of the bed, looks up at the stars, the familiar stars of her past, the ones she traced and counted many times. She shivers. The September breeze becomes cool and strong, turns into a wind, and she feels that she needs to wrap something around her shoulder. She looks at the veil, sitting there in its heavy folds, heaving and throbbing, pulsating like a living thing. She picks it up, gently, and walks to the edge of the roof. She stands there looking down at the square courtyard and the round pool in the middle, the persimmon tree, the lanterns of the ripening fruits and the pansies, sleeping shyly in the dark. She takes a deep breath and thinks about tomorrow, Friday, when Poori will show up at ten o'clock to spend the day with her. They'll sew some, then they'll cook for the week; they'll eat together in front of the television, and take a nap on the porch. They may go out to the market and shop, or they may plant new flowers in the flowerbed. Poori will stay until evening when her husband will come to pick her up. They'll chat all day while doing these things, they'll reminisce, they'll laugh. They'll eat the neighbor's vermicelli soup too, which always tastes better when it sits overnight. The day will pass quickly and the new week will begin—the yard, the chores, the prayers and the folding and unfolding of many scented cloths—the *chador*, the cashmere, the kerchief—and telling and retelling her stories to God.

Reviewing all this in her mind she smiles and feels something lapping inside her, something like a small tide—lapping and lapping, repeating a rhythm that extends to the coming autumn, the winter and the next spring, to many seasons, as long as she wishes. She feels a vague joy, imagining a snowy day, when suddenly the sun comes out and the world glows like an immense diamond. New tides lap in her and make her giggle. Now slowly she shakes the black veil and spreads it open. The wind blows from the west and she holds the veil up in the air, letting it wave and quiver like a gigantic flag. She laughs louder now and says, "I tricked you, little devil, I rinsed my *chador* with the wind!"

She is standing at the edge of the roof now, Sima, a woman of fifty, holding the very end of a wide *chador*, making it dance in waves. Now, in an instant, she feels that she doesn't need this piece of cloth anymore; what if she let it go? She opens her fingers and lets the veil fly into the sky of the night, like a bat, or an ominous bird. She watches it floating and flapping its wings, and she wonders where it will land, or if it will land at all. Wind dishevels her graying hair; she shivers with pleasure, and lets the breeze play in the strands of her hair.

If You Change Your Nose

Leyla Momeny

What isn't part of ourselves doesn't disturb us.
—HERMAN HESSE, DEMIAN

if you change your nose,
you change your destiny

my mother's changed hers twice
my sister, once

I am quietly planning an escape

pacing outside of her bedroom
like a child,
where politics prevent me from entering,
where purple dust clouds land
on what was once a human face

slouching under her doorway
with legs entwined
azaleas
one fist raised
against this oriental plague

I am fetching
ice
water

magazines

yogurt

I am trying *to be supportive*

I am trying *not to judge*

I record phone messages

create excuses

readjust mirrors

and segregate piles

of secondary laundry

the machete hanging on the kitchen wall

displays my mother's initials

and a recipe for miss clairol's

summer of '56

solarium blond

but I prefer

the beauty of Ugliness,

and in between

the post-surgery and celebration,

I rush back and forth

from these two, three, or four worlds

I have my life planned

and if you look closely at my fingertips,

you may see that it doesn't involve

dismemberment

Iranian Women

∞

MOJDEH MARASHI

TAKE I

Hot afternoon, in a city far from home, one hour by train if no delays, she walks back from work to the station. Tired, dragging a computer on her shoulder—hating the computer at this moment, yet appreciating its value at the back of her mind, giving her a job even in this bad economy—wanting to escape the burning sun, she migrates to the sliver of shade on the sidewalk she finds in her path.

Two women, in their fifties or more, who knows, dressed in dark outfits, scarves tied under their chins, covered from head to toe—standing out in the crowd of tank-tops and shorts—approach from the opposite direction, leaving the station, walking towards her.

Eyes meet, eyes of three women, all sharing a common history but not a current state of mind, nature, or belief.

The two women covered from head to toe in dark clothing—must be exhausted with those heavy shopping bags in hand—jerk their necks, not wanting to associate. A sudden withdrawal, eyes moving away, escaping the somewhat surprised gaze of the woman with a computer on her shoulder.

The two women in dark clothing stop their conversation abruptly as if it is not safe to talk as they walk by the other woman, this one not covered from head to toe in dark clothing and a scarf. Instead wearing a pair of jeans, and a white cotton shirt—but wishing she had worn linen in this hot weather.

On the faces of the two women in scarves, one can read: a line of fear, a page of resentment, a chapter of condemnation. On the face of the woman in jeans, one can read: a line of empathy, a page of resentment, a chapter of blame. The book is called *Contemporary Iranian Women Abroad: An Untold Story of Differences and Similarities.*

TAKE 2

Hot afternoon, in the city where she was born—on vacation from a land halfway around the globe where she now lives and goes to school—she walks back from shopping towards home. Tired, dragging a couple of shopping bags—pistachio nuts, sweets fragranced with rose-water and colored by saffron, dried sour cherries, and other wonderful edibles she has been craving for the past year and a half—wanting to escape the burning sun, she migrates to the sliver of shade on the sidewalk she finds in her path.

Two women, in their twenties or more, who knows, dressed in dark outfits, scarves tied under their chins, covered from head to toe—blending in well with the mixed crowd of covered women and women in jeans and baggy shirts—approach from the opposite direction, entering the bazaar, walking towards her.

Eyes meet, eyes of three women, all sharing a common history but not a current state of mind, nature, or belief.

The two women covered from head to toe in dark clothing—must be exhausted with those heavy shopping bags in hand—jerk their necks towards the woman in jeans, roll their eyes, draw angry frowns, not wanting to understand, co-exist, and co-habit the ancient land but wanting to preach, to scold, and force their ways.

A sudden withdrawal, eyes moving away from the painful stares of the two women covered from head to toe. The woman in jeans and white cotton shirt—wishing she had worn a dark shirt today—drops her head and speeds her pace, as if it is not safe to stay close to the dark-clothed women.

On the faces of the two women in scarves, one can read: a line of empathy, a page of resentment, a chapter of blame. On the face of the woman in jeans, one can read: a line of fear, a page of resentment, a chapter full of questions for which one must find answers. The book is called *Contemporary Iranian Women in the 1979 Revolution: An Untold Story of Differences and Similarities.*

Hot afternoon, in a city that is her home, full of memories, stories, and hopes, she walks back from shopping towards home. Not tired, being so young, only fifteen—holding her shopping bag under her arm, loving what's inside—a new pair of platform shoes—she can't wait to try them on again and again at home—wanting to escape the burning sun, she migrates to the sliver of shade on the sidewalk she finds in her path.

Two girls, in their late teens or early teens, who knows, dressed in dark outfits, scarves tied under their chins, covered from head to toe— standing out in the young crowd of jeans, short-sleeve Ts, and miniskirts—approach from the opposite direction, walking towards her.

Eyes meet, eyes of three young girls, all sharing a common history but not a current state of mind, nature, or belief.

The two girls in dark outfits stop their conversation abruptly as if it is not safe to talk as they walk by the other girl, this one not covered from head to toe in dark clothing and a scarf. Instead wearing a pair of jeans and a white cotton shirt—but wishing she had worn shorts in this hot weather.

On the faces of the two girls in scarves, one can read: a line of shame, a page of envy, a chapter of confusion. On the face of the girl in jeans, one can read: a line of empathy, a page of relief, a chapter of curiosity. The book is called *Contemporary Iranian Women in Pre-Revolutionary Iran: An Untold Story of Differences and Similarities.*

Love in a Time of Struggle
(from *Lipstick Jihad*)

✖

AZADEH MOAVENI

In your presence I see the green of my wings,
like the image of grass the feathers of a parrot paint
in the mirror.
In the lines that define your being I seek a hedge
to protect the green clove from being trampled.
I grow in your consciousness like a vine,
with my hair covering rooftops, doorstops, and fences.

—SIMIN BEHBEHANI,
"I SING YOUR VOICE"

To be a young woman in the Iran of the Islamic Republic involved a certain degree of uncertainty over one's identity, or at the very least, over one's romantic priorities. Most of my girlfriends had no idea whether they had a "type." In contrast to California, no one fretted much about being unready for commitment, or the passage from dating to dating exclusively. Perhaps in time, quality of life would improve in Tehran, and along with it, quality of dating. But in the meantime, rather than worrying over arcane distinctions in relationship terminology, or the riddle wrapped in an enigma of "Why didn't he call back?" relationships served a far more vital purpose: taking a fragile identity and anchoring it in a situation or person.

You may think, not incorrectly, that for women relationships the world over involve defining yourself through men. But modern Iran went so out of its way to confuse and complicate the identities of women that this natural tendency became an overwhelming one. The regime fed young people such contradictory messages—women were liberated but legally inferior; women should be educated but subservient; women should have careers but stick to traditional gender roles; women should play sports but ignore their dirty physical needs—that it elevated even basic questions of self (What are my priorities, expectations, needs?) to higher physics.

It was a tough climate in which to be a young woman. It made it hard to know what was truly important to you, what defined you deep down, if all those layers of family/peers/neighborhood/social background/trickle-down dogma were stripped away. In Iran, a society in flux, every single one of those layers was also undergoing transformation. Constructing a coherent personality out of all the chaos was a formidable task. That's why my generation of Iranians was called the lost generation. And that's why for women, searching for relationships was, if not a search for self, a search to anchor a self adrift.

The intensity of life in modern-day Iran added another complication to finding love. You had to find not only chemistry but a partner who wanted the same sort of Islamic Republic experience, both emotionally and logistically, as you. A dating service would have needed to create questionnaires with such questions—Do you want a partner who (check one): is furious and bitter / resigned and placid; externalizes rage / internalizes sorrow; is itching to emigrate / determined to stay; flouts laws regularly / is cautious and obedient; reads five newspapers a day / does not know what year it is; is addicted to opium/heroin / addicted to food, Prozac?

For Tehrani women who dated within their own milieu, such considerations were psychologically complex enough. For those who strayed across borders of social class, the result was something between agonizing and mortifying.

This proved especially true with a distant friend of mine, Fatimeh. She was the very last person you'd suspect would embroil herself in an inauspicious relationship. When she finally did, she had it the hardest of all, because her relationship, or her would-be relationship, really, had to be conducted in secret, away from the watchful eyes of her traditional family.

The first time I met her, we were waiting for a presidential reception outside one of the palaces at Saad Abad—the royal complex built by Reza Shah in northern Tehran. The press pool stood in the shade chatting, and apart from me, there was only one other woman, Fatimeh. It was only the second or third time I had encountered the Tehran press corps, which was full of journalists who had known each other forever, and I didn't feel comfortable smoking in front of them and the ceremonial guard. I moved to the side of the giant fountain outside the palace, only to find that I had made myself more conspicuous. Noticing the tense way I had my arms folded, Fatimeh walked over to keep me company.

I smiled my thanks to the fascinating, black-clad creature that had appeared next to me. She wore the full-length *chador,* with an elastic strap over the top of her head, to keep the fabric in place. Underneath each arm, swinging back and forth amidst the folds, hung a camera. She chirped hello, in her cheery, brusque tone, and inspected me with equal curiosity. When the officials finally arrived, I ignored them. Fatimeh was a far more absorbing sight, as she maneuvered her way to the front of the photographers, juggling cameras, clicking with one then the other, somehow managing it all gracefully—under a hot sun—while swathed in yards of black nylon.

She came from a traditional, pious family that was exhibiting exceptional openness by allowing her this independence, letting her out of the house at all hours alone, to pursue her work. They did not feel entirely comfortable with this, but that they agreed at all was one of the not-so-small successes of the Islamic Republic. You have to forgive me this brief historical point, and an unfashionable one, at that, but it's important to understanding how Iranians were still struggling with the events of 1979. The revolution rolled back the legal rights of Iranian women, but it transformed the lives and horizons of women like Fatimeh.

Under the Shah's regime, traditional parents like hers would never have let their daughters stray out into society. They preferred to keep them uneducated and housebound rather than exposing them to corrupt, Westernized Iranians who drank, smoked, wore miniskirts, and slept around. The revolution erased all those sins from the surface of society (tucking them under wraps, along with women). In the process, it made it possible for young women like Fatimeh to venture out of the home sphere. They were given the opportunity to do something with their lives besides washing dishes and birthing.

A generation of such middle-class, traditional women were educated under the revolutionary republic. But inevitably, their new freedom stalled the day they graduated from university—when they walked out into an ailing economy that offered no jobs commensurate with their qualifications, back to families who expected them to hang their degree on the mantle and stay home. Fatimeh found a job and started working, so she managed to evade the revolving door that had flung so many of her peers straight back inside the house. She was the first woman in generations of her family to have a career, and her work made her feel capable of more. It raised her expectations of what life should offer her. Captivated by possibility, she was trying to negotiate her future within the conventional role her parents still expected her to play.

Fatimeh worked for a new, conservative-owned newspaper, but talked about its stolid headlines and poor design with disapproval. She brimmed with talent. That was obvious from the first time she dropped by to show me her portfolio. She wanted us to work together on feature stories and asked for help getting her photos published in U.S. magazines. In the end, we never collaborated on anything, because *Time* either used wire service images or dispatched its legendary photographers for special projects.

We saw each other constantly, though, because the months I lived in Iran were dense with news, and the press corps spent endless hours together, waiting for events to start, getting bused around with the president. Fatimeh was totally in love with President Khatami, who in turn had a special affection for her. Once or twice at events, he walked over to say hello and praise her, and her smooth, olive features gleamed afterward for days. "You're so lucky," I told her dolefully. The president had never singled me out, except once on his plane, to tell me he had heard I was a very nice girl.

She called me a lot, and it was clear she wanted to be friends. We met for tea during the workday, but beyond that I didn't know how to include her in my life. It might upset my relatives to bring her over in the evenings, because there would be alcohol around and a stranger in full *chador* would make everyone edgy, like having a nun in a habit at a cocktail party. Dariush refused to socialize with her, and his father had banned her from the house, on the grounds of her *chador* alone.

As much as Fatimeh wanted to hang out, she never discussed her personal life with me. She complained about her parents, of course, but about romance she remained silent. I only learned about this side of her when my friend Davar, also a journalist, informed me she had a crush on him. At first I was skeptical. I couldn't imagine Fatimeh, that intense, purposeful whirl of black *chador* and camera lenses, having a crush on anyone. Maybe you're misreading her signals, I suggested to Davar.

But eventually, her ambiguous overtures turned unmistakably forward. Instead of dropping by his office and lingering for hours, she dropped by his office, lingered for hours, and brought teddy bears holding hearts. Flirting with a guy such as Davar was not in her repertoire, and she probably had no idea where it would lead. So she punched him in the arm a lot, and professed to admire his work. She began phoning him on Fridays, suggesting they go hiking in the Alborz Mountains. I hate hiking, complained Davar. And besides, how can I be seen in public with her, wearing that damn *chador*? Turning her into a proper girlfriend would be nearly impossible.

She had suggested hiking because it was one of the very few activities in modern-day Tehran where people of all different classes and backgrounds came together, trooping up and down the mountains, reclining by riverside cafés. A girl in a black *chador* and a young guy in a bright fleece could walk side by side, attracting little attention. But apart from the mountains, where could they go? A relationship could only get so far, when the venues of its evolution were limited to photo exhibitions and newspaper offices. Even cafés would have been tough. It wasn't so common to see a *chadori* woman sipping Turkish coffee with a clean-shaven male in the sorts of cafés middle-class Iranian kids frequented.

The logistics were thorny, but far more complicated was a possible relationship between Fatimeh and Davar. The ocean of difference between them made Davar himself an unlikely choice. He was Christian, secular, middle class, and Westernized, liberal in manner and thought, and an irrepressible partier. Though on paper, and in person, he could not be more inappropriate for her, I understood the attraction.

Tehran was awash with the male equivalent of Fatimeh. They were journalists and painters, writers and photographers, who had fought in the war with Iraq or were married at eighteen, and were now breaking away from their traditional social backgrounds to enter an intellectual, urban milieu filled with people very different from themselves. The men had an astonishing ability to move in and out of these disparate worlds, hanging onto their evolving personas and sexuality all the while. They easily left their wives and families at home, while finding themselves in the new Tehran.

As a woman, Fatimeh had no such mobility. Her identity as an independent woman, a photojournalist, and a professional in her own right was still wholly vulnerable to the undermining traditions of her family. If she agreed to consider the men picked by her parents—conservatives who would require their wives to stay at home—that fragile new self she had worked so hard to create would be trampled. All this exposure to colleagues like us, people who spoke and socialized freely, who related to one another across the gender divide with an easy openness, had changed her. Davar, she knew, would regard her work as an organic part of her identity, not as a phase to be indulged with the expectation that it would end.

How could she not be alienated by that old, familiar world of marriage, babies, and cooking? Yet this other world, to which we belonged, was disturbingly foreign. And Davar was not interested. He wanted straightforward relationships that included sex from the beginning and had no inclination to court a woman like Fatimeh who might never sleep with him at all.

Davar began pursuing a journalist in our circle who was perfectly comfortable going over to his apartment for drinks, and whatever came later. They weren't dating publicly, so it was not immediately apparent to Fatimeh that the object of her affection was embroiled in a side affair. She did, however, sense that something was amiss.

"So you're friends with Davar, right?" she would ask me, tentatively and repeatedly, on the phone. Too timid and embarrassed to go further, she let the question hang, hoping I would pick up the subject, and somehow shed light on the behavior of this young man she was so drawn to but did not understand. I could sense she was already feeling pangs of betrayal, even without knowing the full story. He had spent time with her, and to her, those hours meant something, even if no words had been exchanged.

"Davar has been extremely close to his mother since he was young," I offered lamely. "He has lots of female friends." My answer sounded vague and useless to my own ears. But I didn't know, given the lack of emotional intimacy between us, how to broach such intensely personal matters. In retrospect, I wish I had been less elliptical in warning her about their colliding worlds. I wish I had said, Fatimeh, your conception of a relationship radically differs—in assumptions, substance, and practice —from Davar's. If you judge what exists between you through your attitude, you're going to get disappointed, if not hurt.

I'm certain part of her suspected there was something between Davar and me. In her world, a man and a woman simply did not call each other by nicknames, hang out in each other's houses, go out for dinners and to cafés, unless they were engaged. If they did, their parents would have already met and negotiated their children's potential future. The time alone would simply be a short trial period before marriage, to ensure they did not despise each other.

To disabuse her of this idea, I began complaining about the lack of proper guys in Tehran, making joking laments of my spinsterhood, a refrain in our conversations. Once she realized Davar and I were just friends—that it was possible, indeed natural and common in our milieu, to be platonic in this way—she relaxed. It made her feel less vulnerable to know this was normal, and she sought him out more boldly.

Davar, in his thoughtless but still harmful way, must have mentioned to his new lover that Fatimeh had a crush on him. Though the last person to pose a threat to their new liaison was Fatimeh, uncertain and awkward in her *chador,* the new lover became defensive. I will never forget the afternoon at Davar's office when we all converged. He and I often met there at the tail end of the workday, to walk to our favorite park to smoke *ghalyoun.* Fatimeh called to say she would also drop by, with some photos as a pretext. The new lover phoned his mobile, as she had begun to regularly, and when she heard we were all there, having tea together, informed him she would be stopping by as well. Probably resentful of having her status confined to his bedroom, she showed up to mark her territory.

Painfully unsubtle, she arrived decked out in a glittery evening veil, with lots of eye makeup and a cloud of perfume. She promptly took a seat near Davar's desk closest to him and made a point of touching him with a casual but proprietary air. Fatimeh looked on, stunned and quiet. The moment groaned under the strain of its awkwardness. It couldn't have lasted more than fifteen minutes, but our collective self-consciousness seemed to slow time.

Davar blinked at me helplessly. "Well," I said brightly, rapping my knuckles against his desk, "who's up for *ghalyoun?*"

Fatimeh stopped calling Davar, stopped littering his office with little fuzzy ducks and bears. Eventually, she stopped passing by all of our offices, stopped calling with pretexts of photos she wanted to drop off or stories to discuss. She blipped off our screens, and when I asked Davar a few months later if he had heard from her, he told me she had gotten married to "some conservative guy." But how? I asked. When did she meet him? When did they date? Why had she stopped working? She kept in touch with no one, and we never saw her again.

∽

As an equal-opportunity catastrophe, the revolution had generously confused the sexuality of secular middle- to upper-middle-class Iranian women as well. These girls married for love and professed to oppose the rigid morals propagated by the regime, but found themselves as conflicted as their highly traditional peers in the realm where sexuality, self, and future intersected. Should they try to carve away the influence of tradition and family on their life choices, as Fatimeh was gingerly attempting to do? Should they look for relationships with men who thought every part of them, including the unconventional, tentative parts, was fantastic? Could they afford to be honest about their sexuality (like the fact that they had some), or should they be guarded, and play to the still-traditional expectations of Iranian men (who liked the farce of believing they were the first—to make you breathless, to make out, to go to bed)?

Relationships that were considered successful, that led to weddings and emigration and babies, so often required a total shrouding of a woman's real life and desires. Everyone knew this, because they had watched girlfriends go through lovers, get bored of not being taken seriously, hit upon a suitable prospect, and fake their pasts and camouflage their needs and tastes in order to get married.

Becoming this mercenary—prepared to meet, marry, and live under pretense of being someone you were not—took a while. It took the failure of the relationships where you tried to be yourself, tried to communicate your expectations and passions (hoping they would be adored and encouraged), and watched it all fall apart.

A young distant relative of mine, Mira, grappled with these

considerations at the tender age of twenty-two. We weren't very close, but every couple of months I would drop by for dinner, sometimes staying the night so Mira and I could watch videos and raid her mother's stash of French chocolates. "So what'd we get this week?" I asked her. In Tehran, where Western movies were officially banned, everyone had a *filmi,* a video guy, who schlepped a trunkload of new films around to his clients' homes as a sort of mobile video store.

Mira didn't answer, but she slipped a tape into the VCR, and dimmed the lights. She looked at me with an expectant, abashed smile. I need your help with something, she said, winding her thick, ash-streaked hair into a loose knot. Her skin was like porcelain, and glowed without all the layers of foundation and blush she coated it with during the day. If I had skin like hers, I would wear nothing but lip gloss, ever. But her morning ritual before the mirror took an hour and a half.

When summer rolled around, Iranian girls groomed themselves with a seriousness of purpose I had never before witnessed, even in California, a place dedicated to the worship and pursuit of external beauty. Often, a particular feature was singled out for obsessive attention. Tattooed eyebrows, collagen-plumped lips. For the daughter of my waxing woman, it was the fingernails. She grew them out an inch long and painted them a different technicolor every single day. Sometimes she affixed nail jems, sometimes alternating colors on the tips, for particular effect. When finished, she would blast Mary J. Blige and "Nastaran," that year's Persian pop hit, on the stereo in the living room, and dance around alone, waving her hands in the air to the beat, to dry the lacquer. Exhausted, she would splay her fingers for me to inspect that day's creation—the fruits of an hour's labor—which she would wipe off the next day with acetone, priming her canvas anew. I suppose teenagers the world over were preoccupied with beauty—the aesthetics of being not quite a girl, not quite a woman—but in Tehran the attention seemed extreme.

Mira liked to remind me that because of the country's demographics, each year *one million Iranian women were unable to find a husband.* She repeated this figure, or possibly urban legend, with a grave solemnity and tragic expression.

Mira was distressed over my beauty regimen. Since I was neither looking for a husband nor habituated to overcompensating for the veil with too much makeup, I usually went about with what I called a natural look and Mira called self-neglect. Mira's adolescence had corresponded with the years just before the election of Khatami. This had given her a politically weighted relationship to the products of Revlon that continued to this day, when it really wasn't that big a deal anymore.

"You really need to do something with yourself," she told me with a disapproving glance, as though I had a mustache and walked about in a mumu. "Men are turned on by makeup."

Applied properly, she informed me, makeup is meant to mimic how women look when they are aroused—smoldering eyes, flushed cheeks, swollen lips. I was older and supposed to know these things. They were included in the skills of husband acquisition, which also included: knowing how to make a proper béchamel sauce, being coiffed to gleaming perfection at all times, even when stepping outside in the morning for milk, and smiling pleasantly and disguising any hint of a personality.

The objective of this skill-set was to nab an Iranian software designer from Palo Alto who had flown to Tehran for wife shopping. If I had packaged myself properly, maybe he would pick me. Perfect hair! Perfect sauce! And I would be rescued and taken back to America, to shop at Pottery Barn and get depressed with all the other imported wives (or at least the ones who didn't ask for their divorces on the tarmac).

Deep down, many friends and relatives suspected something was wrong with me. Clearly I had been unable to find either a job or a husband in the West, and that's why I had come to Iran, to toil day and night before a laptop hanging out with clerics. They offered sympathy and helpful advice, like how to pour tea more gracefully and rim my eyes with kohl.

Usually, because she loved me and thought it her duty, Mira was the one giving me lessons, in cosmetics and cuisine, but that night, I was supposed to have the answers, to whatever it was in the VCR.

She hit the play button, and a fuzzy image of two very white, very naked people appeared on the screen. I'm not prudish, but neither have I seen much porn in my life. I *definitely* haven't seen German porn from the seventies, which is what this appeared to be. I rose and shut the door to the kitchen nervously. If someone were to walk in, there was little doubt who would be held responsible for such a session. Certainly not innocent, supposedly virginal Mira.

She expertly fast-forwarded to the next scene. Clearly, this was not her first screening. A towering man, Viking-like, was busily plying his fingers between the parted legs of a frizzy-haired woman.

"Why does he keep doing that?"

I cracked open a pistachio, from the bowl on the table, and studied the shell, encrusted with salt and lemon juice. "He's, uh, pleasuring her."

"But why there? Like that?"

"That's where her, uh . . . that's a very sensitive spot." What was it with young Iranians? How could they be so obsessed with sex, yet know so little about it? Or maybe she was being disingenuous, pretending not to know because she was too shy to straight out say she wanted to talk about sex.

I switched off the video and asked for the real story. I refused to believe she didn't know about her own sex organs, though I suppose it was a slim possibility. As it turned out, her boyfriend had given her a "sex kit" to educate herself with, which included the video and a few lewd magazines. Because their sexual encounters were limited, she explained, he didn't want to waste their time in erotic tutorial. Since Mira was a virgin, and I knew they both lived with family, I asked when and where this knowledge was being put to use. Sometimes we go to the park behind the house at night, or if his parents are out, we'll go to his place, she said. He sounds seedy, I said disapprovingly. I want to please him, she sniffed. Seedy boyfriend preferred the sort of sex that allowed her to remain, technically, a virgin. "Is that a problem?" she asked.

Where to begin? Should I pull up a gynecological site on the Internet, and explain vaginal mechanics? Should I bother asking whether they use condoms, although I was certain they didn't? Should I point out that she is supposed to enjoy sex, too? If Mira started telling her seedy boyfriend what she wanted in bed, he might well consider her loose, acting like a *jendeh,* a whore. Progress in gender relations circa Tehran 2001 meant that men were now willing to marry women who slept with them during the dating phase. But that didn't mean they would marry the ones who had acted like they liked it.

I didn't know what Mira should do. As a starry-eyed romantic, full of passion and dreams of walking into the sunset with her lover, she had to balance her fantasies against her matrimonial prospects. She had to find someone who could accept the many sides of her—the red wine–drinking devotee of flamenco, the bourgeois housewife-to-be with a talent for sauces. On the other hand, as she well knew, Tehran was not exactly littered with suitable guys. Mira had not attended college, had a declining opium addict for a father, and could not afford to let her twenties march by as she worked out what sort of mate would complete her personality and make her an adult and not just a wife.

"Why don't you just go out to dinner more? Are you even friends?"

She rolled her eyes, shooting me one of those exasperated, like, when are you going to get how it is here looks. Curled up in her lilac flannel pajamas, her long lashes sweeping up and down, liberated from all those too-heavy coats of mascara, she looked so innocent.

We sat there silent for a while, occasionally reaching for a square of chocolate. I needed to say something. So I tried to explain that like many men, her boyfriend was intimidated by how much he wanted sex and that it was easier for him to vulgarize intimacy than admit that she (a mere girl/woman) controlled the supply of the most powerful physical experience of his existence. It was kind of an academic point, the stuff you absorb during women's studies classes, and I lost her halfway through.

What an accelerated, demeaning, furtive initiation into sexuality. Their evenings should be spent at clubs, dancing; their afternoons in cafés, ankles lazily interlaced. Of course now they could hold hands in public if they really wanted to. Lots of middle-class couples, who had nowhere else to go, did this freely. But it wasn't nice, being affectionate like that with an eye to your back.

Of all the Islamic Republic's casualties, among the most lethal for young people was the deterioration of platonic friendship between young men and women. As far back as I could remember, the lives of my parents, my aunts, and my uncles had been full of friends of the opposite sex, who were simply friends, nothing more, often not even recycled former flames.

Though highly traditional spheres of Iranian society had socialized along gender lines—with men and women in separate rooms, or separate sides of the room, at parties—platonic interaction and friendship had been ordinary among secular middle-class and upper-class Iranians. The revolution reversed this. It threw up obstacles everywhere to casual coexistence between the sexes: segregated elementary schools and university classes, segregated buses, segregated restaurant lines, segregated passport offices.

Separated most of the hours of the day, young people became

mysteries to each other, familiar but alien. It became easier for girls to spend time with their girlfriends, guys with their guy friends. Being together involved sneaking away, into the dark corners of public parks, into the woods in the Alborz Mountains, into each other's empty houses.

I wanted better for Mira. I wanted to see her pretty face radiant with the silly crushes of early womanhood, her weeks filled with candlelit dinners, unmolested strolls through the park behind her house. My adolescence in the decadent, satanic West seemed bubble-gum innocent in comparison to hers—footsy under a blanket at a winter football game, slow dancing at the prom, sleepovers where we drank beer, giggled over Monty Python, and fell asleep in a pile, like puppies, in someone's living room.

The next day the seedy boyfriend would collect Mira, covered in a dark veil and *roopoosh* (still mandated by lots of offices), from work. Maybe they would go out to dinner, but maybe they wouldn't because you can only get in the mood to do this about half the time, when you know there are eyes always watching you. Probably they would go to the home of friends, and then wait for an evening his parents would be out.

It wasn't always, or at least exclusively, as bad as that. An imaginative couple, with some creativity and luck, could create a sparkly courtship out of these circumstances. Sometimes, all the challenges infused drama and romance into a new relationship. Existing as a couple in the Islamic Republic meant facing the petty, the bizarre, and the sorrowful on a regular basis. You had to trust faster than usual, and situations, rather than your own readiness, determined when you would be vulnerable. Islamic Republic coupledom was almost like being in the military together—you got worn down, built yourself back up, and found yourself bonded to the person who had been right next to you the whole time.

In the West, with online matchmaking services, twenty-four-hour restaurants, and the birth-control patch, dating was fast and easy. There was no struggle (worse than not being able to get a dinner reservation) that might elevate a third date from boring to extraordinary. Since romance thrives on mystery and delayed gratification, I had imagined the Islamic Republic would be conducive to excellent love affairs. I thought nothing could be more romantic than love in a time of struggle.

But like most of the conceptions I bore with me to Iran, it ended up being totally wrong. Confronting hardship together didn't magically turn your relationship, or your life for that matter, into Casablanca. Struggle, it turned out, is about as romantic as leprosy. It makes you emotionally absent. It gives you the most compelling, lofty reasons ever to avoid dealing with your emotional problems (you're too busy with The Struggle, of course). It makes you live exclusively in the present. It makes emotions besides hate a luxury. Because in the end, life in the shadow of struggle is really just life in the shadows.

Becoming a Woman

∽

ELHAM GHEYTANCHI

I grew up and became a woman in Jamalzadeh *koucheh* (alley) in Tehran. My parents, who were both educators, joined the Iranian middle class when they first bought an apartment there. Our neighbors were Zoroastrians, Christians, Muslims, and Jews. It was only later that I found out our street was a unique place in Tehran. As kids, we spent most of our time playing in the street. It would always start with Kia, my Zoroastrian friend, coming into our door and then both of us would go to find Betsy, our Christian friend, and then Annie, our Muslim friend, to play. Later in the evening, our parents would come to gather us and talk to each other. These were the most joyous times of my life.

It was in the autumn of 1979, just as the revolution was taking place, that I became a woman. One day we all came to the street and were ready to play football. I was quite good at the game because I could run fast. But that day, in the midst of the game, the ball hit me in the chest and for the first time I felt an excruciating pain in my breast. Morvarid, who was a bit older than I, and never played football, came to my rescue. As she rubbed my shoulders, she whispered into my ear, "Your breasts are growing . . ." I was terrified of the news! I ran home crying. My mother had just finished the administrative work she had brought home from school, where she was a principal. "Mom, my breasts hurt . . ." I said as I was looking into the mirror. Morvarid was right. I really did have two small nuts on my chest! My mother looked at me and said: "I told you . . . no more football. And you shouldn't run in the street so much. Try to act like a woman." I knew my mother was never quite accepted in her male-dominated workplace as a woman. So, instead of comfort, I felt a threat in her words. Acting like a woman, I gradually found out, indeed meant severe limitations, less presence in public, and definitely no running like I used to.

Kia, however, was becoming a man. Contrary to my experience, his space only widened. He could now ride a motorcycle, shout at us with his big voice; he was certainly running without fear. Later that year, I had to wear *hijab* to go to school. My space shrunk even more. But I couldn't simply comply with the rules. I had my parents shave my head twice that year. I would go into the street without *hijab* and ride the motorcycle with Kia. I would run as fast and kick the ball as hard as I could, knowing that becoming a woman would mean losing all this. I yearned for the freedom Kia acquired upon his passage into manhood. I resented womanhood.

The memories of Jamalzadeh Street haunt me to this day. As an undergraduate at UCLA, still feeling unease with the limitations of womanhood, I wanted to carve out a place for myself as an activist. I was clearly not a "white woman." I tried to join the groups of women of color on campus. But I was never satisfied with the narrow definitions of particular identities such as "Iranian" because the Zoroastrian, Christian, Muslim, and Jewish identities of my childhood friends were somehow blurred. The category of "Iranian" was too narrow to capture my experience. Everywhere I went, I was asked about my "identity"; where was I from? Being an "Iranian American" never quite did it for me because I always had to explain that I really didn't come from a repressed society, that Iran didn't always have a theocratic regime, and that I didn't just find diversity on the UCLA campus! On many occasions, I simply wanted to say that I came from Jamalzadeh Street, where I became a woman, resented it, and struggled to define myself differently.

The World Was a Couple

KATAYOON ZANDVAKILI

Her.
A beautiful word
an undressing word
her and she: her shoulder carried me—
her hair. I am mad for her—
Then:

Sunlight in rooms of afternoon tea, the red and green
laughter over cards—
Grandma's Feraud skirt parts to reveal a fat white knee.
Family, with the drapes pulled aside—*famiglia*—
    their look

                as I am drawn into another's eyes

Don't worry, I say with a backward glance, I will be
the gentleman I was raised to be;
honorable in a female body.
(Honorable *meme* in a *barracks,* as Baba used to say.)

And yet, and yet, *The World Was a Couple*
(Her.)
The World Was a Couple.
Her!

What makes a Girl and what makes a Woman?

The Gift

∽

Marjan Kamali

The morning of her Saturday math camp group, my mother, Darya, calls to say she has found the perfect gift for my twenty-fifth birthday. "His name is Mr. Dashti," she says, almost breathless on the phone. "Two degrees, a Ph.D. and an M.B.A. He is a descendant of the third cousin of Reza Shah. He lives in Atlanta. He has perfect health. The nicest teeth. He'll be here on Sunday afternoon for tea and questions. Please, Mina. No tricks this time. And wear the lavender dress with your new belt." I put down the phone, half asleep. Another potential husband. Another boring afternoon spent nodding at a strange man, with my parents in their best clothes, aiming to please. Waste of a Sunday. I could be preparing for my oral dissertation on the poetry of Chaucer instead.

As I line my coffeemaker with a cone filter and carefully measure out the grinds, the phone rings again. "Yes, Darya," I say, because no one else on this planet that I know is awake this early on a Saturday.

"Mina, it is your maman."

"Yes, Darya. What is it?"

"You haven't heard?"

"No, what? This new guy? Yes, I heard. You just told me. You're inviting him to tea . . ."

"No, silly Mina. Not that. The princess . . ." She pauses. "She died last night. They killed her. She's dead and so is her partner."

Her voice trails off and is soon replaced with tiny sniffles. She mumbles that she cannot talk anymore, she's hosting math camp today, and that I should join them for some tea together. "Together tea," she says in her Persian way of speaking English. "You come, Mina, and we'll have together tea."

Every Saturday afternoon, my mother, Darya, gets together with her two best friends, Bindoo Patel and Lin-Hua Wang, for tea and math camp. The three of them work for Chase Manhattan Bank and live in Queens. They all adore mathematics, though Darya's passion for the subject borders on obsession. When she was a young girl in Iran, she excelled in mathematics. She wanted to study math "forever," she says, but then got married, had two kids, and moved to America in her late thirties after the revolution. My father, a doctor, worked at a pizza shop stirring tomato sauce when we first moved to New York in the early eighties. He couldn't practice medicine with his foreign license. He studied at night for a year and a half and surrounded himself with medical journals at the pizza shop as he patted dough and sliced green peppers, then took his American medical license exam. He practices internal medicine in Long Island now, treating gastritis and ulcers, massaging gall bladders and counting intestine spirals. He's content with his patients, medical library, and daily turkey, tomato, and corn chip sandwiches. He's the one who suggested several years ago that Darya start her own math group.

"You have to do what you love, Darya," he said to her one night while I was still in high school, my parents, my two older brothers, and I all eating dinner. "You cannot push away what you love. Don't you see? You say you love math. You say it is your passion. But where is it in your life? If the mountain won't come to Mohammed, Mohammed must go to the mountain. You have to use your personal action to focus your energy on mathematics. Claim it!"

As he said these last few words, he leapt out of his chair and punched his fist triumphantly in the air. My older brothers and I quietly chewed our stuffed eggplant. In the late eighties my father had discovered the self-help tapes of a self-improvement guru and had since been focusing on self-esteem and self-confidence. He quoted his guru daily.

"But, I haven't done math in years," Darya almost whined, lowering her head and listlessly swirling her fork in the eggplant sauce. She wasn't working at the time and spent most of the day doing housework or watching soap operas.

"No matter!" my father said, punching his fist in the air again, then clapping his hands forcefully. He had learned the motions from the free seminar video that came with the tapes he'd ordered through the home shopping network. "The past is not the future! If you believe it, you can make it happen! You have to use your individual power to make your life a masterpiece!"

Darya had stared at him through bluish tears and nodded gravely like a child as she put down her fork. That night they worked together on various strategies for bringing more math into her life. My brothers and I watched as they sat to work at the dining room table. They stayed up late, scribbling on memo pads, brewing pots of coffee, brainstorming by the fireplace, and pacing up and down. We walked quietly around them to go up to bed. The next morning, my father hit the side of his orange juice glass with a spoon and cleared his throat.

"From now on," he said, "Saturday afternoons will be different around here. Your mother will be pursuing her passion then. Her friends will meet at that time to do math together. They will immerse themselves in that which they love. During these hours, the dining room will be a mathematics think tank. You will respect your mother's space and group. You will not run around and scream and argue during those hours. If you wish you may participate in the workshop, but only if you come prepared, having done the mathematics exercises due that week. No phone calls during those hours. We must support your mother as she takes personal action to live with passion. Do I make myself understood?"

My oldest brother, Ramin, grunted, then left for football practice. My other brother, Houman, said, "Cool," as he listened to his British new wave music on headphones. Darya turned to me.

"Mina-Lady," she said, as she often calls me. "Will you support me?" Her eyes were pleading.

"Of course I will," I said and picked up my backpack to leave for school. As I walked down the block I thought about my father's solemn speech and Darya's request for "support." I thought about math camp, the idea of inviting friends every Saturday to do equations together, and I wondered again, as I often did during my years of adolescence, if maybe my parents hadn't been damaged by some chemical spills when we lived in Iran during the days of the war. Maybe my brothers and I were in a different neighborhood that day and were never told about it. We would never know.

Her small black address book in her lap, Darya parked herself by the phone that afternoon and called all her friends. In the end, of the dozen or so people she called, the only ones who agreed that spending every Saturday afternoon working on algebra and calculus was a fun idea were Bindoo and Lin-Hua, two of Darya's oldest friends in America, and immigrants themselves. From then on, every Saturday afternoon they met over tea and cracked away at equations. They started with the basics, since they were all rusty. At first, I could understand what they were doing, and it matched my lessons in school. But together they whipped through one textbook after another and soon were deep into calculus. Eventually, they lost me. Not that Darya didn't try. "Please join us, Mina-Lady," she would say almost every week. "You don't know how beautiful math is." I would mutter under my breath that they were clinically insane for sitting around and solving calculus equations in workbooks. As their skills returned and the math became even more sophisticated, I stopped mocking them. I just stayed as far away as possible. For Christmas (which none of them celebrated as they were a Muslim, a Hindu, and a Buddhist), my father bought them each a financial calculator. Darya cried as she lifted the wrapping to find the financial machine, the photograph of which she had fingered longingly in technology catalogs. And so the economics and finance learning began to bloom as well. Within two years Darya applied for a job at the bank, joining Bindoo and Lin-Hua at the Chase branch in Queens, where they had both been working. One year into math camp, Bindoo and Lin-Hua had received promotions at the bank.

∽

This morning, as I sit and sip my coffee, I think about how Darya has delivered two blows in the past fifteen minutes. Mr. Dashti, whoever he is, is coming to tea. The princess is dead. Darya must be hallucinating. Of course it couldn't be true. But then a thin man in a dark suit with a leather tie on the entertainment channel confirms Darya's words. The blond princess in the London palace is dead.

I drive to Queens, feeling somewhat sick, refusing to listen to the radio with all its news of the princess's death. I remember hearing about the princess's wedding as a child in Iran, the other girls sneaking in photos of her to school, my friends and I keeping pictures of her short haircut tucked beneath our veils. As I pull into my parents' driveway, Darya walks out wearing a pink and white housedress, her red hair gathered in a bun, hiding the black roots.

"Do you know who killed her?" I ask as I get out of the car.

"How could you ask me who killed her?" she says. "How could you not know? No newspaper, no TV in your apartment? His name is all over the news." She tilts her head to one side and starts to whisper. "It's a Mr. Paparrazi." In her hand she is holding a printout from the Internet with the headline "Paparazzi Killed Diana." Then she adds in another whisper as she glances nervously at a sanitation truck across the street, "I think he's Italian. Maybe even mob-related."

✂

Bindoo and Lin-Hua are sitting at the dining room table, drinking tea and eating coconut cookies. They greet me with hugs and kisses, pinch my cheeks and laugh. I can tell they're on a high from some incredibly challenging calculus. "We did some more integrals today," Bindoo says in her squeaky high voice. "Applying integration to finding total cost from variable cost."

"Yes, but we had to also factor in fixed costs," Lin-Hua says, talking quickly, like a runner who has just successfully completed a marathon. "Don't forget, we had to factor in fixed costs."

"It was beautiful, Mina," Darya says. "So beautifully beautiful. God created calculus so we could find total cost from variable cost."

I stare at the three of them in silence, accustomed to the Twilight Zone that is my parents' house.

"Huh," I say.

"Come, Mina," Darya says. "Come to my office. I want to show you the charts on Mr. Dashti."

I nod at Bindoo and Lin-Hua, who wave at me, giggling as I follow Darya up the stairs to her bedroom, where she keeps her computer and endless files. She is proud of her knowledge of Excel, fond of making graphs. She opens her file drawer and starts sifting through the files with different labels typed neatly with a Persian typewriter: "Mr. Jahanfard," "Mr. Samiyi," "Mr. Bidar," "Mr. Ahmadi."

"Ah, here he is," Darya says as she pulls out a bright yellow folder. "Mr. Dashti."

She opens the folder and shows me its contents. "Look," she says. "Mojgan, your father's aunt's friend in Atlanta, faxed me his resume. Mojgan is a second cousin of Mr. Dashti's brother's wife. See this. He studied biochemistry at Yale, getting a bachelor's and a Ph.D. He then went and received his master's in business administration at Stanford. He likes to listen to Persian music and he plays the sitar. He has a very good job with Kodak in Atlanta now, he runs a research department. You know how the photos are so nice on that paper? Mr. Dashti decides the balance of the chemicals for each roll of film." She folds her arm across her chest with satisfaction, then adds, "His mother was very pretty."

She studies me in silence, then continues to sift through the pages of research that she has compiled using Mojgan's faxes and her Excel program. "See this, Mina. No history of disease in his family. Everybody healthy. One sister got divorced in 1991 but Mojgan says it was for the best. I called Mojgan last month and sent a photograph of you. She met with him and told him all about you and he said he had to be in New York on business anyway and why not come to tea to meet the daughter of the nephew of his sister-in-law's second cousin's friend while he was at it. I mean, why not? So, he's coming next Sunday and you have to behave this time, Mina-Lady, you must behave for him. This time, I know he is right for you, I have read all the information, I have talked to Mojgan and to others in Atlanta, and everybody agrees he is right for you. I know it in my heart, he is the one."

I sit in Darya's bedroom, on her bed, listening to her tell me who is right for me. Downstairs Bindoo and Lin-Hua are munching on cookies and taking a break from integrals. My father is in the bathroom sticking sealant on the cracked tiles. We've been here several times before, down this road for the past six years. Darya finds an available Iranian bachelor of good standing and excellent background. She makes lists of his attributes, researches his family members, his past schools, then transfers the data into her computer and creates charts out of it. She finds someone who knows someone who knows him, then makes endless phone calls and overtures to set up a meeting. She uses the photograph I had made when I was nineteen and thought I would be an actress to land somehow within the sight of these men. Often, they get on planes and trains and into their cars to come to tea. Together tea. They know of my family or hear of its reputation, they learn through the various messengers that all things point to my still being a virgin. They consider the family name, my father's career, the height of my cheekbones, my degree from Columbia. Most of all, they consider that I am twenty-five and still a virgin. And they come.

"Darya," I say, growing hot and feeling my eyes burn. "I don't want to have tea with Mr. Dashti next Sunday. I don't want to meet with him. He is the seventh man who has come to tea so far. I do not want to get married. Is that so difficult to understand?"

Darya stares at me, her mouth in the shape of a perfect zero. She stares at me sadly for a few moments, then starts to talk to the bedspread.

"My daughter says she does not want to get married. My daughter sits here and tells me she does not want to get married. Why? It is her youth. Her complete youth and lack of knowledge. She doesn't know."

Her eyes are solemn as she turns to face me.

"Mina, I want you to meet Mr. Dashti. I want you to meet him because he is right for you. I know that in my heart. I have talked to several people. I know of his family. He really is the one. Forget Jahanfard. Forget Bidar. Forget all those others who came here and made you bored and whom you conveniently avoided eye contact with or deliberately spilled tea on. I am forgiving that, forgetting it. Whoosh! They're gone, who cares. But this time, Mina. This time I want you to know that this man is right for you."

"You don't even know him!"

"I know enough. When I went to Atlanta for Aunt Parvin's funeral, I saw him. That's how I learned about him. My bones told me then, they screamed that he was right for you. They told me he is the father of Mina's children."

I press my fingers into the corners of my eyes. I take a deep breath and try to push back with my fingers the tears that are forming in my eyes.

"Darya, I am so tired of this. Why do you think that you can find a husband for me? Why is it so important to you that I get married?"

"Because you need a partner."

"I don't."

"You need a partner, Mina, and I am not a fool. You are young. You are horny. You need a husband. It is my job to find you one. Why are you refusing him?"

I use all my creativity to snare Darya, catch her where I think it will hurt her old world sensibilities the most. "Did it ever occur to you that I am a lesbian?"

"Lesbian?! Don't think I don't know about lesbians. We had lesbians in Iran. You know how we knew they were lesbians? From their *partners.* They had partners, Mina. You don't even have a girlfriend! You're no lesbian."

She's right. I like men. I just don't sleep with them, the result of a leftover childish promise I made to my grandmother when I lived in Iran. A promise to wait till marriage. I stare at the wall, at the paintings from India that cover almost every inch. Bindoo brought them back a few years ago when she visited her daughters there. Bindoo raised two daughters in Queens, then received a phone call from her father in Bombay and sent the two daughters over to meet their new husbands. They both have children now, live in Bombay with big homes and several maids. I turn to Darya.

"This is so ridiculous. Why do you think you can pick a husband for me? What makes you think I even want one?"

"You need one, Mina. Everybody in this life needs to have a partner."

"I don't need a partner." I am almost laughing.

"You need someone, Mina. What's going to happen when I die? Who's going to take care of you? When you are all alone with your thirteenth-century poetry and books, who will wipe your nose when you are sick?"

"I will. I'll wipe my nose! I'll call one of my friends. I'll hire someone, how's that? I'll put out signs on tree trunks requesting a nose-wiper for my sick days! How's that, Darya? Will that satisfy you? Will that stop you from this ridiculous quest you're on, this absurd research?"

"You need someone, Mina. You need to have . . ."

"Everything you didn't have?" I finish the sentence for her as my body grows hot and my heart starts to bang loudly against my white shirt.

"No, Mina," Darya says quietly, closing her eyes and exhaling slowly. When she looks at me again, her eyes are filled with water. "Not everything I didn't have. Everything I *had.* I want you to taste life the way I have. To give you a fraction of what I was given in this life. I want you to have a passion. I want you to fall in love like I fell in love."

"Your marriage was arranged."

"I fell in love with him."

"You grew to love him. You'd never even known him before."

"I got to know him, Mina. I took the time. I loved my mother. I knew she wouldn't do me wrong. Because my mother . . ."

And she breaks off and cries silently into her hands. Her mother was killed in the Iran-Iraq War during a bomb raid one night. She was buying oranges at a grocer's when the bomb blew the grocer's wooden stalls into grated shreds. Darya always cries when she talks of her mother. I sit up straight on the bed next to her, watching her sob into her hands. Her tears over her mother are nothing new.

"Because . . ." she looks up, her face wet but suddenly calm. "Because, Mina, my mother gave me a gift when I was nineteen. Don't you see? She gave me a gift and at the time I was young too and foolish and couldn't appreciate what she had found for me. I told her I hated it. I attended the wedding reluctantly, only because in those days we didn't refuse our parents' choices. I didn't know any better. It took years for me to realize what she had done for me. The happiness that she placed into my hands."

I think of the man in the bathroom next door, sitting on his knees and squeezing putty onto pink tiles. I think of my father and his few wiry hairs, the dent in his skull where his baldness is most apparent. I think of his uneven teeth and self-help tapes, his silly jokes and ridiculous quotes. I see his bulging stomach, the way he slurps his cereal milk every morning, and the old battered tapes he plays in the car, hearing the lyrics all wrong. Darya holds her head steady and looks at me. That is the gift her mother gave her? That is the happiness she's talking about?

"It's the most ridiculous thing in the world," I say. "You cannot pick a spouse for someone else. How do you know what's right for them?"

"It's been done for centuries. This, the way they do it here, *this* is ridiculous. You cannot pick a spouse for yourself. How does one person, one *young* person know what's right for them? When you were eighteen did you think the way you do now? Well, when you're thirty you'll look back on today and laugh at your thoughts. It's like anything else when you're young. Vegetables. Cod liver oil. A jacket on a seemingly warm day. Your mother says take it, it's good for you. You refuse, you hate it, it seems unnecessary. Then you realize she knew you better than you knew yourself. That is why she is your mother."

I observe Darya in silence, watching her red hair bounce as she talks to me.

"Don't you think I know how you feel?" she says. "I cried like you cry by yourself at night now. I didn't want to marry him, didn't even find him attractive. I wanted to get a Ph.D. in mathematics and become a professor. I always thought I would contribute something big, something huge to academia, that I would be remembered for a theorem or proof or *something*. I never thought I'd be sitting with Bindoo and Lin-Hua on Saturdays solving equations no one would ever see. I couldn't even imagine not being a famous mathematician back then. When my mother introduced your father to me, I hated him. I hated her for pushing him on me. I spent several months, years even, resenting the marriage."

"So? What happened?"

"What happened is I grew up. What happened is your father. He gave to me. Consistently and unselfishly worked to make me happy. One day I woke up and I looked at him and looked at my house and my swollen stomach and his uneven teeth and realized I was happy and didn't even know it. I heard about a woman receiving a prize in mathematics and I laughed. Instead of leaving the room when people talked about successful people in math, I stayed and listened and felt all right. When my mother died I couldn't have survived it without your father. No professorship in math would have saved me then."

She absently picks up her hairbrush and twirls it in her hand. I say nothing.

"Besides," she continues, "remember when you were eighteen and we went to the department store and I bought you that blue denim shirt? Remember how you didn't want to get it and you hated it then? Now, you wear it almost every day."

"Mr. Dashti is not a shirt!"

"He wears nice shirts!"

"Darya!!!"

I feel a tiny tickle in my stomach. A small quiver works its way down to my toenails and up to the cores of my teeth. I feel my body throw itself forward as my shoulders start to shake. Suddenly my face is burning and I cannot keep my mouth closed anymore. It bursts open and a million smiles explode. I am made of laughter. The insanity of our conversation. Mr. Dashti wears nice shirts. My father as a gift. I imagine a huge red bow on his bald head. My stomach starts to hurt and I snort like a pig as tears soak my cheeks. I think of the graphs, Mr. Jahanfard, Mr. Bidar, Mr. Dashti, the slopes of the lines Darya calculated. My sides begin to hurt.

"You should've done a graph for Mr. Paparrazi too!" I burst out as my body melts onto the bed. I think of the gift, my poor dead grandmother's gift.

"Why didn't she just buy you some china and get it over with?" I squeal.

"What?" I hear Darya say. "What? What are you talking about? What china? You want to go to China?"

"Oh boy! Oh man! Man oh man! Go to China!" She is far away now. I am lost in my tears, unable to stop laughing.

"China man?" I hear Darya say. "You want a China man? Fine, no problem. I'll tell Lin-Hua, call her tonight. She has notes on a few."

No! No, no, no, I want to say, but I cannot speak anymore; my cheeks are hurting and my stomach is tight. Through my veil of tears, as I lie doubled over on the bed, I catch sight of Darya. She is standing in her pink and white housedress, her pudgy feet pointing outwards, the Dashti folder in one hand, her hairbrush in another. Her black roots are showing, the fiery red dye in need of a touch-up. As I catch her standing there watching me in frustration, I remember when we left Iran, how she had vowed to dye her hair red if she could ever reach a country where she didn't have to wear a veil. Our first morning in New York she closed herself in the hotel bathroom for thirty-five minutes, then rinsed her head in the shower. I remember how she emerged from the bathroom with her new orange hair, my father clapping loudly for her, whistling and cheering, urging my brothers and me to join in. I can see my father now, the pride on his face as she shyly removed the towel from her wet hair, how he went to the bathroom and cleaned the walls that had been stained orange, just as he had cleaned the clothes on my grandmother's body parts that had been stained orange from the bomb at the grocer's those years ago.

Silence replaces my laughter; my body hiccups slowly a few times as I get up from the bed. I see my mother. She's quiet, her eyes confused.

"Oh, Maman," I say as I take the hairbrush from her hand and sit her down on the bed. "Do you think I should wear the lavender dress with a cardigan or just by itself when I see Mr. Dashti?" And I place the hairbrush on the top of her skull and slowly begin to brush my mother's hair.

The Execution of Atefeh

PERSIS M. KARIM

For Atafeh Rajabi, age sixteen,
executed by the mullahs in Iran, August 2004

She was a tired girl trapped in a woman's mind.
Thinking of cigarettes and sex on tender afternoons.
She couldn't help herself. Her anger
resided at the tip of her tongue, in the color of her lips.

First, she gave herself to the boy next door,
then later to a man twice her age.
The reports say she was mentally incompetent.
When she faced the judges, for "acts incompatible with
    chastity,"
her quiet state of madness grew louder.
She spoke against her accusers, lashing her tongue
100 times against the body of men
wrapped in white cloth and holiness.

Weeks later her body hung from a rope
tied to the bough of a chestnut tree in Neka Square.
Beneath the black folds of cloth that would erase her,
those passing by saw the scorn
in her past-virgin face.
They made themselves feel better
speaking
under their breath.
"She was a whore, a temptress, a victimizer of men."

That night her body lay in the hot, humid ground.
Someone, perhaps the men, dug her up,
fearful that her skin and bones
might eat away at the soft earth
where mortal saviors walk.

She has risen again, some say.
Given her body over
to the flight of souls, to watchful eyes
that entreat us to remember
the body from which we came.

Bad

SANAZ BANU NIKAEIN

I am bad:
to decorate my face with piercings
dye my hair blue
to match my nail polish
pose nude for art students
bad

I am bad:
to hold my lover's hand in public
enjoy watching him sleep
in my bed
before marriage
bad

I am bad:
to disobey my husband
have a career instead of being his cook
control birth without his permission
refuse to wear turtlenecks in Spring
bad

Tradition disowns me as a member
I disown the culture as a follower
still the eyes of my community watch my every move

no regrets
no shame
bad
proud

Summoning

HALEH HATAMI

This is a song about women
This is a dance about respect

Napoleon man, smallish man, squawks into his wife's
corsage, tries to outtalk her in front of the wedding guest.
She takes her cue. Her words fade back, her eyes
glaze. The orchid withers on her silk lapel like the night
he deflowered her.

Tattered man in a chipped blue truck slams on
the brakes in front of Church's Chicken to make his
point clear. His woman can't be seen behind the veil
of black hair hanging, protecting her from his barking. She's
a very bad dog.

Balding man calls his wife of 30-odd years a cretin
in front of her children and friends. Schoolyard bully
stomps on her head and claims he's King of Kings. She
fingers her bracelets and laughs, embarrassed at how
stupid she can be.

> *We dance a dance of respect to summon a force*
> *lying dormant in her breast. Women strength*
> *from mothers' milk*
> *left*
> *the moment she caught his eye.*

Masouleh

∝

PARINAZ ELEISH

There are flies resting on the mantle.
The samovar boils.
My aunt swings by in her brick-red hair,
little blue scarf and click-clack shoes.
There is sun in my cup
and sun on the wall.
The mountain painted with tea plants
and mud roofs ends far below
in a rice field green as an emerald sea.
And we drink tea in our saucers
in this slow afternoon of crimson heat.

Words to Die For

❦

ESTHER KAMKAR

I read that the Russian poet
Osip Mandelstam was ordered killed
because he'd likened Stalin's mustache
to a cockroach.

And I heard that Moosa, my father's cousin,
was executed because he'd sworn
loud enough for the guards to hear
that His Holiness, the Imam
was fathered by a dog
and mothered by a whore.

And I met a woman
who was half crazy.
She'd visited her two daughters in prison
once a month for ten years
and brought them care packages
of birth control pills.
She said: Their faces were yellow like turmeric.
It was all in their eyes.

In my mother-tongue we say
that a desired woman's body
is like peeled peaches,
that she walks like a drunk peacock

and sees with her deer eyes.
We say that a child's body is as pure
as her mother's milk.

Where I come from
these days they don't execute
the virgins.
First they rape them
and then
they shoot them.

Fariba's Daughters

SUSAN ATEFAT-PECKHAM

Iranian law states that once a girl turns nine, she
is of age and must wear the chador *in public places.*

Fariba pulls her scarf off when we are alone,
holds her head taut like a winter oak, dark
and bare. She likes her books under
the mattress, under the wooded tucking
of blankets, between mattress and box spring.
She asks me if it's good to read, and reaches
under white to pull the book from its hiding.

I hear her voice, clear and strong, talking
of school, asking how freedom feels,
asking if I had sex before marriage like girls
in the West, or if I was a good Iranian virgin.
I tell her what freedom is. It is noon
and the prayers outside are loud. I ask her
why she never teaches her daughters
a different way. Her stare is hard. Almost
as hard as the roll of her eyes when someone
wants for *doukgh*, more *bakhlava.*
She is worn from wanting.

This is my favorite—Jean-Paul Sartre, they say
his wife was smart, she says. But I can see her
daughter Attar turning with the scarf, winding it
around her head and loving to see herself as her

mother in the dresser mirror. I ask Fariba why
she wears it. For my daughters, her fingers
catch in her hair, for my daughters.

I remember when Father said I wasn't to wear
a *chador* to the bazaar. I was not old enough
to choose my way, that I would be safe.
So Grandmother pulled me under her *chador,*
wove me into her folds, just me and her under
cloth so *pasdars* would leave us alone. *Bepau,*
she said, Watch it. And I thought it was fun
and safe and soft standing against Grandmother's
lap, seeing from an opening near her hands.
Perhaps there is some joy in being captive,
some comfort in knowing we obey.

Nebraska winter drops in tufts. Does Sartre
still hide in wood? What does Fariba read
today? Attar turning, almost nine. What color
will her first scarf be? Woolen snow drifts
and weaves its way. Daughters are warm
wrapped in their Grandmothers' *chadors.*

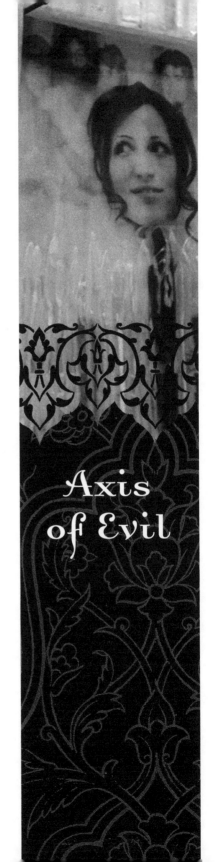

Axis
of Evil

Lower Manhattan

❧

Susan Atefat-Peckham

If you're lost, look for the World Trade Center,
and you'll find your way home.

—A PASSERBY

From the United Nations
International School, on FDR Drive
and 25th Street, Mother and I walked
the wind north fifteen blocks to meet
Father who waited for us at the United
Nations, the Hudson River lapping
its edges, lifting our hair to the brass
of rush hour traffic. And the twin
towers gleamed with western sunlight
if I looked over my small shoulder.
If you are lost, look for this shining,
shadows looming over the bay
as the Staten Island Ferry pushed
its way from Lower Manhattan
through Hudson water, home to
New Jersey, the skyline receding
till the towers slipped between
the closing pinch of my thumb
and forefinger, my eye just behind.
This city, in the palms of my hands,
beneath spaces of clamped fingers,
where I carried it to France, Iran,

Switzerland, Texas, Nebraska,
Michigan, where I still hold it
the years I've left it behind. How
will I find my way home? My palms
burn. If you are lost, look
for my eyes, hot in your hands,
carry me there, bright, burning,
and alive.

Another Day and Counting

ZARA HOUSHMAND

It's routine now:
I drive my son to school,
the sun just breaking through Pacific mist.
Driving home, I listen to the news
and quietly cry.

My son won't listen anymore:
"All opinions, hot air. Call me when they find some
    facts."
Proud and fragile privilege of youth:
demand the truth.

The sky recedes, ashamed.
What passes now for truth on this cold ball?
The sky is pink with shame
beyond the concrete ribbons where commuters crawl.
What's in that microscopic dust
that bends our light to postcard pinks?
Dust of concrete hopes exploded,
dust of homes of sun-baked brick,
complex chains of human dust
and dust of promises to youth.

Tonight my cheeseburger arrives
with a flag poked proudly in the bun.
The tiny paper stars and stripes seem far away,

victory through the wrong end of the telescope,
moon-landing on the circle of my plate.
The waitress smiles broadly,
but the food tastes bad,
or maybe I've just lost my appetite.

Axis of Evil

∽

PERSIS M. KARIM

1.

Soheila puts the *samovar* back on the crowded shelf,
sips the last of her dark, red tea.
Her hands sweep across the *sofreh*
on the floor—gathering empty plates
littered with pistachio shells and sprigs of mint.
Tonight they have declared war on Baghdad.
She worries about her young son,
her mother suffering from rheumatism.
Upstairs her husband listens to the radio,
sometimes the BBC, sometimes Voice of America.
But lately it's the government station.
When he hears the sound of the plaintive *ney*
he turns the volume up,
down when the mullahs address the nation.

2.

In a quiet city in the Midwest
a woman opens her umbrella
at the first sight of a last spring rain.
Lately, she's been thinking about her safety.
What will it take to drive back
the forces of evil in our midst?
She's thought more about the places
and people on earth that live
like she does. Checking their watches,
feeding their kids, dutifully
paying their taxes.

3.

All night Mohammed hears the wail of sirens.
In the morning, he watches angry men
hoist long ropes and topple
statues of the Great One.
Let them erase this history—
so long as he can go to school again,
so long as the rain of bullets
ceases.

4.

Soheila awakens to a glorious sunrise.
How can she have turned in her bed
so much and still feel so rested?
Tehran is a lonely city, she thinks,
gazing out her second-story window
at the sad dirtiness enveloping her city.
She thinks too of her deceased father's
voice. His reminders to look always
for *goodness.*

How Lucky Persimmons Are

Parinaz Eleish

I look out the window
From the corner of one eye,
Past the benches and the lonely crows.
The persimmons still hang quiet and lucky,
When all else smells of decay.
I touch my grandmother's hands,
Hold her love in my eyes
When I know it won't last.
How lucky persimmons are
And the stillness of the leaves,
The silent breeze passing
Through the curtains.
The streets are empty,
The pavements breathe with heat
I long to hold on.
But know with time,
The clock tower will crumble,
Babies will go thirsty
And the pools will grow trees.
I see from behind
My father's shoulders
The neighbor's son writing
His name backward
On the fogged window.
When all else is quiet
I read it silently—

It doesn't take long.
My breasts are hurting,
And my brother's off to war.
How thoughtlessly beautiful the persimmons
Feel in the bloody dusk.
I long to hang from a tree
Watch my grandmother pray in the shade.
For even one more day.

Mamaan-bozorg

❧

FARNOOSH SEIFODDINI

In September 1980, Iraq seized ninety square
miles of Iranian territory in the Shatt al-Arab
but failed to win the swift victory predicted by
many; a bloody war of attrition set in.

When we heard the sirens
my sisters knew what to do.
But I stood
staring at the layered shadows
their arms threw on the wall
fingers pointing at me.
Then she would come grab me
her gray thin strands of hair
a halo in the candlelight
her fingertips
cold and dry
brushing my forehead
nodding
rocking
pressing my face
to a bony chest
that had nursed ten children.
I liked her huddling in the doorway with us.

In the Gutter

❦

SANAZ BANU NIKAEIN

The girl screams across the playground
i—ran in the gutter
i—ran in the gutter
I stand with my legs glued to the cement
my eyes follow the blond hair that flows in the wind
i—ran to squirt you
they all laugh
I cup my hands on my face
pretend to dry water not tears
not tears

Yes Iran in the gutter
when I repeat myself
until out of breath
that we don't ride camels back home
we drive cars
the entire fifth-grade class stares at me in disbelief
one yells:
she lies, cars get stuck in sand
I give up

Yes Iran in the gutter
when four men in Armani suits
offer me a job in a sweatshop
where he says:
you belong next to all the other immigrants

my eyes widen
cheeks burn with anger
fingers turn into a fist
I want to bury his head in his rigatoni
instead I say, *enjoy dinner*

Yes Iran in the gutter
when I get an American passport to travel the world
when I deny my ancestors to get a job
when I'd rather have American friends
because
because
I see no more glamour as an Iranian
Iranian means terrorism on TV
Iranian means bombs in the media

Iran in the gutter
Iran in the gutter

The Witness

∞

ROXANNE VARZI

The cab circles the block for the fourth time.

"Hussein Ziadeh Street?" the cabby reconfirms with the passenger.

"That's the address."

"Are you sure it's in South Tehran? I've never heard of this street."

"I don't know," the passenger curtly replies. "That's what I was told." He runs his hand through his thick gray hair and sighs.

"Maybe it's a new, post-war street?" The cabby drives on, not waiting for a reply.

"The war has been over for two years," the passenger says with another sigh. As if that were news to anyone. It lasted almost a decade.

"It's a *koucheh,* I'm sure. Are you sure the address is *keyaban*★ and not *koucheh?*"

"Yes, that's what I was told," the passenger answers, thinking about how annoyed his wife will be that he's so late from work. Maybe he should just go home. If he doesn't stop by the mosque, it will look rude. After all, it's his co-worker's son.

"Is it a residence?"

"No, a mosque."

The cabby notes his own surprised look in the rearview mirror. He takes another look at the crisp white oxford and well-made suit and decides that there is only one reason a wealthy North Tehran man would be going to a mosque in the early evening: death.

The drizzle turns Tehran's fluorescence into a sad-looking woman in a wet sequined dress, smudged lipstick and runny mascara. She should be covered. The light is fading to neon, a sign that he's late. Circling the busy streets, the cabdriver occasionally sticks his head out the window to call to another driver, "Ever heard of Hussein Ziadeh?" Their heads shake "no," and lips offer apologetic smiles. He stops to ask

---

★ Street.

a man under an awning smoking a hookah pipe on the sidewalk. "Not in these parts," he croaks, the smoke evaporating into the rain.

The streets are decorated in wet shiny plastic banners to welcome returning prisoners of war. They are always decorated for some Islamic commemoration or other, the passenger thinks. Looking out at the blur of lights, he remembers when Tehran nights were pitch black, when the mountains were outside of the city, and when the air was breathable. He sees Tehran as if for the first time in twenty years, because he, like most Tehranis, never pays attention until he has to, until he is lost.

"Tomorrow is the parade for the returning POWs. We have one in my family," the cabby offers proudly.

"God bless him," the passenger offers; he won't congratulate the cabby because he doesn't believe in the sanctity of boy-martyrs. And he doesn't want to be lost in the city in the rain. And he is sick of looking at the billboards with the faces, the reminders of all the martyrs. What he wants is to be at home listening to his children joke about school and helping his wife prepare for dinner.

"Is the person young?" the cabby asks.

"Who?"

"The wake."

Did he mention his reason for visiting the mosque? He's too tired to remember; the ride feels like an eternity.

"Yes," he says, not wanting to talk, trying to see through the steamed window.

"An accident?"

"A skiing accident."

The neon fades as the cab slowly winds its way uphill, away from the city center and toward the mountains. Tacky Greek columns dot the edge of the mountains, where newly built mansions are coming up faster than weeds. Kerosene lamps flicker within tents at each site. Where there isn't neon, there's kerosene, and anything that hasn't become neon soon will, the passenger thinks. He used to play in these hills. The man's thoughts are interrupted by the cabdriver.

"I'm going to ask in this store."

As the cabby crosses the street to the small store, the passenger notices how short the cabby is, bent over like the men who carry street trash on their backs. His blue woolen cap becomes white with flakes of the city's first snow. Streams of steam puff out of the canvas flap as the cabby pushes through it to enter the little room where cigarettes, batteries and gum are sold; the string of lightbulbs that marks its entrance suggests warmth. The thought of whiling away the hours on the other side of the canvas flap, perched on a low stool and smoking a cigarette with the proprietor, staring out at the rain, is inviting, but beneath him.

The passenger's head is pounding. He is tired and afraid of being confronted with everything he has tried to avoid these past eighteen years. They say that in Tehran, if you have money and the right connections, you can avoid it all. But there are times, despite himself and his attempts to avoid thinking about it, that he finds himself face to face with the reality of a never-ending war. The war is over, but its images are more alive than ever. There are constant reminders: a billboard of a little girl holding the head of a dying martyr in her lap; men in wheelchairs advertising the Olympics for war veterans; red roses poking out of the barrel of an AK-47 or red tulips and poppies fertilized in battlefields of blood. Every beautiful image has been turned into one of death. In Behesht-e-Zahra cemetery in Tehran, a fountain flows with red water to remind visitors of the blood spilled in this war. The rows and rows of dead faces—laminated photographs staring out from tombs in the cemeteries—are replicated in billboards around the city.

"I found it," the cabby yells, running back to the car. "We've actually driven past it a few times," he announces proudly.

"How is that?" the passenger asks.

"The name has to be changed; they took down the sign."

"Why?" the passenger asks curtly.

"It was changed just this afternoon, after the news that Hussein Ziadeh has returned. He is no longer a martyr!"

The passenger frowns and turns his head toward the window. It was bad enough when the Iraqis were bombing; it was impossible to find anything in the city. Whenever a boy died in battle, his family was rewarded by having their street renamed for their son. Even after the war, Tehran is still mapped by death.

"*Alhamd'allah,* they were so happy to have him back. There is no shame in trying . . . but they had to change the name, of course," the driver says, as he starts the car. Approvingly, he adds: "Allah commends the intention, but only martyrs have streets named for them."

The passenger is relieved to leave the cab and feel the cold city air. He has no desire to be inside a mosque where the women are wailing and the men crying. Standing outside, he lights a cigarette and tries to clear his head. He glances at the cage-like funerary object that is lighted and displayed both outside the mosque on the day of the wake and in the deceased's former neighborhood for the following forty days and nights.

Announcements of the services dot the frame of the metal cage. In its center, like a canary or a prisoner, lies a framed photo of the deceased: a young, handsome boy who never reached the age at which death could come to him in a military uniform. He died in bright colors that sharply contrasted with the crisp snow surrounding him: no street will bear his name.

The man throws his cigarette into the wet street. He closes his eyes but it does not help. Mixed in the loss, the sense of always being lost, he senses wayward ghosts and thinks of a *shahid*—a martyr, one who bears witness. Entering the mosque, he knows that he has no choice but to bear witness.

American Again

✧

Parissa Milani

I am Iranian
until I open my mouth. Then
I am American.

But if I promise to not even breathe
through my mouth, will you take me in?
Will you take me to the Caspian Sea
and tell me it's always been so close?
Will you take me to Esfahan
and tell me I've been there before?
Will you take me to the bazaars of Tehran
and tell me I have haggled for
ripe pomegranates and sour plums?

Will you forgive me for playing
dodgeball in America
while my brothers and sisters
dodged bombs in Iran?
Will you forgive me for loving
the flag you once hated?
Will you forgive me for
deserting you?

Will you understand when
it gets hard for me to
breathe easy and I become
American again?

Butcher Shop

✑

BY SHOLEH WOLPÉ

Aisha was gunned down
in her father's butcher shop.
She was twenty-four, a virgin,
had a cat named Hanna.

The boys in black bandanas
the ones with large dark eyes
that devour light
wanted her brother.

And what better place for blood
than a butcher shop
where it already covers
the counters, stains the white aprons,
is sold in long red sausages.

Iranians v. Persians

✍

SANAZ BANU NIKAEIN

I am an Iranian
with terrorist tattooed on my forehead
that reminds everyone I meet
of the hostage situation in 1979
my passport gives permission
to every international airport
to escort me to the back room
and strip-search me to the bone

As soon as a bomb explodes—
World Trade Center in New York
Federal Building in Oklahoma—
every news station reports with no shame:
it's probably Iranians again

But you Persians
have the soft and friendly look of a Persian cat
beauty of a Persian rug
you live your lives
without verbal repetition
that your father has one wife
and she is the boss

You live your lives
without restating
that camels live in the zoo
and are not a mode of transportation

When one asks
the difference between Iran and Persia
you mumble
it's the same thing
but forget to mention
Persians don't have enough Iranian blood
running through their hearts
to eat the harsh words of society
to show we carry professional degrees
instead of guns
and try to change our terrorist image
one
by
one

Invitation to the Hungry Ghosts

ZARA HOUSHMAND

There has never been such a good time to be alive:
Fascism digging in like gangrene, the earth abused,
Rolling over to die, the work laid out like a feast.

The piss-stained schizophrenic at the curb holds high
A steaming dainty-plate. Is he not a mother's son?
Am I not mother enough to swallow his feast?

Why do I choke on soldiers?—Lick those babies clean
Of fear. My belly grows—is it big enough yet
To hold Washington? Feast within feast within feast!

Only war gets poets in the door here: Basho
Hid in a body bag. Rumi showed up early—
You should have seen hell coming when he served you his feast.

"My turban is worth two cents," he said, a sly
Loss leader. Now his tattered coat will cost you all
The oil in Araby; his boots, your four-star feast.

Your bloated souls are starving, pounding at the door.
Napa wine won't get you drunk. You've bombed the tavern
Flat with greed. Now you'll have to come outside to feast!

When Toys Are Us

∝

BEATRICE MOTAMEDI

I went to Toys "Я" Us today to see if my brothers were still for sale, and they were.

Neatly shrink-wrapped, they stood straight and tall next to the Navy battleships and the Bradley fighting vehicles. They were toys, with names that echoed the war in Afghanistan and Iraq—names like "G.I. Joe Adventure Team" and "Ultimate Soldier, U.S. Desert Special Operations."

I saw my brothers last Christmas, when I went to my local Toys"Я"Us to buy my nephew a present. Despite my better intentions *(get in / get Elmo / get out)* it wasn't long before I was wandering in a vast waste-land of blinking lights, my mind wiped clean of whatever I was look-ing for.

Eventually I found myself in the section reserved for military toys, where I expected to see soldiers with blond hair and blue eyes, Barbie and Ken in khaki.

But to my surprise, the Joes I found looked just like my bros.

They were slender and handsome, with wavy hair and neatly trimmed beards. Their eyes were dark and intense and totally familiar. They had the curly hair, trim build and coffee-colored skin of my father, who left his village on the shore of the Caspian Sea, and emigrated to the West, more than fifty years ago.

In a word, they looked Persian.

Of course, there were exceptions. Some of the soldiers were packaged with not one but two interchangeable heads, the first a clean-shaven Anglo, the second faintly Arab. One soldier was indeed blond and blue-eyed, though he was from the war before, a U.S. Marine "circa 1944–45."

Of all the toy soldiers I saw, he was the only one who was smiling; obviously he had missed the Long March to Bataan, the bombing of Dresden, the annihilation of Hiroshima. But he was the exception, and my brothers were the rule.

FROM TOM RIDGE TO THE RED CROSS

Sometimes the resemblance between Joe and bro was enough to make me laugh out loud.

A soldier named "Ultimate Soldier: U.S. Army Afghanistan" looked just like my brother Rick, the morning that I rang his doorbell too early and found him standing there in his bathrobe, exhausted from staying up all night with his baby.

The G.I. Joe "Undercover Agent" came with two heads, one that of a grim, square-jawed man who looked like Tom Ridge, the homeland security czar, and the other that of a slightly worried, even less optimistic fellow, who resembled my brother Mike, a former nurse for the Red Cross.

Then there was "Dial Tone," a G.I. Joe whose mustache was embarrassingly similar to the one that my brother Dave grew just in time for my wedding.

Dial Tone, according to the marketing copy, was a radio telecommunications specialist, capable of setting up a mobile satellite transmitter in less than three minutes even under battlefield conditions.

"Nothing stops Dial Tone from doing his job," the bio read; his messages go out "loud and clear."

I had to smile—my Dial Tone, my David, lives in Germany now, halfway around the world. It's been weeks since we talked on the phone, months since I talked to Cara, my niece. It would be great if either of us was a telecommunications expert.

Alas, in the real world, we're not.

The irony of finding my brothers on a shelf was unexpected but delicious.

Like many Persian Americans after 9/11, I dreaded seeing photos of the hijackers in the *New York Times;* but for their dead eyes, their empty gazes, they, too, could have been my brothers, with the same neat white dress shirts, the same unruly hair.

Over the past two years, my brothers—middle names Cyrus, Reza and Davoud—have been searched more often at airports, glanced at more closely on the street. They don't protest; like most Americans, they know that these are troubled times. But sometimes the fears are unreasonable, even racist.

My seventy-five-year-old father, a surgeon who has saved countless lives, was openly stared at recently when he boarded a plane; one passenger, a woman, complained to the flight crew that he looked "different."

When David's son was born a few months ago, the nurses at the hospital called him "the Turkish baby," lumping Johnny in with all of the brown-skinned babies who come from God-knows-where.

So maybe that's why I was oddly pleased by what I saw at the toy store. The fact is that these playthings reveal a serious truth: like all of America, the U.S. military is increasingly multiethnic, with growing numbers of loyal, patriotic Arab and Persian Americans, as well as Muslims of all races.

At the same time, the people we fight also are increasingly diverse. More and more often, our enemies are who we were, before the diaspora that scattered us to New York and Chicago and Los Angeles. They are Iraqis and not Iraqi Americans; the Afghans who stayed versus the Afghans who left; Iranians from Tehran, but not the ones who live in "Tehrangeles."

Sure, Persian Americans sometimes look like terrorists. Then again, sometimes we work for the Red Cross.

Toys have always had an uncanny way of predicting the future. In 1959, four years before the publication of *The Feminine Mystique,* the introduction of Barbie, with her impossibly long legs and piled-up hair, forever banished the myth of the happy housewife. In 1965, the year that Malcolm X was assassinated and Martin Luther King Jr. was arrested in Selma, Hasbro introduced its first-ever black Joe, a symbol of the integration that was inexorably underway in the U.S. military, if not society as a whole.

This year marks the fortieth birthday of G.I. Joe, and Hasbro has released its first Asian American version; he joins the first female Joe (1967), the first Navajo Joe (2000) and the first Hispanic Joe (2001). One day, I hope, there will be an Arab American or even a Persian American Joe, an Abu-Joe, whose face will be that of an ordinary soldier, a common grunt who is trying to build a bridge between the culture of his birth and the country of his future. An Abu-Joe who, like most soldiers, dreams at night of returning to his home and family, wherever they may be.

And that's the Joe I might consider buying for my eleven-year-old son, middle name Henry. Because, like my brothers, he is an American citizen. But as my father always points out, he is the one who was born "with the Persian eyes."

As Good as Any Other Day

❧

PARINAZ ELEISH

As good as any other day
To buy an umbrella,
My mother called to say
Over seas, over mountains
On tapped phones.

Dawn on the Fall Equinox

❧

PERSIS M. KARIM

The shifting light of autumn
has caused an uneasiness.
This morning, I lay beside
my son, listening to his breathing,
finding comfort in the soft bulbs
of his hands, opening
like poppies at first contact with sunlight.

What those other boys
in that place where we've unleashed
war are thinking, I cannot say.
Theirs is a life punctuated by
the *ratta-tatt-tatt* of bullets,
the mud-green of uniforms,
and corpses of bombed-out cars.
Waking at dim first light
cannot be like this. Soft and sweet,

the certainty of their mother's
breath against neck and hair.
In this dream-state here,
I can only think of dressing,
feeding him, caressing his smallness.

I don't like this early darkness,
the falling leaves, the raking

that once provided a kind of order
reminds me of death
somewhere else.

How will I explain *this* to him?
In these hummed hours
before he speaks my name,
I pretend to have a truth
that turns the darkness into light.

Instilling Shock and Awe

❧

Farnoosh Seifoddini

*5:17 P.M. EST March 21, 2003—Fires and huge
plumes of smoke filled the skies of downtown
Baghdad in what correspondent Peter Arnett
said were strikes far larger than what he had
seen in the 1991 Gulf War.*

I hear the news anchors as I wash the dishes
Some bubbles settle on my bare arms
While others drift through sunlight
  a ladybug crawls on the windowpane
    and I think I'm falling in love with J.

I turn off the faucet and listen for voices
There is only a humming and muffled sounds of thunder

In the living room
I find a desert landscape
The thunder: bombs bursting white against the night sky

I stand in my bra and panties
The cat weaving around my ankles with a purr

Summer Day

∽

Parinaz Eleish

Imagine canyons with the slight flutter of bees
as the only echo.
Beyond, three women row down the stream
in canoes of rare crystal.
Their ankles end
in satin shoes.
One cracks sunflower seeds.
The other begins a story:
Once upon a time there was only God . . .
Imagine the sweet taste of pears from Persia
and tea from a tiny field in China,
the lemon sun kissing your skin softly.
On the brown sand the soldiers armored in steel
march away with a breeze.
Such a clear summer day.
Just imagine!
Tigers swimming a pool of ashen waters.

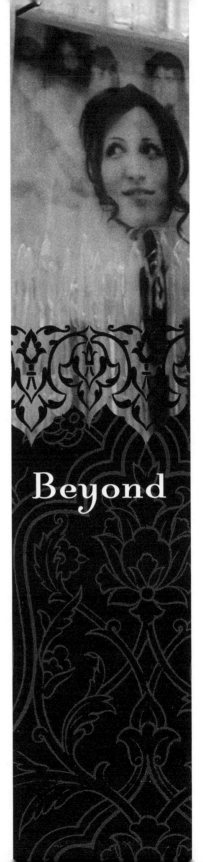

Beyond

Sestinelle for Travelers

∞

SUSAN ATEFAT-PECKHAM

We are bound for the silence of unknown roads
and trails winding red clay hills. And for what we bring
down the paths of this blue world. The traveler knows

the lumber trucks that sway past the mottled nose
of a stabled mare and the folding joint of a heron's wing,
past corridors of mailboxes. Past every home we've ever known.
The logs they haul, like unclothed bodies, shadows
upon shadows, trembling. These trucks ring
down the paths of this blue world. The traveler knows

the fog will part when trucks push through like boats, knows
the circles of cut logs vanish in mist like dying galaxies, these
rings
we are. Bound for the silence of unknown roads

together we wind a universe. We feel it, know it, on these roads,
where fog rises from water like heat from a body that wrings
down the paths of this blue world. The traveler knows
these are the alleys, ravines, side streets traveled all our lives,
shadows
that hang the sun at our backs, the canopy of telephone wire
and wings.
We are bound for the silence. Unknown roads

curve through the heat, where metal clamps of trucks corrode
and life is a falling turquoise pendant flipping from an old, gold string
down the paths of this blue world the traveler knows,

flipping fast, like a lit cigarette tossed from a window, where there is no
stopping. Bark peels, wind-whipped, as if loose skin or wings.
We are bound for the silence. The unknown roads
where strangers' oncoming cars will veer out of reach. And home
is crushed glass gleaming on a street, like stars. Or gold rings
down the paths of this blue world. The traveler knows

    the orange flag that trembles at the end of one long trunk, knows
    that fog won't clear from around this house. Once it clings
    we are bound for the silence. Unknown, rowed

    logs sway, appear and vanish down random roads,
    ready for travel on trucks with smoke stacks, shimmering,
    We are bound for the silence of unknown roads,
    say the faces, lit, as they keep watch at passing windows,
    their eyes, constellations blooming inside, stare sobering.
    Inside our homes we lie like cradled, unlimbed shadows.

This world is ringed by many bodies pressed together. Shadows
we are bound by: the silence, the unknown roads—
down these paths—these blue worlds. The traveler knows.

The Best Reason to Write a Poem Is Still for Love

∽

Farnaz Fatemi

*Phillip Vorlander, an assistant fire chief with the
Madison, Wisconsin, Fire Department, fought
the appointment of Debra Amesqua as chief of
the department, claiming gender and race dis-
crimination, since she was hired at the beginning
of 1996, complaining that she was considered
and hired because she is Latina and a woman.
He amended his complaint in September to
include the fact that she is a lesbian.*

She sees faces in the flames
where she aims the surging jets,
and sleeps with her boots next to the bed,
where her lover trips in the darkness
of their lost sacred hours alone.
She's seasoned.
Here's another fire sparked by ancestry,
her X chromosomes, or love.
Her hands are scarred
by last month's backdraft
and she doesn't know her breaking point.
This time, who will give up first?
Perhaps she'll survive with fourth-degree
inhalation, and recover in time for the next housefire,
months, or weeks, away.

He looks at her and she is flattened,
a life-size cut-out he would buy at the supermarket,

then take his picture next to
like the presidential family or John Wayne.
He sees her body in outline,
no organs or innards,
not the guts it takes to fight these blazes
find a common goal next to men
who will often hate her.
He has no idea how many fires she's put out
or how many still nip at her heels.

Some days she wants him to win
so she can put the hose down.
These are the days
she forgets all about flesh—
scars, softness, the way she melts
next to her lover's skin—
and all about blood—
its diseases, its necessity
its legacies inside her.
She is heatblind
and the faces are gone,
even his before her.

But she wants to step into
the whiteness of this inferno
and search Madison
for someone in his life
with the power to change him:
daughter, father, wife.
She would become that person
undress him in the daytime
stand naked in front of him,
say, look at what we're wrapped in.
See this soft scraped creamy dark thing? It's life.

Perfectly Parallel Mirrors

∞

LALEH KHALILI

For John T. Chalcraft

between two parallel mirrors
as if between two pasts

she stands unadorned
but for the strokes of history upon her flesh
blood sacrifice of dubious origins
tempestuous kisses
in tempestuous climates
and gouged chasms
upon her core

definition is always a precarious enterprise
in twilight—blurring boundaries—

she hunts herself in a persistence of
mirrors and mirages and memories
the naked ambivalence of her breasts
painted
on the interminable canvas of her lineage
and the rebellion of her navel
reflected
on the shoulder blades of her past

between two mirrors
as if amidst intertwined forests of fable and history
the nations persistent in her kaleidoscopic womb

no fact ever verified
no reality ever substantiated
no truth ever proven

Money Buys

SANAZ BANU NIKAEIN

so easy to fall in love
with a man
whose checkbook
makes worries disappear

Once

⤖

ZJALEH HAJIBASHI

once, spread wide
now press them close
so closed they fuse together
for perfect minor scales

play the major ones of course but
play A minor twice
to strip it
of its dolor

mechanical, precise they hammer
harder on the fingerboard (the black paint yields in time) than
on gut strings
that lie between, live,
and forced to sound
up three octaves and back down
all the keys and both A minors
dead steady
in its hollow

so perfectly in tune the tones, so smoothly drawn the bow
flesh turned wood
tap tap tap tap
their blunt ends
ply unlovely notes
refusing all vibrato

deny the stroke and resonance
to music grown so calloused

while captive romance no. 2 in
      what doesn't fucking matter
expiates its sentience

in my deaf, diminished hand.

From *Stones in the Garden*

❧

LAYLA DOWLATSHAHI

CHAPTER I

"Roya! Get up!"

Roya awoke to find her aunt, Khaleh Farah, dressed in a black *chador,* standing over her bed.

"What? What's happened?" Roya asked.

"Nothing has happened, you lazy girl, except that you have missed the *azan* again."

"Oh, Khaleh, I'm sorry, but . . ."

Khaleh Farah held up her hand to silence her. Her other hand rested on her rounded hip, the manteau material tight around her bulky frame.

"Stop! I don't want to hear any of your excuses this morning. Come! Get out of bed, and get dressed. Your cousin has been up for half an hour already. *She* never sleeps through the *azan.*"

Roya lowered her head, black hair hanging loosely about her face.

"Yes . . . I am going right now . . . I am sorry . . ."

"Don't apologize! Just move! We are leaving in two minutes."

Khaleh Farah turned from the bed and drew the black curtain across the partition that separated the two rooms of the apartment. The room had been a storage area, but after they moved in, Khaleh Farah had immediately sewn together the black curtain, making the space the girls' bedroom. "Young girls need privacy," she had said.

Inside the space, they had managed to place a compact double bed and a wardrobe with a vanity mirror hung on the inside left door. On the windowsill were placed a decanter of water and an empty, cracked mixing bowl used for washing the hands and face. There was barely room to move about, and Roya and Shada used the room for only sleep and dressing. On the floor, the girls had spread a large misshapen rug purchased secondhand from the Fabric Shoppe, and on the white walls hung a picture of Imam Reza, along with a tattered poster of the Pahlavi royal family.

Roya leapt out of bed, cursing Shada silently. *She is never late.* For once, she wished that Shada was not always so perfect. In Iran, it had been the same thing: Maman comparing her to Shada and asking her why she couldn't try and be more like her cousin. Shada pulled open the wardrobe doors and grabbed a pair of pants. She caught her reflection in the vanity mirror and sighed. She was not very pretty and felt she never would be. Her eyes were dark and her hair was thick and curly, so unlike Shada, with her blond hair and blue eyes and skin the color of sand. Shada, smart, mature, devout, was always being praised for whatever she did. *Ah, Shada, this kabob is perfect! Ah, Shada, you have been to* mashjed *so early . . . ah . . . you have done so well in school this year.* No one ever told Shada that she had done something wrong and Khaleh Farah never raised her voice to her. There wasn't ever a need. Shada did everything before she was asked. Maman had told Roya for as long as she could remember to be more like her. Oh, how she tried! She threw off her sleeping gown, pulled on underwear, a long-sleeve black shirt, and then the pair of black, corduroy pants. From underneath her bed, she pulled out a folded black *chador* and then, placing it on the bed, walked to the windowsill, poured water from the decanter into the washbowl and scrubbed her face.

Roya sighed as she dried her face. It seemed life was going to be much the same in Germany.

❧

Khaleh Farah walked into the other room, which was both her bedroom and the family living area. In one corner, there was a small sleeping mat and a chest, where she kept her *chador,* her other dress and the Koran. A poster of Imam's Square in Esfahan hung across one wall. In the other corner of the room, their downstairs neighbor, Mohammed, the owner of the *halal* deli, who was also a plumber, had installed a galley kitchen. There was a tiny one-range stove, a sink and a folding table with three chairs that the women used for both eating and studying.

Shada stood at the sink washing the breakfast dishes. Her long blond hair had been tied back earlier into a bun and hidden beneath the long folds of the muslin *chador,* but a few strands of it had escaped and now peeked out at the hairline.

Khaleh Farah walked over to the table and sat down in one of the chairs.

"Has the box come?"

"Yes, Maman," replied Shada, not turning around. "It is over there by the door."

Khaleh Farah walked over to the front entry, picked up the small cardboard box and carried it easily back to the table. She sorted through the box's contents and removed four loaves of bread, a sack of oranges, a sack of potatoes, half a carton of eggs, a pound of cheese and one pound of pork, wrapped in plastic foil.

"I don't know why they would think that we can survive for two weeks on this kind of food. If I didn't work at the *kiosk* we would starve, I think."

Shada, her hands still in the water, turned to face Khaleh Farah.

"Do not forget, Maman . . . they do give each of us forty Euros per week."

"Forty Euros? What is that to feed two growing girls and buy clothes with?"

"Don't worry, Maman. We will pray to Allah to make things better for us in this country. HE will hear our prayers."

Khaleh Farah nodded, staring into the empty box. Shada, not getting an answer, turned around.

"Maman?"

Khaleh Farah did not answer, her eyes still on the inside of the cardboard box.

"Maman . . . ," began Shada, "the water is ice-cold again. What shall we do?"

"You would think we have always been in Germany the way that girl forgets that Friday is our day of prayer and rest!" Khaleh Farah said suddenly.

Shada looked away and continued washing the dishes. She was familiar with this topic of conversation.

"Ah, Maman . . . leave her alone. We start school on Monday and she is nervous and that is what makes her sleep and forget. She is a good girl," replied Shada, turning off the water and drying her hands on a dishtowel.

"Yes . . . but will she remain that way if she keeps putting her own thoughts before the thoughts of Allah?"

Shada wiped her hands and folded the wet dishtowel. She sat down next to Khaleh Farah at the table, placing her smooth, white hand on the other's dark, rough hand.

"We have only been in Germany six months. It is hard for her to . . . adjust. *Inshallah,* she will be fine once we get to know the other Muslims in the neighborhood. We are still strangers here."

Khaleh Farah stared thoughtfully at Shada. Although the two were mother and daughter, there was very little resemblance between them. Khaleh Farah bore the looks of a desert warrior, fierce, strong and wild, her eyes the color of night and the shape of Arabian almonds, her skin the dark olive of people from Southern Iran. She was heavy and stout, her body that of a woman built for hard work and used to it.

"Yes, that is what she needs. She has yet to meet any of our neighbors and refuses to talk to any of the young people after the prayer sessions. She seems . . ."

"Distant?"

"Yes," replied Khaleh Farah. "These are her people. We are all Muslims. There are Iranians, some even from our province, and Afghanis . . . the . . . what is their name? . . ."

"Gholobis."

"Yes, that is them. They have a daughter who is sixteen, Roya's age. She will also be starting school."

"Fereshteh . . . I think."

"Yes," Khaleh Farah replied. "Your cousin must learn to be more sociable and not always look into herself. My sister, Allah bless her, told me often that she was so quiet as a baby that she would have to shake her to see if she was alive!"

Shada laughed. "Unlike me, who kept you up with my screams? We are so different."

"Yes . . . but Maman saw that you two would be close and she was right. Now, you are her only friend. She never had any in Arak."

"She is just shy. She has always been, can you not remember? In Arak, when there was a party, she would hide underneath Khaleh and Amu's bed until the guests went home."

Khaleh Farah smiled and nodded her head.

"Yes . . . I remember . . . it was not so long ago . . ."

Roya walked in then, her *chador* hanging from her arm. Both women turned to look at her. She swallowed nervously before walking over to the table. She kissed Khaleh Farah on both cheeks. Khaleh Farah crossed her arms and stared at Shada, taking her in from head to foot.

"Go . . . od . . . morning. I am sorry that I am late."

"Why are you not wearing your *chador*? Do you wish to make us later than we are?" Khaleh Farah demanded.

Shada stood and laughed nervously. She grabbed the *chador* from Roya and unfolded it, helped her to put it on. "Here . . . let me help you, cousin."

Khaleh Farah walked over to the chest and removed the tattered, gold-leafed Koran from inside.

"Let's go . . . we don't have time for talk."

Shada and Roya nodded their heads, glancing at one another nervously. Khaleh Farah walked back over to the table, placed the pork back inside the box and then carried the box to the door and out into the hallway.

"Be careful . . . she's not in a good mood . . ." began Shada.

"I know, you don't have to . . ."

"Girls! Come on! Hurry up!" yelled Khaleh Farah.

They both grabbed the ends of their *chadors* and followed Khaleh Farah out, shutting the door behind them.

The hallway was empty, as most of the residents of the Shule Heim had already gone to *mashjed* or were still asleep. The striped walls, half white and half black, had the musty look of having been without sunlight and soap for a very long time. The tile floors were dingy and covered with streaks of dry mud, urine and old food. The kitchen, to the right of the bathroom, had six range-top stoves and two sinks for those unfortunates in the building who could not get a room with a kitchen. There were twenty-one apartments in their building, seven on each floor, each with only two or three rooms. They occupied one of the apartments on the second floor. Next to them lived a Pakistani man, Ahmed Khan, who worked at the government's check office. Upstairs, two more Pakistanis, Singh and Naral, brothers from Karachi, shared a one-bedroom apartment. Across the hall lived Khanoum Nomani and her son, Ali. He was very handsome and about the same age as pretty Shada. Next door to them, in a two-room apartment, lived a family from Kurdistan, Amir and Leila, and their four boys. They had arrived the previous week and were seen only when they had to use the bathroom or kitchen facilities. Except for the two apartments downstairs, one occupied by a Yugoslavian woman from Foca, Marta, and her two children and the other by Mohammed, who was also the caretaker of the building, the rest of the apartments were empty.

The bathrooms, one on each floor, had a sink, two toilets and two shower stalls and were unisex. As they made their way down the dimly lit hallway, a cockroach scurried across in front of Shada. She leapt with fear and clung to Roya.

"Ah!"

Khaleh Farah swiftly stepped on the black insect.

"Ah . . . that cursed Ahmed Khan!" said Khaleh Farah as she hurried past the dead roach. "He and that bunch of Pakistanis leave their garbage all over the place and the bugs come to torture all of us!"

They continued down the rounded staircase into the main foyer of the building. There was a lounge in a separate area to the right of the exit/entrance doors, with an old television set and a rack full of used magazines in various languages, their corners torn and bent. A few chairs, once part of complete sets of furniture, were spread about the room. Khaleh Farah's shoes made click-click noises as she and the two girls crossed the tile floor to the exit doors, next to which was a stone bench. Two boys with blond hair and black eyes sat playing with a piece of yarn. Their dirty feet hung from the ends of the bench and one of them, the smallest, sat shivering near the door in his cut-off shirt and shorts. Khaleh Farah bent down and patted the smallest one's head with her hand.

"Where is your mother, Isak?" she asked in German.

"In the room."

Khaleh Farah gave Shada the Koran while she walked over to the apartment. Shifting the box to one arm, she knocked at the door, twice. There was no answer.

"Marta? Marta, are you there? It's Farah from upstairs!" called Khaleh Farah in German.

There was still no answer. Khaleh Farah placed her ear against the door to listen, but hearing nothing, walked back over.

"She must have fallen asleep. Are you sure she's home?" Khaleh Farah asked Isak.

Isak turned to the older boy, who kept his head lowered, concentrating on the piece of yarn.

"She said to stay here, didn't she, Yuri?"

Yuri nodded.

Khaleh Farah shrugged her shoulders and, leaning down, addressed Yuri.

"Yuri, give this box to your mother, okay? Tell her she can bring the cheese up later today, okay?"

Khaleh Farah placed the box next to him, and then she and the two girls walked past the security camera and out the heavy front doors. Outside, Shada turned back to look in at Yuri and Isak sitting on the bench.

"It is a shame . . . the way she carries on . . . leaving those boys alone all day!" began Shada angrily.

"What can we do? It is none of our business if she wants to sell herself. She must deal with Allah," replied Khaleh Farah.

"Yes, Maman. You are right. Her fate is up to Allah," Shada said quietly. "Come. Let's go."

They walked into the warming fall morning. Streaks of sunlight fought to get out from behind several rain clouds in the sky. Roya stared at the Ruesdandt Mosque, sitting illuminated in the forthcoming sunlight. *Did I imagine it?* she thought. She hurried to follow Khaleh Farah and Shada into the mosque.

Stripes

∞

Katayoon Zandvakili

that psychic businessman in Paris in a three-piece brown suit
who stopped outside the Ritz
where the wind rose up, in Paris, and with it my raincoat;
I was nineteen then

and his friend stood a few feet behind, laughing,
shaking his hand with the cigar in it, a rich black briefcase in the
      other,

(the man talking to me had a brown alligator briefcase)

saying his name, saying to come on, let it
go, it's just a girl, *laisse-la, oh la la;* but the man in brown
kept looking me in the face, impassioned, alert,
speaking softly, urgently, saying, *Grace a bon Dieu qui m'a donné ces*
      yeux (he looked
like Rilke, with his pince-nez, his thin frame)

        and I was
trying to follow him, I wanted to, in those phrases like half gasps
    I emitted,
forgetting all my French in the gathering rain; and watched him,
realizing how far behind the sense of his words I was
even though I understood him and wanted to.

        He looked at me with Rilke's eyes and said
with a sweet, resigned sadness, Even though you do not understand,
you are the most charming person, woman, I've ever met,
he wanted me to know, and if things were different—under different
    circumstances—

his friend had stopped guffawing here, stopped swinging his
    rich black briefcase and
turned to look at Cartier's jewelry cases; this was serious—he would

            leave all that he had behind, leave it all, and follow me
            to the ends of the world.

I was nineteen and stared at him on that cobblestoned corner in
    Paris, my hands finding the
lining of coat pockets, and going cold.

I can't remember how we left it, except I think he grabbed my hands
    to further make his point.
I have tried speaking about this three times. Each time my listeners
    laughed until I saw the joke
in it too. *Yes, of course, how ridiculous. Yes, a pickup. Yes, I see your point.* So
    I believe I
have never spoken about this. Now periodically, when things aren't
    working out for me, I stop
and think back to my man in brown in Paris, how he saw me when
    I couldn't see myself.

And I think of my husband Tom,
whom I call Your Grace, who cares
what happens in this world,
about his children, the news—they lay garlands at my feet, he called
to say after a meeting—and I love him for it.
        Your Grace,
I fling out on occasion, all the while thinking of
things I saw in a stable years ago
when I owned a black horse,
the grass and green, the late afternoon
light on the hay bales flooding them like honey,
while the anxious horses nickered for their meal

And then the horse named Stripes
whom they had castrated that
morning
      (I'd never kissed a boy and my hair was long)
         Stripes running from one end
of the arena to the other, Blood running down
his legs (I thought at first he missed his pony friend,
because they were never apart), but the blood ran down
his legs and Stripes shrieking hollow and thick, but there was
no one to hear
(I was at the fence now, fingers in my pockets)
         the jiggling blood as I followed the toss and snort
         of his head,
he ran up to the fence and away again as if there were no one
there to hear
         or as if he were a ghost, reckless and abandoned,
his neck and eyes swollen as he ran, not stopping,
like a wooden horse of infinite feeling, infinite pain.

Magical Chair of Nails
Becoming a Writer in a Second Language

❧

ROYA HAKAKIAN

Less than a year ago, I made one of the most important decisions of my life: I quit a prestigious job in the world's hub—the coveted New York City—for the quiet of the country. I chose a writer's life. Happily I emptied my desk, neatly leaving sharpened pencils and boxes of paper clips for that unknown successor, with what I hoped would convey the sentiments of my happy departure. The place had been good to me and I wanted to leave good behind.

The employee directory and several office handbooks stood on the shelves as I filled my boxes with novels and notepads, and my mind with the certainty of the ease with which the words were to flow through my fingers and onto my keyboard. I left the skyscraper into which I had walked so anxiously every Monday morning for years and drove away with the thrilled speed of the car of a Just Married couple, except that I was Just Unemployed.

And thus began the hermetic life I had always believed to be my destiny. Day after day I awoke, went down to the kitchen and poured myself a cup of tea and expected ideas to flood my head as I ascended the stairs to my study. Why wouldn't I have such an expectation? I come from a culture in which writing is a metaphysical act.

In Persian, a poet doesn't write poetry, she "tells" it. That subtle shift from writing to telling had long defined my expectations of how writing should feel. Telling seems as natural and effortless as casual speech. Picking up a pen—or typing as I do—becomes the same as opening one's mouth and humming a tune.

Telling has no trace of sweating. It goes against the swelling feeling of an exhausted head that has wrestled to fine-tune a thought. Telling has a hint of a biblical miracle: an ordinary shepherd finds himself on the mountaintop to discover the flame of divine inspiration or an illiterate man suddenly realizes that he can indeed read.

Persian lexicon aside, there was the example of all those

formidable role models who never spoke of writing as anything less than magical. The poet Ahmad Shamlou has always been portrayed as a possessed man. He is alleged to have been struck with inspiration in the middle of parties, where he would simply abandon all company to be alone in a corner, jotting down notes. His urge would have such immediacy that he would find himself unable to postpone it by waiting for a more appropriate time or locating a notebook or piece of paper. He wrote on the flap of matchbooks and on cigarette wrappings.

Forough Farrokhzad referred to her own creative bouts as "happy sicknesses," thus doing her part to mystify the act. In a collegial tête-à-tête, the poet Mani whispered the question in my ear, "So, Roya, when does it come to you?" and quickly proceeded, "It kills me when it doesn't come." He too talked about writing like some unstoppable human urge, like desire or hunger.

With the wisdom of such literary predecessors, I sat down to write my tome some nine months ago. Day after day, no muse leapt before my eyes, only a solitary cursor on a blank monitor screen in a most ordinary landscape of File, Edit, View, Insert, Format, Tools, Table, Window and Help. In that lineup, Help was the only word that stirred my imagination. I wrote an uninspired line and then stared at it. I bolded it, italicized it, underlined it, and it still remained as uninspired as ever.

One by one, I pulled down the menus, like a lone woman in a bar, hoping for an uplifting song to come out of a broken jukebox. And when weeks went by and my lines did not shed their flatness, I could do little but think about my predicament. Nights went by without a wink. And still, I descended the stairs day after day, poured myself a cup of tea and reported to my desk. Some days, I had the same anxious feeling of my New York Mondays.

Lightning finally struck, but not in the way that I had expected. It was not among a party crowd that I first sighted the muse. Nor did my sickness, my insomnia, feel happy at all. And the natural "coming" that Mani spoke of, alas, never blessed me. But I made a wholly new discovery. I learned that the push to write is against human nature. The process I underwent on a daily basis was best captured by a professional athlete, who likened her daily running routine to exposing herself to getting hit by a hundred nails. To subject my mind to the rigors of true writing is to choose to sit on a chair of nails from nine to five, every day.

Physicists describe it best by saying that the inclination of all objects is to be in a state of chaos. That goes for writing too. The mind prefers not to examine every word, not to write a sentence and examine the relationship of the new sentence to the one before and ask itself, at every period, whether the latest sentence tells with utmost clarity what the writer meant. The mind would rather not have to inspect whether one paragraph follows the logic of another. If forced, it would much rather spew a few metaphors here and there and leave it to pretty ambiguities to finish the job of an unrefined idea.

To do the kind of writing that I needed to do, I had to first unlearn most of my Iranian education. Writing is not telling. I stopped looking for inspiration to come from some superhuman heaven. The seat of writing is in the human mind. Its manifestation expresses not only the passion of that mind but also its fashion—how a mind sees and deciphers the world and how it presents that learning with clarity and simplicity.

Though they never articulated it, masters such as Forough and Shamlu must have known this truth. They knew that only the artisan can give birth to the artist. And yes, writing can be both magical and miraculous, once that unmentionable part reconciles with the daily touch of a chair of nails.

Us Four

❧

Sanaz Banu Nikaein

she sits across from him
but his head follows
another woman
whose curves dance
as she walks by
his sudden stillness confirms lust

but she refuses to accept
she is not the only *other woman*
his wife does not know of

The Eglantine Deal

⤎⤏

KATAYOON ZANDVAKILI

We're both on our knees to someone only we see.
There is a gold coffin suspended in space,
haze like a soft and distant drumroll
                    (Schumann's nocturne)

                              the purpose: to get to Noah's Ark

Cowboy and Dog and Horse, of course—spots of white paper along
the freeway
spooking the Horse. Coffee and poncho and cups with the face cards
all
over them.

This person feels safe in the world, this person is a boy becoming a
man, an owl evolving
in the hum and singsong arms of redwoods. He is astonishing
because he knows you
will forgive him, because he knows it isn't up to you to forgive.
Covered in a clear-white
layer of goodness the other side of his mind has created, he troubles
you by bringing
your weakness into the circle of light his arms pretend, telling you in
an offhand way that
you, too, are received—

The white butterfly
        bridge dream: he rode
        to tell us something before
        he changed.

                    And we find what by the riverbed?

Kneeling in the church—this could just as well be a bench off a
park trail—(the
intangibles, cherries and goblets)—he relates his dream. It is of being
licked
on the side of the head by a large wolf-dog. On burial ground.

The girl would like to play Hansel to his Gretel.

He meets his supplier friends and after, walking through the hills, he
sees her. At first, he thinks she is a vision. She isn't. She sits on the
side of the hill with her knees drawn
up, scent of azurine and a cream-white dog. Later she takes him to
the magic circle of
wishing trees. She lives in the hills, has no other home.

She believes in the butterfly,
in the eye of the wolf-dog
at her feet, in the smoke trailing
from her hut/cabin in the woods.

He dances in the rain for her
one night, flapping his poncho
to make a point, making wolf
and turkey sounds. Other times,
he is nothing so much as
a deer. She watches him
as he watches her.

She wears a Maya of the Wolves/Raquel Welch top the first time,
made of animal skin
and tan. She tells him almost right away about her dream of the perfect trail, how it
wound around past the bend, past the familiar boulder she and the
horse knew.

We also need a character dedicated to sheer, strong laughter—not a fool but one with
a bird's-eye view, a this-too-shall-pass wisdom.

He says, "I don't know why I am doing this for you, but . . ."

Last shot would be of him in a Little Prince scarf, a hint of cigarette, his frame long and skinny,
standing with a blue–white globe at his feet—a bouquet of flowers off to the
right.

The Sandcastle

FIROOZEH KASHANI-SABET

Waves wash away Hamid's footprints in the sand. He wanders toward the dregs of a wooden boat, and I follow him. It's early in the morning, and except for our presence, the beach is devoid of human life.

"How did you find this place?" I ask.

He doesn't answer.

I repeat the question, this time with an edge in my voice.

"My college roommate," he says. "He spent his summers here. Do you like it?"

"Yes," I lie.

"I'm glad," he continues, staring at the sky. "I thought you would."

I don't know what Hamid sees beyond the thick clouds. The sky makes me impatient. Its gray expanse confines the coast, closing off the ocean. I'd have preferred somewhere far south instead of this abandoned New Jersey resort. Most of the stores are out of business. Even the residential block contains more "For Sale" signs than it does inhabitants.

"Did your mother object to your coming?" he asks.

He reaches for my arm as we walk along the beach.

"No," I say. "Why should she?"

He smiles and squeezes my hand.

A seagull's cries echo in the air as we reach the broken boat. Cycles of rain and wind have evened out the edges of its scattered boards. Though the enamel has been stripped off the exterior, three letters painted in red remain legible. H—R—M. I try to make out their meaning: Harmony. Heirloom. Harem. But I can't decide which sounds best to my ears. We climb into the detritus of the boat's interior. A flattened life support jacket sags in a corner. Two yellow ropes dangle from the side of the boat, their braid damp and unraveled. Underneath the seat cushion there's a plastic bag, but when I look inside, I find nothing. "Disappointed?" Hamid asks. I nod. I'm disappointed that the bag contains no hints about the owners of the boat, that its past remains as mysterious to me as its present.

"I wonder why it's here," he comments.

"Who knows," I say.

"These beaches are usually free of debris."

"Maybe this is a private beach," I add.

"Maybe. But I didn't see any signs."

Hamid descends from the boat and chooses a suitable position for himself on the ground. He bends over slightly to begin digging, and the moistened sand quickly takes form in his hands. "Come here," he says, creating a small sandy hill near the boat.

"In a minute," I answer, looking around. I try to imagine Hamid as a young boy, free of his guarded emotions and bureaucratic aphorisms, playing on the shores of the Caspian Sea. Instead, I see the placid waters of the sea repelling him. I leave the boat to join Hamid. The earth cools my skin as I remove my leather gloves and start digging. My hands follow Hamid's and I let him direct our movements. This is the first time I've seen him in casual clothes, unshaven and soiled. His hair, though still moussed, has fallen out of place.

"What are we building?" I ask.

"Guess."

"I don't know. A tunnel."

"Wrong. Guess again."

"A dungeon."

"Close . . ."

"Oh, forget it," I say. "I'll just wait and see."

Driving up to the shore was Hamid's idea. I didn't know he'd be bringing me here, although I should have expected it. This was his way of making up for lying to me about his plans to move to Tehran after the wedding. I can't say I was thrilled about coming, remembering the lackluster dinners we'd already shared together. But here, away from the pressures of the city, there may be something more.

"Remember?" I ask, taking a break from the digging.

"What?"

"That summer at the shore," I say, removing sand from his forehead.

"Uh huh," Hamid mumbles.

"We went to that old cottage."

I can tell that Hamid is neither listening nor remembering. He focuses solely on his digging, reaching deeper and deeper into the sand, as though convinced that his search will lead to some overwhelming discovery. But there is nothing hidden beneath the ground, not even a single seashell. For miles and miles, the oceanfront extends to the coast, barren, without a seashell in sight.

This isn't the way I remember the beaches in Iran. There, shells rose to the surface of the sea, leaving a busy trail along the shore. During the summers, tourists came from around the country to the Enzali port to collect the rarest of seashells. Every year was the same, except one when a severe drought kept the visitors away. That summer, the sun raged overhead. There were no rains throughout the month of Mordad, just sparing drops of water. On the streets girls complained about the blisters on their feet. "And the rice fields?" they grieved. "What will become of the harvest?"

That was the summer I met Hamid. At a family luncheon he was introduced to me as a successful engineering student at Stanford, which at the time meant nothing to me. I was fifteen. For the most part, the luncheon, like all the luncheons my mother dragged me to, was boring. To pass time, my cousin and I decided to explore a secluded locale several homes away from my uncle's villa, and Hamid offered to accompany us. We meandered along a path strewn with thick weeds. The miasma of dying vegetation subdued the salty smell of the sea. Beyond this moribund terrain we spotted a little cottage with broken windows. Hamid quietly opened the door, and we saw an old man draped in a navy robe, sitting cross-legged before a torn prayer rug. In slow motion he turned his head around in circles, speaking to himself.

"*La illaha illalla,*" he recited with each rotation of the head. As we listened to him, his iterations drew us into a trance. *La illaha illalla, la illaha illalla.* We linked hands and one by one repeated his phrase: "*La illaha illalla, la illaha illalla.*" When he noticed our voices outside the door, he stopped.

"Who is it?" he asked, rising from his seat.

"We didn't mean to disturb you," Hamid said, shutting the door behind him.

Scraps of a battered prayer book covered the wooden floor of the cottage. The dervish brushed aside fine specks of Caspian sand as he made room for us on his *kelim,* but the grains remained imprinted on the rug like nagging transgressions upon the mind.

"How did you find me?" the old man asked.

"It was by chance," Hamid answered.

"Have you ever heard her story?" the old man asked.

We shook our heads.

The old man then started to pray. His words rang familiar. They were prayers I'd heard before, but the dervish recited them to a different tune. He told us about a woman imprisoned at the bottom of the sea. As though awakened by the tale, the waters of the Caspian seemed to bubble for an instant. "She's listening," he said. "Can you hear?" We lied and recited the *fatiha* after him. Then the dervish told us to leave. "Do not come back," he said. "You will not find me again." His words were prophetic, though we didn't realize it at the time. My uncle sold his villa that year and we never visited the Caspian shore again.

∞

"I wonder what happened to that dervish," I say.

"Who?" Hamid asks.

"Never mind," I say. I knew he had not remembered.

Hamid sculpts the sand with moist fragments of wood, smoothing over bumps and carving angular indentations. The amorphous clod of earth in his hands has gained life. I recognize what he is building now. The form expands, acquiring the rugged features of a stately edifice —regal, ageless, and reaching splendidly toward the sky. He does not notice that I've moved out of his way until I begin etching stick figures with curled hair in poor imitation of the ancient Persian ruins.

"It's finished," he announces. "What do you think?"

Hamid climbs inside the boat behind me to get a better view. I stand next to him, on top of the life jacket, watching him admire his artwork, and for a minute I ask myself whether life with him will be as horrendous as I've envisioned it. Maybe I haven't given him, or my fate, a chance. In that minute Hamid kisses me. I close my eyes and for once try to welcome the intimacy. I imagine us sailing away upon this boat, somewhere distant and warm, but his touch constricts my breathing, and I feel faint. Before me I see the shadow of a woman. I can't tell who she is but she looks familiar. Gently, she runs her hands across my face until I can breathe again. When I open my eyes, I watch the waves crest onto the shore. Hamid stares at me, unaware that a wave has flooded his sandcastle.

Ghazal

Mimi Khalvati

If I am the grass and you the breeze, blow through me.
If I am the rose and you the bird, then woo me.

If you are the rhyme and I the refrain, don't hang
on my lips, come and I'll come too when you cue me.

If yours is the iron fist in the velvet glove
when the arrow flies, the heart is pierced, tattoo me.

If mine is the venomous tongue, the serpent's tail,
charmer, use your charm, weave a spell and subdue me.

If I am the laurel leaf in your crown, you are
the arms around my bark, arms that never knew me.

What shape should I take to marry your own, have you
—hawk to my shadow, moth to my flame—pursue me?

If I rise in the east as you die in the west,
die for my sake, my love, every night renew me.

If, when it ends, we are just good friends, be my Friend,
muse, lover and guide, Shamsuddin to my Rumi.

Be heaven and earth to me and I'll be twice the me
I am, if only half the world you are to me.

Mandala at Manzanar

∽

ZARA HOUSHMAND

May the mountains witness;
Williamson, Whitney, Lone Pine, look:
> *To the East, a sea of strangers.*
> *Each one wears my face.*

Erase the shame, the fear, the witless hate,
Witness now, too late:
Each stranger wears my fate.

Let the winds watch:
> *To the South, a million mouths.*

Each tongue speaks my own hope,
Each foreign tongue my own, one taste,
Each hunger, one I've known.

Let the earth feel:
> *To the West, a friend unfound yet.*

Embrace the lover yet to be discovered.
Unmake the bed you've made; go free.
How like you is the other: simply see.

May the sky see:
> *To the North, a need so endless deep,*

That only one whole heart can offer
Ever to console or feed. Then offer this one:
Ever watchful never to repeat.

Beyond

ॐ

PERSIS M. KARIM

Beyond this body,
the weathered edges
of the tent we live in
you'll find me.
Not moored to the language
of my father and mother
but creeping,
spilling over,
seeking the blue light
of the spaces between.

Only the Blue Remains Unchanged

✧

Parinaz Eleish

And so the trains passed me by.
Winter arrived
and fall left me standing still
in a twilight of flames.

Who was it that came
to rescue
these slippery vowels from disgrace,
and the four luminous geranium leaves
from leaving my dreams?
And was it again winter?

And who was it that came
by that gray mass of iron
into this broken station
to spread red paisley carpets
in the lost rooms of my eyes?

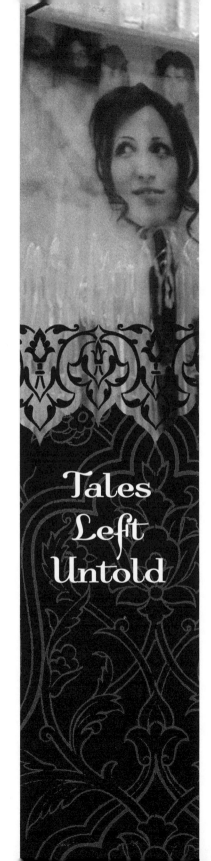

Tales
Left
Untold

Night Conversations (Deep Are These Distances)

❧

Susan Atefat-Peckham

Star said to Palm: How far
would I fall to your knots
and root? Palm said: Thousands
will kneel before you.

        Star: I am
just white dust behind rippling
firelight.

        Palm: See how
my green blades wear you
like rings.

        Star: What will I do,
erased at sunrise?

        Palm: Breathe
from my temple.

        Star: How
do you see my burning path
yet not my face?

        Palm: How
do you beg to travel such
unknown distances?

Star: Friend,
clap the blades of your leaves
into these black hours, for deep
are these distances between us.

Do You Miss Me?

❧

ROYA HAKAKIAN

You ask
and I ponder
that fog of a question
—if fogs were ever to grow
in the skies of sentences.

I do miss February
                     —desperately
the way the bolt of longing
cracked the month in half
leaving an abbreviated occasion
                     on one side
and on the other
the purifying jolt of our tide.

I miss March
the way you kissed the mar away
with unhesitating lips
and what remained
—a blazing arch
was the cat-back of desire
over a trampled torso
in a clawed tangle
we wished to never unravel.

I miss the certainty
the June-blue clarity

of your eyes.
But most of all
I miss the soaring sensation of possibility
the love-ignited sound of the implosion
                   of all impossibility.

I miss the glimpse
of that elusive
but sure bliss
and the spectrum of our promise
—if colors were ever to render
all the intrigue
all the tender
range of a rarity.

Lost Karbala

❧

HALEH HATAMI

For my dear Ladan

I'd forgotten about the flies,
the muck fires, mosquitoes, the relentless
reptiles squirming, swimming in the laden
humidity. Spurts of gaseous flame lick
the roadside—Shaytan's tongue.

Spanish moss hangs low over the
tombstone, drawn down by afternoon
heat. The gnats distract your mourning
parents. Fire ants form a mass of tears
at their feet—Mary and Joseph.

Disease scorched your vibrant body
not unlike the field fires that combust,
consume, and die in a span of days.
Fumes linger on reminding us of her
unjust rule—Mother Nature's pyre.

You sacrificed for the very ones
that drained you dry and now
the vultures gather. Relentless. Was the air so fetid at the
Martyrdom—lost Karbala?

Sing

FARNOOSH SEIFODDINI

In the lunch room
Mahmood points at an article
posted on the corkboard
next to Chef Jamie's Smart Recipes
  members of Iranian soccer team
  caught in scandal
  underground prostitution ring uncovered
  100 lashes per encounter
he tears it down, crumples it
  they will think we're barbarians

I sit
voice in a cup
staring at Chef Jamie's picture

The space between
  if only this had the larynx of a bird.

Earth and Water

∞

ZARA HOUSHMAND

You don't ask anything of me, you say.
(How can I ask anything of you?)
And yet we face each other empty-eyed
like two unanswered questions.

I am brittle twigs on the floor of the bare winter woods.
They snap under your shoes as you walk away.

I am blossoms, fragile beyond late returning winds,
fragile beyond the slow, slow melting ice,
fragile beyond time
in the cup of your hands.

You are tides,
and fickle as the moon returning,
reams of silver and smiling fish,
and tales of voyages beyond.
You are silver through my fingers, and light,
and now you are gone,
beyond the memories that have burned away like morning mist,
beyond.

You are silver through my fingers, and sweet.
You have come a thousand miles underground
in summer's heat
and still you taste of melted snow.
Why here, why now?

You smile once and seep into the hungry sand
where roots grope blind.

I am roots, I am bark, I am hardy.
I am dry sand under your feet.
I am twigs, I am sand, I am blossoms.
I am nothing so real as hope.
I am nothing, but hardy as blossoms
the wind probes,
the fragile cup of a seed.

Tales Left Untold

∞

APHRODITE DÉSIRÉE NAVAB

*To my beautiful parents, Dr. Ali Navab and Katerina
Armenakis Navab. Both their hands and their feet, I kiss.*

PROLOGUE

To tell a tale is all that's left
To those forbidden passage home
It's in the telling
Not the tale
That the untold pieces get re-sewn
To pick them up
One
By
One
And then throw them in the air
Is this storyteller's mad hope
That one piece will make it there

TALE #1

These are the bags I bring with me
Suitcases burdened with memory
I'll put them down and open them
To let them breathe before they speak
To tell a tale that needs to be
To travel with these bags and me
Back in time
Watching signs
Marking

Mapping
Who I am

I am Iranian, Greek, American
Not just one
But all of them

How I've tried for consistency
To be one of them
Complete
Just one of them
Please
Just to make things neat
How I've tried all my life to be
No messy ambiguity
No ambivalent loyalty
To be
One
Whole
One
Identity

The flag of each nation
In me, stirs little sensation
No nationalism shouts loud in me
Even after living in all three
To see one flag burned
In the other country
There's no going back for me

My people held my other people hostage
The weight of this I carry in my luggage
A criminal in reverse

Hypocritical

Perverse

Even a blaming finger

Becomes a hollow gesture

Pointing at them

Yet right back at me

Because them

Is me

I am all three

Both the beauty and the blood they've shed

All three

TALE #2

It is not fear of planes I feel

A different crash takes place in me

I thought that time would pass

And so would too

The suspicious eyes

That sort me through

How did you become American?

The interrogation begins

The airport official's eyes

Questioning me up and down

First at me and then at it

In my passport

In black ink

Disclosing where it is I'm from

Born in Esfahan, Iran

Passport, all-American outside

But a potential terrorist inside

Permitting them to terrorize me
Picking points to punish me

I was fifteen with a group of girls
On a trip from the U.S. to Canada
Please don't give me trouble
In front of them all
Don't single me out
Away from them all
Don't hold me long
Remember that age?
You want to belong
Don't stop me
Search me
Steal me
Why do the others all prance through?
When my passport is just as blue?
Official eagle, stamped and sealed
So much prejudice revealed

How did you become American?

I sweat, I sweat
Again that dread
I've done nothing
But what's in his head

My mother is American
My father, sister, brothers, me
We were all born in Iran, see
That is it
That is why

No that's not right, he said
Not at all
That's not right
Try again

Here he makes me go again
My mother is American
By birth she is
But I am not
By birth I am Iranian

That's not right, he said
Not at all
You've got it wrong
Try again

I sweat, I sweat
Again that dread
I've done nothing
But what's in his head

I've told you all I know
That's all
I'm hiding nothing
Let me go
Check my body
Check my bags
Check my soul
Just end this show

Don't sneak around me here and there
Don't twist and turn me while they stare

I know where it is I'm from
And I can see where it is I've come

The correct answer
Anger rising in his voice
Impatient at my persistence
You are American by your own birth
Not your mother's or anyone else's
This is the only answer that's correct

He stamped my passport
He let me go
Humiliated like this
I was never before

TALE #3

You have a nice tan
But I was born with this skin
You have a nice tan
But this is my own, my palest skin
No sun it's seen in seven months
No soap can wash this color off
They call this olive skin
They do? I eat olives, yes I do
Like candy, it is true I do
Does that make me an olive too?
I am not greasy
I am not green
Greasy hair and greasy skin
Every day I wash my skin
Every day I wash my hair

Sometimes twice within one day
Just to make it go away

They also call this sallow skin
Sallow, shiny, greasy, green
Yellow, oily, dirty, mean
I scrub my forehead dry, inside
I rub it again and again, outside
I look both ways, though, before I do
You never know who you'll run into
I cautiously raise the back of my hand
Carefully gesturing with my hand
Pretending to be wiping sweat
Pretending the oily skin was wet

A dot, a spot, a speck on the wall
Anything not to stand out at all
Twenty years I've dealt with this
Twenty years I've rubbed it raw
Oily, olive, oily, skin
Oozing oil that burns within

I am not black
I am not white
And never, ever am I green
I am an unremarkable gray
In between

TALE #4

My tongue is twisted
My tongue is tied

My tongue is torn with all the lies
Each time I turn it this way and that
An unfamiliar sound spins its way out
One half screams for the other to come
The other half stands there completely numb
One half knows not what the other half speaks
One half scorns what the other half seeks
My tongue, it trips me
Leading me there
Trapping me in the storyteller's snare
One half leaves while the other half stays
One half sees what the other betrays
One half gestures in meaningless motions
The other half squints to make sense of these notions
But all she sees is spit in the air
From that storyteller
Standing
Ridiculous
There

TALE #5

I am not a Persian Carpet
You may not wipe your feet on me
You may not rest or lie on me
You may not sip your tea on me
With a cube of sugar
Between gold teeth
Hiding
What is
Rotten
Beneath

I am not a Persian Carpet
You may not do your prayers on me
You may not
Trade me
Wheel or
Deal me
No embargoes can be placed on me
No children weave eyes blind for me
My value does not increase with age
No pattern can contain this rage
Rubbing your greedy hands
Imagining how to fill your land
Measuring with an abacus in hand

No sticks can beat the dust from me
No streams can wipe the stains from me
No sun can make my dampness clean

I am not a Persian carpet
But for you that is all in Iran you see
An Oriental commodity
A decorative oddity
An object for your pleasure
At your leisure
Never
Ever
Will I let you
Make me

TALE #6

At times I need to go away
Deep within my memory

And travel to the land
I've lost
My childhood there completely
I cannot see
We cannot touch
We haven't talked in twenty years

Across the sky
The night is hung
I toss
I turn
No longer dreaming
In my native tongue

A stranger to my homeland
Even if you should take my hand
Even if we should exchange sand
Strangers we will be
The home you were
You are not now
The child I was
I put away inside
All these years and years
Outside

And with which tongue can I tell her tale?
Of a revolution which came and went
Tearing up her home
Forbidding passage to her father
Sequestering him alone
That from her airplane window
She watched him

Until she could see

No more

I pull these images out

Wrapping them around

Getting lost and then found

Defying time

Who's tapping his foot

Waiting

And

Wanting

Me

To

Forget

TALE #7

There will always be time

To wonder why and where

There will always be time

To imagine ways of going there

There will never be a way

To make up time not spent together before death

There will never be a way

To make up

Not seeing

Not touching

Not loving

Your parents

Before

During

And after their death

Because you could not mourn their death
Baba, I will mourn for you
Because you chose life for us
Baba, I choose this too for you
Because your exile has been death
Baba, I will travel there for you

I will kiss their eyes for you
I will beat my chest for you
I will tear my hair for you

Walking in the funeral procession
That none of us did see
Singing songs of dispossession
That no one there did hear

An ululation
A lamentation
A scream released from its frustration
To do the things denied to you
Baba, this space, here
I've made for you

I've let it grow
To sweep the floors
My hair collects
The exiled days

It was through his back
I saw him crack
It was from behind
I saw him break
First stone

His father's death
Second stone
His mother's
Third stone
Forbidden to honor them
Trying to topple him
Until I stepped in then

I've let it grow
To sweep the floors
My hair wraps itself
Around the stones

His silent suffering
Not shown
Not shared
He stood there
Staring out the window
At an Iran that was not there
He stood there
Trembling out that window
This kind of grief I could not bear

A silent shiver went down his spine
An aching
Unaware
Seen from behind

I've let it grow
To sweep the floors
My hair hides eyes
Too hurt to stare

There will always be time
To wonder why and where
There will always be time
To imagine ways of going there
There will never be a way
To forget the aching of an exiled man
There will never be a way
To justify why for you
Your father is that man

An ululation
A lamentation
A scream released from its frustration
To do the things denied to you
Baba, this space, here
Is all I can do

EPILOGUE

To tell a tale
When there's nothing more
Is when meaning itself
Has shut its door
It is then
The uninvited guest
Comes in
Breathing life into the rest
It is then
That the untold tales
Begin
Resurrecting that old quest

Because of Hands and Bread

❦

ESTHER KAMKAR

Left hands out of the bus window
Wrists, palms, fingers
Cannot reach the loaves of bread
Offered by a right hand. Where are your
Bodies, your faces, your mouths?

Your hand   hand   hand
Reflected on the side of the bus like
A forest in the river.

Soon the bus will leave
Go home now.
This will be the beginning of your exile
You will lose the keys to your houses
You will forget the names of trees and flowers.

Your hands cut off at the wrists
Will float in the Great Blue River;
Tree trunks, split buses.

Downstream—under the Memorial Bridge
Your hands will wave to other hands
Hands   hands   hands
Like your own
Swollen and toy-like.
This is the beginning of your exile.

Soleiman's Silence

❧

MEHRI YALFANI

Why did all Iranians in Toronto know Soleiman? No one knew. Soleiman wasn't wealthy, he wasn't a poet, a writer, a musician, a singer, he didn't boast university or scientific titles. Soleiman was an ordinary person who chose to be quiet. But Soleiman's silence spoke volumes and people read words into his silence. Some believed Soleiman had never opened his mouth to speak. He was always quiet when they saw him. But it wasn't true. Others heard him tell the story of his past, a past as vague as his silence.

Some believed Soleiman was raised in a city at the edge of a desert; a city full of impatient, gloomy and thirsty people. A city printed into Soleiman's face and eyes. Soleiman told many stories about the city's long, burning, boring summers; bitter and sweet stories. People retold these stories in Soleiman's presence with the hope that he would confirm or deny them. He listened and said nothing.

Others believed Soleiman came from a mountainous area. They believed they had heard Soleiman describe the cold winter, gusting winds, hardworking people who didn't think about anything but how to conquer the summit hidden under the clouds. It seems that Soleiman had nice memories of this city, which, unlike the desert city that dragged energy from people, made people struggle. The mountain, which sheltered the city, frightened people. The people believed there might be a monster hidden on the summit of the mountain, a monster that should be killed. People thought about how to climb the mountain, reach its summit and find out about the monster.

Others knew Soleiman was from a city in the North, close to the Caspian Sea. They said that Soleiman had described tall poplars, willows, cedars and plane trees whose brimming greenness in summer was like a dream in a siesta. Winter was rainy, days turning quickly to nights filled with sincere memories. Soleiman spoke so elegantly about this city, listeners could feel the breeze passing over their skins and hear the waves.

Everyone who knew him believed Soleiman was a good listener. Many witnessed the hours he spent by the lake laid down at the south end of the city, listening to the waves or seagulls. When he strolled in the verdant parks of this city, he sometimes stopped walking to listen to the birds' song, or the breeze. At those moments there was ecstasy in his eyes, excitement at the sounds. So Soleiman wasn't deaf or mute; many had heard him talking, many had listened to his stories as well.

But why did Soleiman choose silence? A mystery! Even though people didn't know why, they didn't admit it. They considered their own lack of knowledge a fault, so everyone claimed that they knew, everyone had their own reason; a reason that might have nothing to do with Soleiman's silence.

Some believed Soleiman was bored by living in exile, that he was homesick. These people had a strong reason for their own silence, not for Soleiman's. They said exile pushes people into isolation, seclusion and finally silence.

More than a few believed Soleiman chose to be silent because he hadn't been able to learn the new language. These people attributed their own problem to Soleiman, and cried sincerely for him. But wise persons knew, theirs were crocodile's tears. Soleiman's problem, if he had one, wasn't that he didn't know the language. He could speak it before he left Iran, because he had started learning it in kindergarten. On arrival he'd had some problems understanding because of the accent, but when he heard the words clearly, he had no problem with comprehension. Soleiman's problem wasn't language. Moreover, Soleiman had lived in this country for years. He had attended school, learned new skills and worked here. He'd had relationships with people of this country. There'd also been TV, his night-and-day companion. Many remembered that Soleiman had listened carefully to the news, and read the newspapers. Soleiman wasn't deaf, or illiterate in English.

But if Soleiman chose to be quiet, other people, people who liked to comment on everything, spoke too much. They made such a hubble and bubble, filling the air with words, that even the most patient became impatient and forced them to be quiet. These busybodies talked and talked about Soleiman's silence. Sometimes they spoke right in front of him. He heard them, and strangely, didn't show any reaction.

Some people believed Soleiman should visit a psychiatrist. He might have a complex or something, forcing him to be silent. A psychiatrist might help. Soleiman might be mentally ill, couldn't assimilate in the exile society. But these people forgot that Soleiman had been living a long time in this exile society and then had chosen suddenly to be quiet. In answer to these people, others said Soleiman was an egoist and too proud of himself. They said words are the only way relationships happen among human beings. If someone doesn't answer questions, stays quiet when facing others, it means he doesn't respect others. Otherwise there's no reason to leave questions unanswered. These people believed human beings are talking animals. One who doesn't speak denies humanity. These people ignored Soleiman. They were hurt by Soleiman's silence. They even wished him dead because Soleiman's silence, no matter what the reason, was an insult to all people who liked to offer a point of view on every aspect of life. These people were like fish, opening their mouths incessantly and issuing words. Only when they were sleeping did they cease.

Some people who were taciturn and usually struggled with words, unable to explain their own ideas, believed that Soleiman chose to be quiet because he was exhausted by many agonizing sounds. These people too were at risk of Soleiman's sickness, at the threshold of becoming silent. But they had to speak, because of the necessity of living in a human community, even though they said less than one thousandth of what they really had to say. But who really knew whether this last group was right? One thing was clear: no one really knew the real reason for Soleiman's silence. Soleiman, like all immigrants, had left his own homeland and landed here, thousands of kilometers away; in this city. Soleiman had once spoken like others, laughed, cried, joined in discussions. Some people said he told jokes, and made people laugh, talked about his memories, his family, but now nobody knew what happened to them, or they knew and told it differently. Because Soleiman said nothing about this either. What happened to Soleiman? Why did he become quiet suddenly or gradually?

Other Iranians in the city didn't stay quiet. They continued to express their opinions in any gathering. Sometimes these discussions were so hot the most patient people became impatient. Interestingly, if Soleiman was present, he said nothing and showed no reaction. As time went on, Soleiman became a permanent issue. As if they all had nothing to do but argue about Soleiman. Strangely, Soleiman became more disappointed, skinnier and more reserved. There were people among the immigrants who had pity for Soleiman and wanted to cure his illness, if he had one. And they always kept the discussion about

Soleiman hot. It's said that once the argument was so hot, it ended in cursing, kicking and fighting. Soleiman too, was present, watching them without reaction, when he suddenly burst into flame, and in an instant was a handful of ashes on his chair.

The flame lasted for a few seconds and many couldn't see it, especially those busy fighting and disputing. Only a few saw Soleiman changed into fire. Those who didn't see the flame didn't believe the witnesses. These people trusted only their own eyes. They saw the ashes, but doubted they were Soleiman's.

Again there was much discussion. But as the majority agreed that Soleiman had been changed to ash, and as Soleiman wasn't seen at any gathering, they thought about burying Soleiman's ashes. They believed that if the ashes were really Soleiman's, they should be buried in the soil, as all deceased are buried in soil for their eternal sleep. As usual, there were different opinions on this matter. Some people said the ashes shouldn't be buried in soil, because they had already been changed to soil. From their point of view it was better to add Soleiman's ashes to the lake at the south end of this city, which gave the city its historical identity and sent life to the veins of the city; this could be the eternal home for Soleiman. Then many compatriots who knew Soleiman would remember him on seeing the lake, think about his silence and create thousands of reason for it.

Others had different ideas. They said Soleiman had spent most of his spare time in one park located in the heart of the city. They said Soleiman was familiar with all trees, paths, bushes and weeds, high and low lands of the park. He spent long hours on a bench, dissolving his presence and memory into the bench and trees. They said Soleiman was close to the swans, ducks, geese, squirrels and hundreds of birds that made the park a magnificent place for him. So it was better that Soleiman's ashes be spread in this park. Some on leaves or on a bench, some distributed in the park's lake with swans, geese and ducks.

As people never agreed on this matter, the jar of Soleiman's ashes was left intact; taken from one place to another. There were many meetings to decide about Soleiman's ashes; a great deal was discussed. Every time the meeting finished without an agreement and again Soleiman's ashes were left on a shelf in a house.

The presence of Soleiman's ashes bothered the residents of each house like a difficult question. And because of that the residents invited immigrants to a meeting, immigrants who felt responsibility for any problem, and discussed it for long hours. In fact, endless speaking and the sharing of ideas had become a way of life for them, the result of an unwanted immigration, of living in an unfamiliar land and struggling with problems that had no ending, but appeared in different shapes and forced people to try to find solutions.

The guardian of Soleiman's ashes changed after every meeting, and each new guardian felt more responsible toward the ashes. The presence of ashes made him or her feel guilty and disturbed. So each looked for a solution more than the others had and invited people to another meeting. And again, after hours of discussion and exchanging ideas, the meeting would end without any agreement, and sometimes with fighting and kicking. The ashes would be moved to another house.

This didn't last forever. While the ashes were being transported, through downtown, through a busy, crowded intersection, where all the world's races crossed, with a skinny old man always playing trumpet, the jar of Soleiman's ashes fell, and broke into pieces. On each corner of the intersection is a huge high-rise, and the wind which always trots through this city is more unbridled, slapping pedestrian faces. The savage, cruel wind grasped Soleiman's ashes and disappeared in the big city.

The carriers of Soleiman's ashes hurried to collect them, but they got nothing. Some stuck to the soles of pedestrians from all around the world, pedestrians of different races and different nationalities, and walked away. Then at that very moment a strong rain shower began and washed away the ashes that had stuck to the street, into the sewer, then into the lake, the symbol of life in this city.

Those who had been carrying Soleiman's ashes breathed easily. They described the accident to all the immigrants in a big meeting. They believed that Soleiman had dissolved into the heart of the city, the heart of life in the city and the heart of all races and nationalities. He was in the lake, the high buildings, the parks and fields around the city; he had traveled to the Pacific, Atlantic and Arctic oceans surrounding the three sides of this country. Flowing in the world waters or frozen like a particle in an ice mountain.

Yes, it was like that. And the story of Soleiman and his reasonable or unreasonable silence is still a mystery to our immigrant community.

Standing in a Mosque Contemplating Faith

∞

Farnaz Fatemi

Slices of the ground between these walls
soak up the sunlight
as if to allow the shaded parts
their pleasures.

I feel the space I take up with my body
a small part of the distance
to the bricks, the tiles,
the solid epic each wall knows.

When I open my palm
to the wide-tiled wall
my hand reads the colors of effort—
times which happened
leave traces in shapes of flowers,
in words, God is great,
like the rest of me,
my hands aren't faithless.
They believe in the deeds
of other hands,
suffering can't be avoided,
only hands bring relief.
That the thing that is bigger
than all of us

is what grows out of gratitude
for this relief.

Sometimes what grows is joy,
the cool ceramic tiles
in the blister of summer noon.

Sometimes what grows
inspires. My capable hands
might fashion these patterns.
I am part of a species
that does this: leaves
stunning reminders
which say, we are less than God
but aspire to such splendor.

I believe in aspiration,
inspiration, honesty.
in finding each other
in these walls.

Sabze

ZARREH

new seeds
a familiar plate

i plant it
every year

and on
the thirteenth day
i throw it
into a river

any river will do

and i hold on
to the memory
of

Hope

until next year

Years Later

❧

PARINAZ ELEISH

Is it a mild case of fever,
a slight pain of the vertebrae
or just dust on the velvet cushions?
Is it regret?

True, the mattress sinks
slightly in the middle
the curtains sag
and my lover's car no longer goes by—
but to sleep all day!

I lie here remembering
the nightingales of Suza
narrow alleys and wooden doors
with heavy doorknobs,
leading to hidden gardens.
I remember my lover's limping hawk
stunted trees in tiny pots,
the day I left
with a promise I would not keep.
And suddenly, I want to sleep all day.

So we drank pomegranate juice
under the mulberry tree when the whole house slept
and we touched secretly after the last prayer

but to let my hair curl
an umber cloud, as he liked it
when I have aged
and he is getting married
to someone else?

Native

⚮

Amanda Enayati

Perhaps it's from having spent a lifetime
on the outside
looking in
on those fortunate enough to belong.

Perhaps it's best to follow the advice of those who, through the
       years,
have spat at me
"Go back to where you belong!" (Where is that?)

Perhaps it's the failed marriage
made of legendary love
but too many differences—
cultural, racial, national, religious—
to be bridged.

Too young to be embittered.
Too idealistic to be cynical.
Too hopeful to be in despair.

Hoarse from hollering that the commonalities
trump the differences
my limbs ache from pointing at the successes
and predicting the moment of critical mass.
When will we reach it?

I need a home, but my map to get there is blurry.
Every day I have more trouble and
I could never read maps anyway.
The home I left doesn't want me back.
And if I were to return
my old home wouldn't unlock
the gate for me. It wouldn't recognize me.
My elements changed along the path.

My new house is no home.
I realized a bit late—
it has conditions
I do not meet.
Now, I feel like a stranger
all the time.
Afraid to impose,
afraid of breaking something.

Everyone's paradigm shifted, but mine
only taunts me,
revealing the potential and possibilities
only when
no one else is looking.

So I bid the demons goodnight
and go to sleep
only to meet them again.
In the morning, I awaken fresh,
young, idealistic and hopeful.
I brave my new house and continue
reading the map
home.
I await—anxiously—that critical mass.

Unpacking

∝

ZARA HOUSHMAND

We opened crates in the barn.
Shipping crates. Crow bars. Bales of hay,
the sun in the open bays and the summer air charged
for a storm.
My son, who did not exist
when these boxes were packed
twenty-three years ago,
helped with the heavy lifting,
shifted that nail-studded chipboard lid
as if it weighed no more
than a withered old revolution.

Blessing

❦

Mimi Khalvati

For Hafez

Between the living and the dead,
may your memory be green.
In the book beside my bed,
may your signature be seen.

May your memory be green
for every lover, every spring.
May your signature be seen
inscribed on every living thing.

For every lover, every spring,
breathing clouds against the frost
inscribed on every living thing,
sees how every breath is lost;

breathing clouds against the frost,
because breath is always warm,
sees how every breath is lost
in the one beloved form.

Because breath is always warm,
Hafez, yours ignites the dark.

In the one beloved form,
it is still a living spark.

Hafez, yours ignites the dark
in the book beside my bed.
It is still a living spark
between the living and the dead.

Green World through Broken Glass

✧

HAALE

Mama had a shoebox for every decade
she endured. Enough space to keep anything
worth keeping, she'd said. Behind old vacuum parts, a frayed
curtain, she hid them—misshapen, dog-eared, bulging
boxes I never opened. I'd just sit in front
of their stunted tower, wondering when it struck her,
this urge to hold, only things. Mama, with her blunt
endings, leaving half-diced carrots on the counter,
returning seven dinners later, no words. I
pictured her riding open roads, trapped by burly
men in some pool hall, dead in a ditch, or on a beach
in daylight stopped by a seashell or by the green world
through broken glass she decides to keep
clenched in her fist, letting it cut, on the edge of the tide.

A Return

✼

KANDI TAYEBI

A thirsty April night, shrouded in black *chadors*
Carcasses slung across windows
The call to prayer—God is everywhere.

Watermelon juices cool my throat
A tress of hair escapes, sliding softly above siren eyes.
Googoosh floats through the hyacinths.

Smoke ring halos encircle white bearded men
"I sacrifice myself for you."
Bazaar owners offer up barters.

Traffic tangles refuse the boundaries
Taxis pressed five people deep
Honks sound revolution through the smog.

Remote controls snuggle in plastic sheaths.
Family encloses miles of land.
Farsi breathes into my lungs.

Hungry vines devour red patterns on the rug
Crisp, cleansing tiles paint an ornate sky
I return to the land of contradictions.

My blood runs through the soil.

Blood

AZIN AREFI

My sister and her husband had left Iran for Eshgh Abaad as a newly married couple, he filled with the hopes and promise of becoming a successful merchant, and she filled with the satisfaction of having a husband capable of such a task. Now, after two years, they were coming back, she as the heavy-hearted wife and mother of a two-year-old daughter, and he as a dying man. My sister had sent word that her husband had contracted tuberculosis and the doctors had advised him to go back to his birthplace, so he would not die on foreign soil. It was her wish that they come home to us so that she could take care of her dying husband with the help of her own family; she too had decided against the foreign soil of in-laws.

Their homecoming was bittersweet for my parents. Their daughter was coming home, but under what circumstances? My mother was as steadfast as always and went about preparing for their arrival as dutifully as she approached any task. She cut and sewed new bedding; she sewed a flowered praying *chador* for my sister; and despite the approaching summer months, she knitted a sweater for her first grandchild. But there was no joy in her work, as if she were welcoming in-laws and not her own flesh. My father was more vocal, muttering curses under his breath, and inveighing against the young man for going to "cold, infested Russia." Hadn't he heard that tuberculosis was rampant in Eshgh Abaad? "Money may be strewn about on the streets there," he'd say, "but is it worth your life?"

I, on the other hand, had to hide my true feelings. I knew that my appropriate feeling should have been one of somber reflection and pity for my sister and her dying husband. But inside I felt a twinge of excitement about my older sister coming home—life without Sooreh had not been difficult, just dull and uninteresting. I could not help but be happy that I would reclaim my sister when I thought I had lost her to that unfamiliar land forever. Moreover she was bringing home a child, on who was at that perfect age: past her burdensome infancy and into engaging toddlerhood.

As for my brother-in-law, I *tried* to feel sorry for him, but frankly he was a stranger to me. He and my sister had moved to Eshgh Abaad shortly after their marriage. My sister hardly knew him then. What hope was there for an attachment on *my* part? If anything, he was that man who had taken my sister away. I felt sorry for him, but sympathy? That was not there. I had to fake it. At night when we sat around the *sofreh* to have dinner, my father would mention the young man and my mother would shake her head as she handed out bread to us and I—I would lower my head and focus on the crumbly yellow of a hardboiled egg and appear appropriately solemn.

⨍

The day they arrived it was unusually breezy for the middle of summer, but we were grateful for it. My father marched in and out of the house like a rooster in heat, praising God for drying the glistening sweat off his brow as if it were *he,* and not my mother, who had been cooking over a hot stove all morning. I had finished sweeping the yard and was throwing water down on the dust and chicken feces when I heard the clunking sounds of donkey hooves on our dirt road. I put down my bucket. I heard the donkey driver whistle and command the animals to stop. I ran across the yard to open the door.

I saw *him* first, as he got off the docile animal. To my surprise he did not look ill. He was slimmer than I had remembered and more pale, but he was not the yellow sickly man I had been picturing. The driver helped Sooreh climb down from the donkey, which was complicated by the sleeping child in her arms. "Khanoum, let me take the child and then help you," he said to my sister with outstretched arms. "No, no, we can both come down at the same time," she insisted. Before her feet were firmly on the ground, my brother-in-law was at the door. His eyes fell on me.

"Salaam," I said and opened our pale yellow door wider. The customary follow-up of "How is your health?" almost tripped off my tongue, but I thought it unsuitable. I was at a loss for words. I simply stood there, eyes locked with his, until he finally acknowledged me with a nod and headed into the yard, carrying a small bag. I watched his back as he went toward the house. Even the customary formalities that people exchange were somehow problematic. True, he was my brother-in-law, but he had also been marked by death. There was nothing to say to him. If I had known then what I know now, I would have understood that a man living with the complete awareness of his impending end is precisely the man one needs to exchange words with. But I was young, and also a girl; I had no business conversing with a man. I don't think I said more than twenty words to him for the next four months while he was at our house and slowly wasting away in front of our very eyes.

My father came out to greet him. He took both his son-in-law's hands in his and welcomed him with an enthusiasm and cheerfulness that I found it embarrassing. Then he yelled for my mother, "They are home, woman! Come!" He bombarded my brother-in-law with questions about their journey without allowing him to answer. "How was the train ride from Eshgh Abaad? Did you have a hard time at the border? The donkey driver, have you paid him yet? I hope he did not overcharge you. They do that, God be watching them. You must be thirsty. Who wouldn't be in this heat? Thank God for the breeze. Nargess!" He yelled at me. "Go and make some cherry sherbet for our guests. And my other daughter, where is Sooreh?"

I turned to see my sister at the door, holding her daughter, awake now, in her arms. The driver had been unloading the donkeys and set the suitcases at my sister's feet. Standing there, surrounded by her belongings in neat packages, she looked like a wanderer dejectedly returning home. If someone had asked me what I planned on doing when I first saw my sister, I would have told them that I would scream in delight and wrap my arms tightly around her. But I didn't even touch her. I hardly said *salaam*. I was staring at the child in Sooreh's arms. Like her father, she looked different than I expected. "Oh my God, Sooreh," I said. "Your daughter is beautiful!" She had very white skin, almost see-through, as if you could puncture it with a finger. Her eyes were gray and she had yellowish, curly hair. She looked like a Russian doll.

"Say thank you, Auntie Nargess," my sister said to the child in that high voice mothers always use with their babies. "Say thank you, Molouk."

The child stared at me with her intensely gray eyes, the recognition of unfamiliarity piercing from them. "Will she come to me?" I asked and stretched out my arms.

"Maybe not at first," Sooreh said, as the child coiled herself further into her mother's bosom. "But she will soon."

"What are you two girls doing by the door?" my father yelled from the porch, craning his neck. "Come inside! Is that my grandchild?" Then he turned to his son-in-law. "By Allah, you leave two women alone for a minute and they just go on talking and talking. And only Allah Himself ever knows what it is that they talk—"

My mother came down the steps, and walked toward us. Without saying a word to one another my mother and sister embraced, much like I had imagined myself doing. My mother's momentum forced my sister back, the way a tree bends modestly in the face of wind. The child looked from her mother to this strange woman with slight terror and I could tell she felt crushed, caught in the middle. The three of them stood like that, frozen. When they came back to life I could hear muffled crying. "What is going on over there?" my father inquired from the porch. "Why don't you come in?" My mother peeled away from Sooreh and wiped her red eyes. I was confused. Why were they crying?

"Salaam, Pedar," said Sooreh. Her voice was shaking. "Are you well?"

"Let's go," my mother said. "Nargess, help with the bags, my child." My sister and her husband had come home with suitcases, three of them, all the same size and all a deep burgundy color that had faded into brown at the edges. They had two huge buckles on them, magnified versions of my father's belt buckles. I had never seen suitcases before. I remember feeling proud of my "foreigner" sister for coming home with such luxuries as suitcases, and also feeling that this meant she had had a life in Russia that I could not possibly imagine; a modern life involving suitcases and—and what else? A life that had surely changed her. We each took up a few bags and headed toward the house, one after another, like a caravan.

"*Masha'allah,* is this my grandchild?" My father seized Molouk from Sooreh's bosom and kissed her cheek. "What a pretty child my granddaughter is!" I believe he fell in love with her that very moment. It took the rest of us little time to fall in love with her as well. Looking back, I can't decide if it would have been better if we had loved her less, or if we did not love her enough. As I have grown older, I have come to realize that this is the revolving ball upon which most mistakes and miseries of the world spin: loving someone too much or not loving them enough.

℮

In the corner of our courtyard just opposite the outhouse, under the majestic willow tree and the carefree grapevines, my mother made a haven for her son-in-law. She set up a wooden bed there, topped it off with one of our carpets, one bright with deep hues of red and orange, and propped up two or three pillows on it. She laid out a straw fan and a plastic pitcher and glass, and made sure it was filled with water every morning. This was to be my brother-in-law's resting place. We thought it was the best spot for him, outside in the kindness of the summer sun, under the shade of the willow tree that invited a breeze to rustle its languid branches. More importantly, the place offered him solitude. It was easy to surmise that he did not desire any of our company. Later, I would question whether we also put him out there in the corner so that he would be out of our way. Perhaps we had little desire for *his* company as well. Who wants Death staring at them all day long?

He would sit out there all day. Then at dusk, my sister would go down and gently ask him if he wanted to come back inside. He would remain exactly as he was for a minute, then swing his legs off the bed and walk slowly to the house. My sister would follow. During the day he didn't do much besides fan the flies away and eat what we brought him. We served his meals there, around the same time we fed the sheep and chickens. Once, as my mother was cutting up a watermelon, my father commented on how lucky we are to be human; we get to enjoy the juicy sweet belly of the fruit while the sheep only get the dense shell. My mother, dexterously cutting out the red flesh, said, "And yet some sheep are luckier than some people."

My job was to serve my brother-in-law his tea, one cup for breakfast, another after lunch, and another in the late afternoon. I often wanted to bring him something cold to relieve the heavy heat, a tall glass of cherry sherbet perhaps, but it wasn't allowed. Every time I asked if he needed anything, he'd shake his head no and say his thanks in as few words as possible. He did not make any demands of us. But his curt answers and evasive glances told me he was not grateful or gracious about what we were doing for him.

His eyes would never meet mine as I served him his tea, but as soon as I would turn around I could feel them on my back. I could feel two holes burning through my dress every time I walked away. I was old enough to know how a man might look at a woman; I had felt it every time Jafar Agha would come to our street bringing his vegetables on his donkey, insisting on touching my hand when he gave me back my change; I had known about it when my mother forbade Sooreh and me to walk through Bayat Street, where sweaty dark men built houses brick by brick. This was not that kind of a look. It was the opposite of desire and wanting to hold someone close. This gaze was something more like hate. It was a wish for my invisibility.

⚇

My brother-in-law, banished, as it were, to the far corner of the house, could have easily been forgotten if it was not for one thing: his coughing. His incessant cough. It would start in the morning in full force, like the sun, and by evening, it and my brother-in-law would start to give up and the coughing would subside with the sunset. No matter where you were in the house you could hear it. It was a constant reminder of his presence, of his illness, and of his impending doom. Whoever passed our door in the street could tell sickness was living in our house. Soon the neighbors all knew what was happening and the word spread like the disease itself. Our house was marked, the same as my brother-in-law.

The first time I saw him cough up blood I thought he was going to die right then and there. He had been coughing more than usual that morning, and by noon, when the sun was scorching hot, he began coughing and did not stop. My father told Sooreh to take him some warm water. But the coughing did not relent. He then snapped at me, "Go give the man some water, for the satisfaction of Allah!" My initial reaction was to say that Sooreh had taken him some. But I said nothing.

Outside I saw my sister hunched next to her husband, her face scrunched up like paper, holding out the cup of water to his face. His whole body was shaking with each phlegmy cough, and I thought his bones might all shatter and fall into his guts. He held a handkerchief to his mouth and coughed yellow mucus into it. Then it happened. Blood began to bloom on the handkerchief like spring flowers. This is it, I thought. He is going to die. I had often thought about how we would find out about his death; for some reason, I imagined myself being the one to find him. I could see myself coming down to bring him his afternoon tea, and then discovering him lying still, no coughing. And I'd know. I would drop the tray of tea, shattering glass, spilling steaming liquid, sugar cubes rolling, and I'd go inside the house, shrieking.

But now, standing there and watching this man spill his insides onto a rag, I was frightened in a way I had never been. The drama did not belong to death or the dead body, but to the *process* of death. I realized it was not going to be calm and serene, one of us stumbling upon him when he had passed on. It was going to be messy, perhaps violent. Death was not silencing him, but making him more present and shrill. It was going to be a battle of wills, he and Death, both stubborn, but the winner predetermined. And we were to be the spectators. We'd watch with morbid curiosity, transfixed by the blood and gore and noise and every other thing that signifies life, and we'd watch it spill out until nothing was left.

I saw all this in a flash—and I was frightened. It took me a second to realize that Sooreh was yelling at me to get our mother. I had to tear myself away from the scene, like a reluctant audience member who's being asked to leave the show right before the climax. I found my mother in the main room and could not find the right words. I just said, "Sooreh needs you." I was dazed, listening for the coughing to stop suddenly with a last breath, and for my sister to cry out. But, of course, the coughing did not stop. It would not stop for another three and a half months.

⸙

If it were not for the child, I don't know how any of us could have endured those months. She was the only one unfazed by what was occurring around her—she had no concept of death or illness, and therefore no opinion or feeling regarding the matter. All she could understand was that her father seemed no longer to love her. She never gave up trying to win back his affections; and it broke my heart to watch her try and fail every day.

Every morning she'd run to his corner in the backyard and talk to him in her two-year-old tongue and he would not say a word. His only reply was coughing, which was the same response he gave to the sheep and the hens and the flies. Then, finally, he would push her aside and tell her to go play. She'd smile and run off. The next morning the ritual would begin again. This time he would send her away a bit sooner and push a little harder; and she would smile a little less, and run off a little more slowly. No matter how much the rest of us doted on her, she still craved attention from her father. To her we were strangers, newly discovered relatives, and she had no bond with us. She wanted to be with the one person that wanted her the least.

∝

Aside from having a dying man in the corner of the yard, we did not do things differently that summer. We tended to our usual duties. My father cautiously and life-lovingly climbed the ladder and picked unripe grapes to make vinegar as my mother stood below him with a large tray. We bought lots of peaches from Jafar Agha and my mother recruited my sister and me to help her make *miyanpor*. We sat on the floor, the three of us; my mother pounded the almonds in a mortar and then emptied the contents onto my tray. I mixed in the sugar and made a paste, and Sooreh stuffed the peaches with it. This summer Sooreh stuffed the peaches like she was trying to keep them from talking, forcing the paste down their throat with no mercy.

But nothing signified summer more to me than when my mother would make jams: sour cherry, fig, apricot, and my favorite, rose petal. Every summer it was my task to collect the rose petals, and this summer, despite the dying man, it was no different.

We had three rows of Mohammadi roses in our yard, two white ones and one pink one, all reliably abundant and beautiful. On the day our Mohammadi roses seemed to be bursting in bloom, their intoxicating sweet scent wafting through the yard, I tied my white *chador* around my waist and went outside to pick rose petals. Each flower easily came off as I cupped my hand around its petals, releasing its scent, and I placed them in my *chador*. They were like silk. Molouk had come out too, wanting to "help." At first she placed the petals in my *chador*, but then she just threw them on the ground. She then found amusement by gripping a cup in her chubby hands and dipping it in the fountain water, and then dumping it back out. She'd spill the water out, making dark patterns appear on the ground. She was laughing in a high ecstatic pitch, expressing pure delight. I laughed right along with her. Whoever was with her had license to laugh and express elation without seeming insensitive or inappropriate. I saw her as our little savior— joy in the face of misery, as life in the face of death.

She dipped her cup in further and further each time. She threw the water up and made it rain down in huge droplets. I was startled at first by the cool water on my dress, but it was refreshing in the heat. She was laughing so hard that she almost, just for a moment, drowned out her father's cough, and everything associated with it. Suddenly his voice came from the corner, louder than I had ever heard him speak:

"Child! Be quiet!"

I was paralyzed, my hand transfixed on the flower. The child ran over to him, still laughing, and the water spilled out after her, making a trail like she was going to find her way back with it. "Baba, Baba! Look!" She was finally getting what she had been seeking for weeks: acknowledgment of her existence. All she knew was that the father who had forgotten her suddenly seemed to remember. I tried to go back to my rose picking, but I watched her out of the corner of my eye. She ran to his bed and showed him her cup and what she could do with it. I watched as he tried to push her away, yelling, uttering more words in that instant than he had in weeks.

"I told you to be quiet! Get away from me, you little wretch!"

But Molouk seemed to see all of this as a good thing. Did she think her father was playing with her? I thought about calling her back to me or going after her myself, but I was numb somehow; the flowers felt like air in my grip. I could only watch. And I watched as he reached down next to the bed and picked up a willow branch from the many strewn about. He lifted it up above his head, held it for a second, and brought it down. My fingers tightened around the petals at the sound of the branch striking flesh, followed by the sound of the cup falling to the ground. The water spilled out like ink. My breath was trapped in my lungs, and the flower in my hand turned to thorns. I was sure that if I looked at my palm it would be bloody. It all happened so fast and then slowed down to an agonizing pace. The blow seemed to turn the child into stone. She stood still for what seemed like minutes, staring at her father. He, too, seemed to be stuck in time, staring back down at her, the branch still in his grip, and a fury in his eyes. At that instant he did not look like a dying man. "Get lost!" he finally said. That breathed life into Molouk and she suddenly turned on her heels and ran toward me.

I let go of my *chador* and the flower petals fell out in a heap of pink and white silk. Molouk stood in that fragrant pile and stretched out her red arm to me. She was shaking like the leaves of the willow tree. I took her fleshy arm into my cold hands. Her eyes were searching mine, beseeching me to explain to her what had just happened. I wanted to be able to hold her, to caress her, wrap her entirely in the soft rose petals at her feet and tell her that it was all right. But I was paralyzed. Her chin started to quiver. Her crying crescendoed to a shriek and soon she was screaming as loudly as she had been laughing a minute before. With every one of her screams came her father's booming voice: "Shut up! Shut up!"

Sooreh came running out of the house. "What is it, what has happened?" Sooreh repeatedly asked me, and when that yielded nothing, she began asking Molouk. Then she saw her arm. Instantly, horror clouded her eyes. She looked over at the corner where her husband sat.

"Keep the child away from me," he said. "Do you hear? Keep her away from me!" His voice matched his awful eyes.

He is going to get it now, I thought. Sooreh is going to yell and scream at him, tell him never to strike the child that way ever again. She is going to pay him back not just for today, but for the last month he has been neglecting the child. But she did no such thing. The look in her eyes faded as quickly as it had come. She collected her screaming child in her arms as calmly as if she were picking up broken pieces of an inexpensive plate, and without saying a word, took her inside, trampling the petals underfoot.

My brother-in-law set the branch next to him like a treasured sword that had saved his life in battle, and lay down with his back to me. I felt weak in the knees. I stumbled to the steps and sat down, replaying what had just happened in my head. Little had met my expectations since the moment my sister and her family walked back into our home. But this? This was beyond anything I had imagined. How could he punish a child for being just that, a child? And doesn't a mother's own flesh throb when her child is wounded? Should she not retaliate? I did not claim to know much, but in that moment, sitting alone on the steps on that summer noon, I felt that everything I knew was wrong and that nothing made sense. But that was just the beginning.

∽

When I finally went inside the house, Molouk was in the room with her mother, eating a *miyanpor*. Her arm was rosy red with a throbbing indentation in the center of it. I stood watching for a second. Sooreh would not look at me. My mother called me from the kitchen.

"Here, take this out." She had set out the usual tray of tea and sugar cubes for my brother-in-law. I could not believe it. How could my mother expect me to serve this man tea? I glanced at the tea, half hoping that perhaps my mother, in her resourceful way, had put something in there; something to end his misery and our own. After all, she knew how to get rid of rats.

"I'm not taking that out there," I said.

"What, child? You're afraid he's going to hit *you* too?"

"But Maman—"

"Nargess, stop it. Your sister is with the child and I still have more peaches to stuff. Go give the man his tea and do not cause me a headache."

I could not fathom why my mother and sister did not protest in any way. I thought perhaps they were waiting for my father, waiting for the man to deal with the man.

I carried the tray out as slowly as possible. I was not afraid, but I did not want to be near him. When I walked up to the bed he still had his back to the yard, facing the wall. The long branch lay next to him. As soon as he heard me approaching, he turned around and sat up cross-legged, waiting to be served. He seemed more vigorous; his cheeks had color. Perhaps if I had detected remorse in him, if he had shown his shame by not turning around I could look at him—but now, I hated him. I placed the tea and the sugar cube holder on the wooden bed. Wait till my father comes home, I thought.

Nothing changed when my father came home. No one said a word to him about the incident. I kept waiting for my mother or Sooreh to say something. I thought, they'll tell him after he has rested a bit, after his tea, after his dinner—but nothing. I half expected the child to go up to him, show him her bruised arm and ask to be avenged, ask for redemption; but she was as passive and hopeless as the women who preceded her.

∽

"Nargess! Nargess!" the next morning my father shouted from the door. "Come take the bread from me, child, before my arms go limp."

I walked past my brother-in-law and helped my father unload the bread he had bought. "God bless you," he said. You would think the bread was made out of bricks rather than flour. "Now I have to go buy some parsley your mother requested." My father always made it sound like he was the only man alive subjected to such physical labor. I was ready to hear more when suddenly a smile broke on his face. He reached into his side pocket and pulled out a wooden comb. It was shaped like a rooster, painted a vivid orange, blue and red. "And look. Look what I bought for Sooreh!"

"Wow. It's beautiful," I said.

"Sooreh!" he shouted. "Go give it to her. I have to go buy parsley before all the fresh bunches are gone. Allah give me strength so I can carry it home and feed my children."

I closed the door as Sooreh came out. "I thought I heard Pedar call for me."

"Come here. Come look at this."

I handed her the colorful comb. "Where did you get this?" She held it with the tips of her fingers.

"Pedar bought it for you."

"Did he? It's very pretty." I could tell she was pleased. "Why didn't he buy you one? Are you sure he bought it for me?"

"Yes, yes, I'm sure!"

I had not seen her smile for a while. "It's very pretty, delicate. It reminds me of one I used to have. Do you remember? That one was not as—"

"What has he bought you?" my brother-in-law asked. Sooreh and I were startled. "I said, what has he bought you?"

"Nothing," Sooreh answered. "Just a comb."

"A comb," he said slowly. He paused for a minute and looked up.

"A comb? So that you can comb your hair and make yourself beautiful after I die, so you can secure yourself another husband."

Sooreh's face crumpled again. I had the uneasy feeling I was intruding on something I should not be privy to, something marital. "For God's sake," Sooreh blurted and rushed inside.

I stood there for a minute, the weight and the heat of the bread on my arms.

"And you," he addressed me. "Did you eat your *salaam* this morning?" He had never spoken to me that way before. But, since yesterday, he had become bold, as if hitting the child had awoken a sense of insolence in him. Something in me jumped and I had the urge to throw my burden of bread at him. Instead I just walked inside.

I had never wanted him to die before that moment.

That day Sooreh kept Molouk busy inside the house and did not let her go outside. That was admission enough on Sooreh's part. But the next day the child wanted out and there was no point in keeping her locked indoors. She was as happy as always, less irritable now that she was out. But she was wary of her father. She did not go up to him all day, and when her eyes would fall on him she'd stand still, take him in, and then go on with her play. I was proud of her for that. The adults may not have had any sense, but at least she did. But it did not last. Molouk seemed to have the memory of a goldfish and, by the third day, she was hounding her father for attention. My stomach would tie up in knots every time she went near him. He still had not relinquished the branch. I wanted to believe that he held on to it so that he could threaten the child—that all he had to do was grip it with his fingers and it would bring back to Molouk the terrifying memory of pain, and scare her off. But somewhere in my gut I knew that he was not sorry he had used it and that he would not be ashamed to use it again.

And for once, since the day my sister and her dying husband and their unfortunate child arrived at our house, I had predicted something right.

He hit her again. And again. He hit her many times and I never got used to it. Every single time that branch fell on Molouk's flesh, I felt like I had stepped on broken glass, as though all the petals shed that first day had turned into glass where they lay. There were marks all over her arms and legs, and there were invisible marks on me that would never go away. Yet Molouk went back for more. I even saw her dodging his slashes as if it were a game. I could have sworn that, instead of shrieks of pain, I heard shrieks of joy. Every time I tried to pull her away, she resisted and even resented me for it. Inside I was screaming. I could not say anything because no one else did. Not Sooreh, not my mother, not my father. Who was I to say anything? It was not my place. All I could do was watch and walk on that field of glass. Day after day, the broken shards of glass pierced my body and crept closer to my heart.

※

And I would have thought I was going insane if there were not subtle hints that showed me that, yes, others could see what I could see, that Molouk really was getting a beating from her sick father. But no one else seemed to feel the same way about it. Or at least not outwardly. And it took me a very long time to figure out why.

I knew that Sooreh did her best every day to keep Molouk out of the yard. But the will of the child was stronger. I once heard my mother say to Sooreh that perhaps she should keep her daughter away from her father—so that she did not get sick from him. My father exploited the changing weather, suggesting the child should wear more layers of clothing since fall was on its way. But no one ever mentioned the hitting. No one.

※

The days got shorter, the sun became lazy, a breeze interrupted the stagnant air and my brother-in-law began to melt away. His clothes now hung on him as if on a hanger, with no indication of meat on his bones. One day when he stepped off the bed I saw his bare ankles, and they were smaller than my wrists. The end was near. He coughed more persistently, and the sight of blood was as much a part of him as the willow branch. He was more sedentary. The only time I saw movement in his eyes was when he forced himself up to hit the child. He never gave that up.

∾

One night toward the end of summer while the rest of our world slept, Sooreh hurried into the room and woke me up. "Nargess, Nargess, get up, for the love of Allah."

"What is it, what has happened?"

"Wake up and help me," she said in a loud whisper. "The bedclothes, I need to change them."

"What? Why?" I sat up.

"What does it matter? They are wet. Where does Madar keep the other sheets?" she said as she rummaged through my cupboard in the dark. "Do you have any in here?"

"They're not in there. I'll get them for you," I said, trying to wake up. "Sooreh, what is happening?"

"It's nothing. It's night sweats. He gets them a lot. Just help me. And try not to wake everyone up, for God's sake."

I sneaked into my mother's room filled with sleep and darkness and took out clean sheets from the trunk. Sooreh came out of her room with the wet sheets piled in her arms. "Here, just hang these out to dry." One side of her nightclothes seemed damp.

"Is this why you are washing sheets all the time?" I asked.

"Sooreh!" I heard my brother-in-law.

"Shush, I am coming! You'll wake the child." Then she turned to me. "Just hang them outside. I'll wash them in the morning." For one second, perhaps two, Sooreh stood there and looked at me in the dark. I could see fear and fatigue swim in her eyes. Then I saw that she wanted her husband to live and to die at the same time, and that she felt guilty and selfish for wanting either scenario. Maybe she realized that I had seen through her torn feelings, and felt violated, exposed; she ran back to the room clutching the clean sheets to her bosom. But she must have felt relieved, even for a second, to let someone else know that, yes, she sometimes wished death upon her husband.

Outside the night was chilly and the moon was wide-awake. I

began spreading the wet sheets on the balcony rail and wondered what was happening inside my brother-in-law's body that made him sweat through his sheets. Afterwards, I went down and washed my hands in the fountain. I looked up at his bed, now empty, and thought that soon it would be empty forever. I can't say I was saddened, but it was not something I was looking forward to as I had been for the past few weeks. Perhaps Sooreh, changing sheets for the seventieth time while the man stood above her and told her to work faster and worrying about the child waking, she alone carrying the shame of waking her sister and the shame of burdening her parents—perhaps *she* at that moment looked forward to his end more than I did.

And what about him? It must be awful knowing not only that you are going to die but that others are wishing it upon you. Until then I had never, not even for a moment, considered how my brother-in-law felt. I must've had my reasons, but I can only attribute it to one: fear. I did not want to imagine what it felt like to know that you are dying—soon. I wanted nothing to do with that feeling.

I walked over to his bed, and after a moment decided to sit down. The yard looked blue in the moonlight. Sitting down I realized that the bed mostly had a view of the outhouse. What a view! I thought. What a *last* view. This is what my brother-in-law is looking at during his last months, days? Even if it were the most beautiful garden, with more flowers and fruit trees and no outhouse in sight, it would still be a last view and he'd be sick of it. Even if it were the Garden of Eden itself, he would start to resent it, wouldn't he? He might even hate it. He must hate everything, I thought, even the good and the beautiful. What good is beauty to him now? What use? He knows he won't look at it again. How can you love the taste of a ripe melon and let its juice drip down your forearms, knowing that soon you will not taste it ever again? How can you appreciate the intoxicating scent of the jasmine, knowing that it will go on smelling sweet long after you're gone? How can you love anything? And then it hit me: the child. How can you love your own child, knowing that you will never watch her grow up, that you will have no role in molding the person she will become? He resented her. Molouk was so full of life and energy. She was everything that *he* was not. He hated her precisely for the same reasons that I loved her.

Hence the willow branch, the relentless beating. She did not belong to him, or rather he no longer belonged to her. He did not belong to anyone. Since the moment the fatal disease crept into his body, he had stopped being a husband, a father, a person. Everything had been taken from him: wife, child, youth, life. He was still alive (not well, but alive) with feelings and fears and hopes like the rest of us; yet everyone—yes, everyone—had discarded him as if he were already dead, told him to go home and die, die in a corner facing the outhouse.

Why had I not seen it before? I had never once tried to put myself in his shoes and walk around on his two feet. I had been too busy wanting my sister back for myself, too busy picturing how and when our guest would die, too busy hating him for hitting my niece, too busy seeing the world through my own mind and heart, until there was no room to see as *he* did. And yes, I was afraid to feel an ounce of what he felt. From the moment he walked into our house I had wanted nothing to do with him. I had been cruel like others, like Fate herself; and cruelty had bred cruelty.

I sat there on his bed in the chill of the night under the blue light of a smiling moon and felt shame and remorse. I felt small. My brother-in-law was only behaving like a human, one of those imperfect beings who wish to be and pompously think they *can* be so much more than their nature allows, that they can be noble and strong and courageous when tested by the gods. But in the end their true human qualities pour out of them.

I sat for a long time. When I finally got up to go inside, dawn was licking the sky. And for the first time in a long time it felt like our yard had been swept of the broken glass and I was back on the cold, real concrete.

My brother-in-law died on a Wednesday afternoon. His death was quiet and not very dramatic. He died in the room where he had been bedridden for three nights. There was a sense of calm around the house, a relieved silence. None of us said anything to each other, and we tried not to meet each other's eyes. When evening approached, our neighbor Akbar Agha came to our house with his Qu'ran, and Sooreh lit a single candle and took it to the room where her husband's body lay. They did not come out till the next morning. My parents kept vigil as well, reciting the Qu'ran along with Akbar Agha, asking God to be merciful and forgive him his sins. My father only lasted an hour before going to bed. He and Molouk were the only two people who slept that night. I was keeping my own vigil: I could not fall asleep. The muffled verses of the Qu'ran reached me through the walls but failed to comfort me. The calm of the afternoon was gone, and as much as I tried to push away the thought, I knew life had fled that afternoon and left behind an empty, morbid shell.

In the morning, the men of the neighborhood carried my brother-in-law out in his wooden coffin, and the women, dressed in black *chadors*, followed. They chanted God's name as they took him out of the house, down the street, all the way to where his body was washed and shrouded, then to his final destination, deep in the earth. I stayed behind with Molouk, but their voices reached me long after they were gone: *La illaha illalla, la illaha illalla.*

That night the neighborhood did its duty and did not leave us alone in our time of grieving. They brought *halva* and dates and helped make and serve tea, while someone recited the Qu'ran in the background. At the end of the night some offered to stay and lend a hand, but my mother refused. When the last mourners left, the four of us stood in the middle of the room, silent. "Well, God rest his soul," my father finally said. "This is all of our ends, as they say. God rest his soul."

We nodded. A minute later we said good night and retreated to our rooms. No one would ever admit it, but we had all been feigning grief to others and perhaps more so amongst ourselves. We were exhausted—not from the day's pretensions but from the weight of propriety during the last few months. That night my dead brother-in-law was not the only person who finally rested in peace.

∞

The peace did not last. The real tragedy for us happened a month later.

When little Molouk died of the same disease that had killed her father, there was no all-night vigil, no chanting men and mourning women following her tiny coffin, no *halva* and dates, since children need no help finding their way back to God. And this time there were no pretend tears.

After the death of her only child, Sooreh became my harshest critic. Suddenly I was the most inept person: I washed the dishes wrong, I didn't fold sheets right, I certainly could not make rice to save my life. I never defended myself. I already knew why she did it. And when one innocent afternoon we paid a visit to Akbar Agha's house for *aash,* and a friend of his, a middle-aged Baha'i widower visiting from Eshgh Abaad, said hello and smiled at Sooreh, I knew right then that my sister would not stay with us much longer. She was married and back in Eshgh Abaad less than a year from the day she arrived. She had two sons. She never came back home.

❧

It was so easy, catching tuberculosis.

Business must have been good, and my brother-in-law must have been spending a lot of time at work. He must have been unusually tired and weak the day he came into contact with the bacteria. He probably had some business dealings with someone who had it; perhaps they shook hands to consummate a deal and the hand held the infested handkerchief. Perhaps he was conversing with someone who was ill (maybe even visiting the sick, although imagining him free with compassion does not fit), and as the man talked and talked, a droplet of infected spit landed on my brother-in-law's lips; that was all it took. Maybe some poor infected passerby had moments earlier unburdened himself of the phlegm in his throat and spit out onto the street. Then the tiny droplets found their way up, up into the air and into my brother-in-law's nostrils the instant he passed by.

It must have been a simple gesture, nothing to warn of its fatal potential. The bacteria indifferently performed their task, fulfilled their destiny, devouring his lungs, in turn devouring his dreams, his life, his family and a piece of all of us.

I don't suppose my brother-in-law could have known that he affected me, that I saw him and life differently toward the end. But if what they say is true, that those who have passed on before us are somehow amongst us, privy to our thoughts and actions, then he knows now that I did not forgive or excuse him at the end, but I understood him.

13 Days

%

PARISSA MILANI

13 Days after the Iranian New Year
we gather separately together.
The sun beats down on
bumpy-soft tablecloths as
uncles and dads laugh
at whispered jokes.
Moms and aunts gossip
and break pumpkin seeds
between their teeth. They
speak the tongue with
such ease, breaking the seeds
as though it were something they did
"back home."

Ari
(1979–1981)

Mahru Elahi

troublemaker
twelve-year-old palm strikes buckle before
squeezing
a story about a blowjob he got
delivering pizza
cast out to a circle of smirking boys
his booming voice thick as borderlines
stretches to catch me in its embrace
mark me immigrant
a neat dotted line down the middle
born here
no more american than he
(iranians make such good italians)

he bellows fire
from the streets of Tehran
gently stokes embers burrowing into crabgrass lawns
Torrance, California
as soot falls unsuspecting into the eyes of our science teacher
tears stuck in a corner of the room

it starts to consume us
once the embassy is taken
frenzied broadcasts foreign trouble
four hundred and forty-four nights
of grainy beams pointed at gauze-covered faces
this boy and i we sit huddled
watching nightly news quiet blocks apart

waiting
alone for the hostages to be freed
a giddy silence in small living rooms
barking dogs the motor growl of garages opening
our only interruptions

mornings bring another kind of heat
blacktop yawns again
we perform calisthenics in neat lines only an arm away
teacher turns her head
they pounce on him the ones who ate his hungry stories
small fists connect gasping between gleeful shouts of
iranian faggot
i know i'm next

they don't touch me
fall away into jumping jacks
he stumbles upright
pupils catching light
my gaze yellow as smoke
we who know the stench of homes burning
how they create unmake you

sinking now
our knees prepare for pushups
deep gravel pink impressions
a study in relief short-lived
whistle empties busy ground between us
quiver of my voice pulling arrows aiming words
whistle
as i move closer hissing
we are the same
hit his mute gaze
hold it

Let Me Tell You Where I've Been

❦

PERSIS M. KARIM

Some have stamps in their passports,
emblems of official entry.
But the places charted
on this invisible map
are etched softly
in the curve of my spine.

Some women go deaf with the sound
of children crying and weep
at the thought of more
togetherness. And I keep looking
for a way to belong.

When you have traveled far
you begin to long for that particular thing:
the sweet mustiness of a childhood room,
the mix of cumin and freshly chopped parsley,
the dull, but knowable color
found in the joining
of four walls.

Conversations about children and debts
have detoured this longing.
Still, I want to speak names
of places with worn roads and blue-domed mosques:

Tehran, Shiraz, Esfahan—
places I want to say I've been.

I keep the box of inlaid enamel and wood—
its pattern of irregular triangles and stars,
the lid that fits a little too tightly—
purchased at a crowded bazaar.
I carry it with me, like a passport
not from this place
where I was born,
but from the other
I think I have been.

Cardamom and Hell

HALEH HATAMI

What we don't expect steals the day.
On a journey this befalls the traveler frequently.
The steppe spreads for months,
I stop for tea at a roadside outpost.
The Uzbek serves a brewful of calamity
Without mentioning loss.
Both of us displaced with no thirst for home.

Nazr

Zara Houshmand

It has been so long,
how will you know me?

I am the one standing still in the rush
scanning the screen again and again
trying to find
a believable destination.

I am the one who has spread her skirts on the grass
like a picnic cloth, saying:
Here is trust.
And honesty.
And kindness.
Come feast.

I am the one tying poems
to the branches of a tree
whose leaves have fallen.

CONTRIBUTORS

AZIN AREFI was born in Iran and moved to the United States when she was eleven years old. She studied English literature at the University of California, Berkeley, and received her master's in creative writing with an emphasis in fiction at UC Davis. She currently teaches English literature and composition at De Anza College in Cupertino, California. Her fiction has appeared in a number of publications, including the online magazine *Iranian.com*.

GELAREH ASAYESH moved to the United States with her family just before the Iranian revolution. She is the author of *Saffron Sky: A Life Between Iran and America* (Beacon Press, 1999). She has worked as a journalist for the *Miami Herald* and the *Baltimore Sun* and contributes articles and commentaries to such publications as the *Boston Globe,* the *Washington Post*, and the *St. Petersburg Times,* as well as National Public Radio. She lives in Florida with her family.

SUSAN ATEFAT-PECKHAM was born to Iranian immigrants in New York City in 1970 and lived there until her father's work with the United Nations necessitated the family's move to Switzerland. She returned to the United States to study medicine before turning to poetry in the early 1990s. She was the 2000 National Poetry Series Award winner, and her book *That Kind of Sleep* was published in 2001 by Coffee House Press. Though initially and primarily a lyric-narrative poet and essayist whose work was driven by story and character, her later poems were influenced by Rumi's mystical lyricism in particular and Sufi mysticism in general. The 9/11 attacks and the resulting American backlash against the Middle Eastern world led Atefat-Peckham to poignant dissatisfaction with American foreign policy, spurring her to become a more public voice and to teach at the University of Jordan in Amman on the Fulbright program. On February 7, 2004, she and her oldest son, Cyrus Atefat-Peckham, were killed in an auto accident on a highway near the Dead Sea. *The Soul Lives There, In the Silent Breath,* a posthumous collection of her poetry, will be published by Coffee House Press in 2006.

TARA BAHRAMPOUR is the author of the memoir *To See and See Again: A Life in Iran and America* (Farrar, Straus and Giroux, 1999), which traces her family's migration from Iran to the United States after the

1979 revolution and her own journey back to Iran fifteen years later. She has written about Iranians in global limbo for the *New Yorker,* the *New York Times,* the *American Scholar,* the *New Republic,* and other journals. She is a staff writer at the *Washington Post.*

LAYLA DOWLATSHAHI graduated from UC Berkeley and received her MFA from Goddard College. Her play *Joys of Lipstick* was staged at the Producer's Club and had a reading at the Lark Play Development Center; *Waiting Room* had a staged reading at the Annenberg Studio Theatre at the University of Pennsylvania. Both these plays will be published by Temple University Press. She has also written two pulp fiction novels. She teaches writing at the City University of New York.

FIROOZEH DUMAS moved from Abadan, Iran, to Whittier, California, with her family when she was seven. She is the author of *Funny in Farsi: A Memoir of Growing Up Iranian in America* (Villard Books, 2003), which was selected as a finalist for the PEN award in the creative non-fiction category. She is a frequent commentator on National Public Radio and is currently touring California with her one-woman show, "Laughing Without an Accent." She lives in Northern California with her husband and two children.

MAHRU ELAHI, the daughter of an Iranian father and an American mother, grew up in California. After many years of teaching in New York public schools, she returned to California in 2003. She is currently an artist-in-residence with WritersCorps, a project of the San Francisco Arts Commission. She is particularly proud of her work with incarcerated women. Her poetry has appeared in the Canadian feminist journal *Fireweed.* She is the author or *The Thorn Garden,* a graphic novel.

On paper and legally perhaps, PARINAZ ELEISH could be categorized as an Iranian American. In reality, she is seeking a new identity that is neither American (which she has not yet become) nor Iranian (which she no longer is in the purest sense). She wrestles with her identity as a poet and the image her children have of her as a mother. And so she travels on paper in search of this identity. She loves writing travel poems and searches the world to discover a new reality that is none of the above and all of it at the same time.

AMANDA ENAYATI is an attorney and a writer. She was born in Iran and raised in Europe and came of age in the United States. She has written widely about issues of education, race, culture, ethnicity, and identity. She is currently at work on her first novel. She lives in New York City with her husband, Jaime Uzeta, and daughter, Mina.

FARNAZ FATEMI is an Iranian American poet and freelance writer living in Santa Cruz, California. She teaches writing at UC Santa Cruz.

TARA FATEMI, currently residing in Northern California, has lived in Los Angeles, Santa Cruz, San Francisco, and Austin. At one point, she left her heart in San Francisco, but now she takes it with her wherever she goes, including her first trip to Iran as an adult. This journey illuminated one fact in particular: she felt like an outsider in Iran, not just in the United States. She is working on creating a sense of belonging from within.

ELHAM GHEYTANCHI is a sociologist teaching at Santa Monica College in Santa Monica, California. She has published numerous scholarly articles on Iranian women's movements in several academic journals and books in the United States and Germany.

HAALE is a New York–born musician, composer, and vocalist who weaves Persian melodies and poetry through a soundscape of tribal beats, sci-fi guitars, and a twanging sitar, creating a unique sound that simultaneously reflects her Iranian and urban American roots. She lives in New York City.

ZJALEH HAJIBASHI teaches Persian language and literature at the University of Virginia. She is currently working on a study of post-revolution prison memoirs entitled "Writing Confinement: The Limits of Autobiographical Expression in Iran." Drawing on this research, she is also writing a novel that she hopes will communicate not the gap between the repressive world of post-revolution Iran and the United States, but the creeping coalescence.

ROYA HAKAKIAN is the author of *Journey from the Land of No* (Crown Books, 2004), a memoir of growing up as a Jewish teenager in post-revolutionary Iran, as well as two highly acclaimed collections of poetry, including *For the Sake of Water*. She writes for numerous publications and is a regular contributor to National Public Radio's *Weekend Edition*. She is a founding member of the Iran Human Rights Documentation Center and a term member at the Council on Foreign Relations.

HALEH HATAMI lives in Oakland, California. Her poems have appeared in *ZZYZYVA, Phoebe,* and *Fourteen Hills.* Upcoming work will appear in the *Indiana Review, Chain,* and the *International Poetry Review.* Her translations have been published in *26* and *The PEN Anthology of Contemporary Iranian Literature.* She is the recipient of the CPIC Life Poetry Award from San Francisco State University and of the Ann Fields Poetry Award.

Iranian-born TARANEH HEMAMI is an installation artist and painter based in the San Francisco Bay Area. She received her MFA from the California College of the Arts (in Oakland) in 1991 and since then has exhibited her work locally and internationally. In addition to being the 2006 artist-in-residence at CCA, she is the director of *Hall of Reflections,* a collaborative art project that documents, collects, and visually displays the stories and photographs of the Bay Area Iranian diaspora community. *Hall of Reflections* (from which the cover of this book originates) has been exhibited at the San Francisco Arts Commission Gallery, the Berkeley Art Center, and other national and international venues including the Sixth International Sharjah Biennial in the United Arab Emirates. For more information see http://www.hallofreflections.com.

ZARA HOUSHMAND is an Iranian American writer and theater artist living in Austin, Texas. Her translations of plays by Bijan Mofid and Bahram Beyzaii, as well as her own plays, have been produced in Los Angeles, San Francisco, Berkeley, New York, and at the Spoleto Festival. She has been involved in pioneering the development of virtual reality as an art form and also, as publications director for the Mind and Life Institute, in facilitating a long-term dialogue between Buddhism and Western science. She is a contributing editor for *Words Without Borders.*

NILOOFAR KALAAM grew up in Tehran and now lives in Toronto. She has studied engineering, mathematics and clowning. Her poetry and essays have appeared in *Shahrvand, Peace Magazine,* and the *Iranian Times.* Her collection of poems, *In Relation,* will be published by Lyrical/Myrical Press in spring 2005. She is currently at work on her first novel.

MARJAN KAMALI was born in 1971 and grew up in Turkey, Iran, Germany, Kenya, and New York City. She holds a degree in English literature from UC Berkeley, a master's in business administration from Columbia University, and a master's in creative writing from New York University. Her first short story, written when she was only eighteen, received a National Scholastic Award. She has acted with the Semi-Circle Theater Troupe in Basel, Switzerland, and recently moved to Sydney, Australia, where she lives with her husband and two young children. She is currently finishing her first novel.

ESTHER KAMKAR was born in Iran and came to the United States in 1972 after a seven-year stay in Jerusalem. She was one of the recipients of the 2001 Peninsula Community Foundation Artist Grant, which supported the publication of *Hummingbird Conditions* and the project *Poetry and Bookmaking,* part of the Ecumenical Hunger Project in East Palo Alto. A minigrant from the Clay and Glass Arts Foundation in 2003 allowed her to create *Personal Narratives in Poetry and Clay* at the Boys and Girls Club of East Palo Alto. She lives and works in Palo Alto, California.

PERSIS M. KARIM was born and raised in the San Francisco Bay Area by her Iranian father and French mother. She is coeditor and coauthor of *A World Between: Poems, Short Stories and Essays by Iranian-Americans* (George Braziller, 1999). Her poems have appeared in *Reed, Caesura, HeartLodge,* and *di-verse-city.* She teaches literature and creative writing at San Jose State University and is currently writing "In the Belly of the Great Satan"—a study of literature and the emergence of a public Iranian American identity. She lives in Berkeley with her husband and her two beautiful sons. She can be reached at persisk@yahoo.com.

FIROOZEH KASHANI-SABET is an assistant professor of history at the University of Pennsylvania. She has worked extensively on nationalism in Iran, and her book *Frontier Fictions: Shaping the Iranian Nation, 1804–1946* (Princeton University Press, 1999) examines the centrality of frontiers, land, and geography in Iranian nationalism. Her current interests include the study of hygiene and U.S.-Islamic relations. She enjoys writing fiction and exposing her daughters, Neda and Ariana, to the eccentricities of Persian culture, particularly their Gilaki heritage.

LALEH KHALILI grew up in Iran and moved to the United States in 1985, when she was sixteen. She is currently a lecturer in politics at the School of Oriental and African Studies, University of London. She lives in England with her husband, John Chalcraft, and her baby daughter, May.

MIMI KHALVATI was born in Tehran and grew up on the Isle of Wight. She was educated in Switzerland and in London at the Drama Centre and the School of African and Oriental Studies. She has worked as an actor and director in both the UK and Iran, founding Matrix, a women's experimental theater group, and cofounding Theatre in Exile. She is coordinator of the Poetry School, running poetry workshops and courses in London. Her poetry collections include *In White Ink* (1991), *Mirrorwork* (1995), and *Entries on Light* (1997), all published by Carcanet Press, which also published *Selected Poems* in 2000 and a new collection, *The Chine*, in 2002. She is also the author of a children's book, *I Know a Place* (Dent Children's Books, 1985).

NIKA KHANJANI was born in Iran, raised in Texas, schooled in New York City, and now lives in Montreal, Canada. She is an independent filmmaker currently working on her first feature-length narrative.

MICHELLE KOUKHAB currently teaches English and creative writing in Los Angeles. She earned her MFA in poetry from the University of Maryland in 2001. She was a waiter at the Bread Loaf Writers' Conference in 2005.

MOJDEH MARASHI is a San Francisco Bay Area writer and visual artist who came to the United States in 1977. Her work is deeply influenced by the ancient and modern history of Iran, where she grew up. Marashi holds an MA in interdisciplinary arts and is working on her MFA in creative writing at San Francisco State University.

Born in Tehran, PARISSA MILANI grew up in Northern California, where she arrived at the age of four. She has a strong connection with her heritage and culture. Her poetry speaks to the struggles of growing up Iranian in the United States. She attended San Jose State University, where she earned a BA in English. She is currently pursuing her MFA in creative writing at San Francisco State University.

AZADEH MOAVENI grew up in San Jose, California, and studied politics at UC Santa Cruz. She won a Fulbright Fellowship to Egypt and studied Arabic at the American University in Cairo. She worked as a reporter for *Time* magazine before joining the *Los Angeles Times* to cover the war in Iraq. She is the author of *Lipstick Jihad: A Memoir of Growing*

Up Iranian in America and American in Iran (Public Affairs, 2005). She is coauthor, with Shirin Ebadi, of *Iran Awakening: A Memoir of Revolution and Hope* (Random House, 2006). She lives in Beirut, Lebanon.

LEYLA MOMENY studied philosophy at UCLA. She plans to teach high school before pursuing graduate studies in philosophy. She is currently obsessed with photography and cultural studies. She lives in California.

FARNOOSH MOSHIRI is the author of two novels, *At the Wall of the Almighty* (Interlink Publishing, 1999) and *The Bathhouse* (Beacon Press, 2003). Her collection of short stories, *The Crazy Dervish and the Pomegranate Tree* (Black Heron), was published in 2004. Her third novel, *Against Gravity,* will be published by Penguin Books in 2006. She has received numerous fellowships and awards, including the Barbara Deming Fiction Award for Peace and Social Justice and two consecutive Black Heron Awards for Social Fiction. She teaches literature and creative writing at Syracuse University.

BEATRICE MOTAMEDI was born in Paris to an Iranian father and a French mother and came to the United States via Canada at the age of seven. She attended Northwestern University and the Stegner Program in Creative Writing at Stanford. She is a former reporter for the *San Francisco Chronicle,* and her work has appeared in numerous publications, including *Newsweek, Health,* and *Salon.com.* She lives in Oakland, California, with her husband and two children, middle names Henry and Elika.

AMY MOTLAGH, more or less a native of Southern California, is presently a doctoral candidate in the Department of Near Eastern Studies at Princeton University. Her dissertation focuses on the mysteries and wonders of the literature of the Iranian diaspora.

APHRODITE DÉSIRÉE NAVAB is an Iranian-Greek-American artist and writer. She is an assistant professor of art in the College of Fine Arts at the University of Florida. She received her BA in visual and environmental studies at Harvard University in 1993. In 2004, she completed an Ed.D. in art and art education at Teachers College, Columbia University. With her camera and her pen, Navab interrogates the visual productions and politics of the competing cultures forming her identity. Through her camera, she also writes her own story as an immigrant within, alongside, and against the grain of the documented story of North America.

NEGIN NEGHABAT was born in Tehran in 1979. She grew up in Germany and moved to the United States to attend university. She holds a BA in international business from San Diego State University. Currently, she lives in Chicago and works in corporate marketing. She is pursuing an MBA at the University of Chicago, and she also plans to attain a degree in international law. She credits her accomplishments to the selfless and unconditional support of her mother.

SANAZ BANU NIKAEIN graduated from UC Berkeley with the highest distinction in general scholarship and highest honors in her major. At twenty-three, she was one of the youngest attorneys to join the legal profession and is currently a deputy district attorney in Modesto, California. In 2003, she was appointed president of the International First Aid Society, an affiliate of the United Nations; she also served as the campaign manager for Badi Badiozamani, a candidate for California governor. She dedicates these poems to her confidant, Feysel Nuri, who is her writing inspiration.

MITRA PARINEH was born in Palo Alto, California, to Iranian immigrant parents. After receiving her BA and MA in English at San Jose State University, she decided to take time off to complete a collection of short stories and pursue her MFA in fiction. She can be reached at missparineh@yahoo.com.

SHARON L. PARKER received her Ph.D. in 2005 in the Comparative Cultural and Comparative Literary Studies Program at the University of Arizona, where she wrote her dissertation on contemporary Iranian women artists. She moved with her parents and two sisters in 1958 to Iran, where she lived for nine years, returning again in 1976 and 2001. Fond memories of Persian gardens led her to surround her Tucson home with jasmine, roses, pomegranates, and potted geraniums. She is currently an assistant professor in the Department of Art and Design at Zayed University in Abu Dhabi, United Arab Emirates.

PAZ is the pen name of thirty-two-year-old Iranian American performance artist "Dirty Phoenix." She currently has a queer, Middle Eastern burlesque comedy show called *The Asses of Evil* in New York City. In both her performance art and her writing, PAZ pushes boundaries and explores the complex and frail layers that make up the modern Iranian American female identity and experience.

NASRIN RAHIMIEH is dean of the Faculty of Humanities and professor of comparative literature and English at McMaster University. Her research has focused on intercultural encounters between Iran and the West, modern Persian literature, literature of exile and displacement, women's writing, and post-revolutionary Iranian cinema. Her publications include *Oriental Responses to the West: Comparative Essays on Muslim Writers from the Middle East* (Brill, 1990) and *Missing Persians: Discovering Voices in Iranian Cultural Heritage* (Syracuse University Press, 2001).

FARNOOSH SEIFODDINI recently graduated from San Francisco State University with an MFA in creative writing. Her poetry has appeared in the *North American Review,* the *Kennesaw Review,* and *Transfer Magazine.* She is the recipient of the Ann Fields Poetry Prize and the Mark Linenthal Poetry Prize and a finalist for the James Hearst Poetry Prize. In her free time, she fulfills her incurable obsession with salvaging and reviving old furniture. Seifoddini dedicates this publication to the many muses who have blessed her life with inspiration.

LAYLI ARBAB SHIRANI is presently a law student at UC Hastings in San Francisco. When her studies are completed, she looks forward to reading through the piles of novels and *New Yorker* magazines she's compulsively collected and returning to a world where thoughts arrive in fragment form and stay that way.

SHEILA SHIRAZI lives, works, and writes in New York City. Born in Washington, D.C., she spent several vivid childhood years in Indonesia and is an unapologetic Francophile. She is still searching for home but suspects she may find it in literature, where individual human experiences fill the fissures caused by politics, religion, and cultural convention.

KANDI TAYEBI is an associate professor of English at Sam Houston State University. She has published work on women writers, technology, writing, and issues of race and gender in the classroom. Currently, she teaches Romantic literature, world literature, and literary theory. Her creative writing has been published in journals such as the *Georgia Review.* Her most recent project is a book of creative nonfiction focusing on the intersections between cultures of the East and West.

ROXANNE VARZI was born in Tehran and moved to the United States after the revolution. She has spent the last fourteen years traveling back to Iran. She has a Ph.D. in anthropology from Columbia University and is currently an assistant professor of anthropology at UC Irvine. Her book *Warring Souls:Youth, Media and Martyrdom in Post-Revolutionary Iran,* will be published in 2006 by Duke University Press.

Poet and translator SHOLEH WOLPÉ was born in Iran but spent most of her teen years in the Caribbean and Europe, ending up in the United States, where she pursued master's degrees in radio-TV-film from Northwestern University and public health from Johns Hopkins University. She is the author of *The Scar Saloon* (Red Hen Press, 2004), and her poems and translations have been published in numerous literary journals and anthologies. Her translations of a selection of Forough Farrokhzad's poetry will be published in the near future. She is the director and host of Poetry at the Loft, a popular poetry venue in Redlands, California. She can be reached at http://www.sholehwolpe.com.

MEHRI YALFANI was born in Hamadan, Iran. She received her degree in electrical engineering from the University of Tehran. She left Iran in 1985 for her children—first going to France and then later to Canada. She has published five novels and five collections of short stories. Two of her collections, *Parastoo* and *Two Sisters,* are available in English. Her novel *Afsaneh's Moon,* first published in English (in Canada), was recently published in Iran by Roshangaran Pubications. Her stories have appeared in many anthologies. Her latest novel, *Tahmineh's Silence,* will be published in Persian in 2006.

TARSSA YAZDANI is an author and editor who frequently writes on contemporary art, music, and popular culture. She lives in New Jersey with her husband, artist Ron English, and their two children.

SHAHRZAD ZAHEDI was born in Iran but moved to Switzerland at the age of ten, later coming to the United States. She is currently a doctoral student in French studies at Brown University. She has presented papers at conferences on Christine de Pizan, as well as Froissart. She served as coeditor of the online journal *Equinoxes*. She enjoys writing poetry, which she began doing during her three-year stay in Switzerland. Though most of her poems are in French, she has recently begun writing in English.

Born in Tehran, KATAYOON ZANDVAKILI currently lives in the San Francisco Bay Area. *Deer Table Legs,* her first collection of poetry, won the University of Georgia Press Contemporary Poetry Series prize in 1998. The book's title poem appeared in *The 2000 Pushcart Prize XXIV.* Her work has appeared in the *Massachusetts Review,* the *Five Fingers Review,* the *Hawaii Review, Rattapallax,* and *Caesura,* as well as in the anthologies *A World Between: Poems, Short Stories and Essays by Iranian-Americans* and *American Poetry: The Next Generation.* She received an MFA from Sarah Lawrence College and a BA from UC Berkeley.

Born in Tehran and raised in London, ZARREH received a BA in sociology and literature at Essex University and a BA in Arabic and Islamic studies at the School of Oriental and African Studies, followed by a Ph.D. in Islamic mysticism, also at the School of Oriental and African Studies. She currently resides in Vienna, Austria, where she is working on her first volume of poetry and nonfiction prose.

SHADI ZIAEI, a poet and fiction writer, is currently directing her creative energy toward her alternative rock band Tomgirl. She is still hoping that at some point she will publish some sort of a collection of something. Her shoe size has gone up from eight and a half to nine. She is a proud resident of the San Francisco Bay Area and still geeks in IT. She thanks the few exceptions who support her in her odd and unpredictable creative jolts.

PERSIS KARIM was born in the United States to an Iranian father and a French mother. She is an assistant professor of English and comparative literature at San Jose State University in California and coeditor of *A World Between: Poems, Short Stories, and Essays by Iranian Americans.*

AL YOUNG is the poet laureate of California. Young has a long list of publications ranging from novels and poetry collections to musical memoirs and screenplays. He is working on a new novel called *A Piece of Cake,* a sequel to his *Sitting Pretty.*